D0875213

Urban Protest in Mexico and Brazil

Why do social organizations decide to protest instead of working through institutional channels? This book draws hypotheses from three standard models of contentious political action – POS, resource mobilization, and identity – and subjects them to a series of qualitative and quantitative tests. The results have implications for social movement theory, studies of protest, and theories of public policy and agenda setting. The characteristics of movement organizations – type of resources, internal leadership competition, and identity – shape their inherent propensity to protest. Party alliance does not constrain protest, even when the party ally wins power. Instead, protest becomes a key part of organizational maintenance, producing constant incentives to protest that do not reflect changing external conditions. Nevertheless, organizations do respond to changes in the political context, governmental cycles in particular. In the first year of a new government, organizations have strong incentives to protest in order to establish their priority in the policy agenda.

Kathleen Bruhn is a leading expert on the Mexican Left. Her first book, *Taking on Goliath,* analyzes the emergence and early consolidation of the primary Leftist party in Mexico, the PRD. She is also the author, with Daniel C. Levy, of a textbook on Mexican politics, *Mexico: The Struggle for Democratic Development.* She has lived for extended periods in both Mexico and Brazil. She has three times won fellowships to write at the Center for U.S.–Mexico Studies at the University of California, San Diego, and once won a fellowship at the Kellogg Center at the University of Notre Dame, also to write. Her research has been supported by the Stanford Institute for International Studies, the MacArthur Foundation, the UC Council on Research, the UC Faculty Senate, and the Institute for Social and Behavioral Research at the University of California, Santa Barbara. She is currently an associate professor of political science at UC Santa Barbara.

in loving memory of William Harry Bruhn

Urban Protest in Mexico and Brazil

KATHLEEN BRUHN
University of California, Santa Barbara

CAMBRIDGE
UNIVERSITY PRESS

CAMBRIDGE UNIVERSITY PRESS
Cambridge, New York, Melbourne, Madrid, Cape Town, Singapore, São Paulo, Delhi

Cambridge University Press
32 Avenue of the Americas, New York, NY 10013-2473, USA

www.cambridge.org
Information on this title: www.cambridge.org/9780521881296

First published 2008

Printed in the United States of America

A catalog record for this publication is available from the British Library.

Library of Congress Cataloging in Publication data

Bruhn, Kathleen, 1963–
Urban protest in Mexico and Brazil / Kathleen Bruhn.
p. cm
Includes bibliographical references (p.) and index.
ISBN 978-0-521-88129-6 (hardback)
1. Protest movements – Mexico – Mexico City – Case Studies. 2. Protest
movements – Brazil – São Paulo – Case Studies. 3. Municipal officials and
employees – Labor unions – Latin America – Political activity – Cross-cultural
studies. 4. Citizens' associations – Latin America – Cross-cultural studies.
5. Political parties – Mexico – Mexico City. 6. Political
parties – Brazil – São Paulo. 7. Mexico City (Mexico) – Politics and
government. 8. São Paulo (Brazil) – Politics and government. I. Title

HN120.M45B78 2008
303.48′40972 – dc22 2007030674

ISBN 978-0-521-88129-6 hardback

Contents

List of Tables

List of Figures

List of Abbreviations

AB	Asamblea de Barrios
AP	Antorcha Popular
ARENA	Aliança Renovadora Nacional
CEB	Comunidades Ecclesiais de Base
CGH	Consejo General de Huelga
CMP	Central de Movimentos Populares
CNBB	Conferencia Nacional dos Bispos de Brasil
CT	Congreso del Trabajo
CTM	Confederación de Trabajadores de México
FPFV	Frente Popular Francisco Villa
FSTSE	Federación de Sindicatos de Trabajadores al Servicio del Estado
MMC	Movimento de Moradia do Centro
MOCO	Sindicato dos Motoristas e Cobradores
MST	Movimento dos Trabalhadores Rurais Sem Terra
PCB	Partido Comunista Brasileiro
PCdoB	Partido Comunista do Brasil
PMDB	Partido do Movimento Democrático Brasileiro
POS	Political Opportunity Structures
PPB	Partido Popular Brasileiro
PRD	Partido de la Revolución Democrática
PRI	Partido Revolucionario Institucional
PT	Partido dos Trabalhadores
SINDSEP	Sindicato dos Servidores Públicos Municipais de São Paulo

SUTGDF	Sindicato Único de los Trabajadores del Gobierno del Distrito Federal
ULC	Unificação das Lutas de Cortiço
UMM	União de Movimentos de Moradia
UNT	Unión Nacional de Trabajadores

Acknowledgments

Like all books, this one could never have been written without the help of many people and multiple academic institutions. Portions of the research were funded by the Institute for Social and Behavioral Research, the UC Council on Research, and the UCSB Faculty Senate. During the initial writing phase, I was supported by a fellowship at the UCSD Center for Mexican Studies and a Kellogg Fellowship at the University of Notre Dame; UCSB also helped by making up the difference between the fellowship and my normal salary. In Mexico, Celia Toro and Soledad Loaeza at different times made it possible for me to have access to the library at El Colegio de Mexico. In Brazil, George Avelino at the Fundação Getûlio Vargas and Fernando Limongi of the Universidade de São Paulo and CEBRAP made it possible for me to get academic visas and were generous with their knowledge, their contacts, and their time, all without laughing once at my evolving Portuguese. I am deeply indebted to – and spent a great deal of time with – the professional archivists working at the National Autonomous University of Mexico's hemeroteca, the Biblioteca Nacional de México, the Arquivo do Estado de São Paulo, and the congressional hemeroteca of the Congresso Nacional de Brasil.

Several people tried very hard to keep me from making mistakes and to point me in the right direction. To all of them, I owe my thanks, but especially to Michael Coppedge, Wayne Cornelius, Cynthia Kaplan, Scott Mainwaring, Luis Hernandez Navarro, Sidney Tarrow,

Jeff Weldon, Chris Woodruff, the Fellows at the Center for U.S.–Mexican Studies and the Kellogg Institute, and the two anonymous reviewers for Cambridge University Press. I have seldom received such thorough, thoughtful, and constructive critiques, and I am sure the book is much better for their advice. Several graduate students also commented on portions of the book or project design or provided research assistance, including Joe Gardner, Richard Huizar, Stuart Kasdin, Russell Kellogg, April Rapp, and Patricia Rodriguez. None of these people can be held responsible for any errors that remain.

Indispensable to the project were the activists and organizers who shared their thoughts and experiences with me, allowed me to attend their meetings, and even invited me into their homes. I wish I could list them all by name, but I promised I wouldn't.

Finally, I want to thank those whose support and encouragement have made this journey not only bearable, but enjoyable. In particular, I want to extend a long-overdue thanks to Maria Celia Toro, for her steadfast friendship over these nearly twenty years since I first showed up in Mexico City to start my dissertation research. My thanks go also to the entire *familia* Navarro, who took me into their hearts and their home more than fifteen years ago, and especially to Doña Michelle, *mi mama mexicana*. Last but not least, I must recognize the unfaltering love, support, and encouragement of my mother, Charlotte Bruhn, and my father, Bill Bruhn. I was too slow: he saw the beginning of this book but not the ending. I dedicate this book to his memory.

Riding the Tiger

Popular Organizations, Political Parties, and Urban Protest

One who rides a tiger will find it hard to dismount.

Chinese proverb

Madero has unleashed a tiger! Let us see if he can control it!

Porfirio Díaz, ex-dictator of Mexico

On October 27, 2002, a man who first came to public notice when he led a major wave of protests against Brazil's military regime was chosen as its third democratically elected president. Luis Inácio da Silva, more familiarly known as "Lula," ran a campaign that downplayed his radical roots and his connections to some of Brazil's most militant and disruptive popular organizations. Beautifully produced and heart-wringing television ads depicted him as a man of the people, emphasizing his working-class background, his struggle for education, and his status as an outsider uncontaminated by the stigma of association with Brazil's often corrupt political class. He formed an electoral alliance with a conservative party, said he had learned to value moderation, and pledged not to renege on promises made to the International Monetary Fund (IMF) – promises he had strongly criticized in prior presidential campaigns. Downplayed were references to his militant unionist background, his long-standing support of socialist economic policies, and his role in the formation of Brazil's most powerful Leftist party, the Partido dos Trabalhadores (Workers' Party), or PT. He campaigned, in the pungent Brazilian expression, as "Lula Light."

Yet even as he tried to calm the fears of economic elites and international investors, his electoral success depended on harnessing opposition to their neoliberal economic program – much of it coming from organizations linked to his own party who repeatedly staged general strikes, demonstrations, and land seizures throughout 2001 and 2002. Elites expected him to rein in these protests while leaving previous economic agreements intact. The protesters warned that he could not expect unconditional support if he failed to implement real policy change. Yet his honeymoon was painfully short; in a matter of months, long before any positive changes could have been expected, the celebratory banners of his inauguration day were replaced by banners proclaiming him a traitor to the cause of the workers and peasants who elected him. This was due in part to his effort to pass a controversial pension reform plan that hurt public-sector unions within his political base. However, other groups seized upon his election as an opportunity to increase their demands. For example, the Landless Movement (Movimento dos Trabalhadores Rurais Sem Terra, or MST), a PT supporter, more than doubled its rate of land invasions in the first year of his administration (Comissão Pastoral da Terra, http://www.cptnac.com.br).

What factors best account for variation in the propensity to protest? Do organizations channel demands through state institutions when their partisan allies gain power? Do they increase their rate of protest when their political opponents assume power and the threat is greater? Does protest vary cyclically with budgetary or electoral cycles? Or do organizations decide whether to protest based on incentives coming primarily from within rather than changes in the political environment?

This book examines patterns of protest in two large cities, comparing the protest strategies of organizations without partisan alliances and organizations that at some point enjoyed special access to the government by virtue of a political alliance with a party in power. Much of the party literature has argued that parties with deep roots in civil society stabilize political systems. As organizations develop an alliance with a political party they become more likely to trust the party as an interlocutor. When the party wins power, they transfer this trust to the government. Therefore protests will not be necessary for the organization to achieve its goals. Moreover, protesting can be costly, not only to the organization that mounts the demonstration, but also to the ally in power. From this perspective, we should see organizations protest less when an ally takes office in order to avoid damaging the very ally they sought to have elected.

Conversely, when political parties unsympathetic to the interests of a social organization win power, their preferences threaten the interests of the organization and its members. Hard-won benefits may be lost unless protests and other pressure tactics can discourage the government from attacking existing privileges. Fears of harming the party in power would not constrain the organization, but instead encourage it to discredit the enemy and undermine its ability to govern. Consequently, the protest level should rise when one's political antagonists gain office.

An alternative view is that organizations may see their political allies as softer targets, already prone to support them and therefore more likely to respond to protest than an enemy. As the efficacy of protest increases, organization leaders gain prestige and power with their members for delivering the goods.

In each of these three scenarios, shifting political opportunities produce strategic shifts in behavior. But even though much of the political science literature focuses on political opportunities as the main incentive for protest, there may be other motivations. Sociological approaches often point more toward the nature of organizations in order to explain strategic choices. Protest as part of a tactical repertoire may become embedded in an organization's structure and political culture. In this case, the structural, cultural, and organizational characteristics internal to protesting groups may constrain their strategic flexibility.

Finally, there may be a temporal dimension to protest propensity that is generally overlooked in the scholarly work on long waves of social protest and demobilization. Specifically, to the extent that protest plays a role in setting the political agenda, influencing budgetary cycles, or framing electoral competition, it may be advantageous to protest more at some times during a given administration than at others.

This book builds on a large body of work on social movements and protest, but departs from most previous work in three ways: (1) in its explicit focus on the intersection between movements, the state, and political parties; (2) in its systematic and quantitative analysis of urban protest by a wide variety of organization types; and (3) in its focus on protest in the context of new democracies rather than the advanced industrial democracies, which have claimed the attention of the majority of researchers up to this point.

Most work on protest has focused on either the micro-level (individual behavior or individual social movements) or the macro-level (aggregate changes in protest over time). The first approach focuses on individual participation, using survey data to predict the likelihood that a given individual will take part in protest (e.g., Opp, 1988; Lewis-Beck and Lockerbie, 1989; Sussman and Steel, 1991; Norris, Walgrave, and Van Aels, 2005). These analyses have provided us with rich evidence about the elements that lead individuals to participate in collective action. They tell us much less about how organizations make tactical decisions regarding whether and when to call for protest. Yet this decision by organization leaders is usually what triggers individual participation in protest: you have to be asked.

Case studies of individual social movements focus on the decision to protest, as well as the question of how movements use symbolic and material resources to mobilize support from members. The majority of works in this tradition are concerned with social movement emergence; however, strategies of rhetorical framing, selective payoffs, repertoires of action, identity formation, and so forth have implications for the role of protest in movement reproduction. The challenge for this approach lies in how to draw generalizable conclusions out of the particularities of a handful of cases. Individual case studies do a better job of developing the (long) list of factors that facilitate mobilization than of determining their respective weight.

Finally, cross-national statistical analyses isolate aspects of the institutional context that can have systematic effects. For example, research on protest cycles pays less attention to the calculations of individual movements than to the factors that may create or deny opportunities to many movements at the same time (e.g., Tilly, Tilly, and Tilly, 1975; Francisco, 1996; Moore, 1998). However, this kind of analysis is not well-suited to uncover the factors, such as party alliance, that differentially affect specific movements in the same institutional context.

This book does not attempt to explain individual decisions to participate in protest, or – except in general terms – cross-national variation in protest patterns. It focuses on individual organizations, but not exclusively or even primarily through the lens of in-depth case studies. The core of the book is an extensive and original dataset of protest in two Latin American cities, with a sample from a third for comparative purposes. The two primary cities – São Paulo and Mexico City – are two of the largest cities in the world. Each experienced two periods of Left municipal government, which are contrasted with data from two non-Left municipal governments. For each city, I coded newspaper accounts of protests from two major daily newspapers according to type of protest, target, sponsoring organization, demands, location, and attendance (if available). The Mexico City database contains entries for 4,501 events over a twelve-year period and 846 separate organizations. The São Paulo database contains entries for 2,485 events over a fifteen-year period and 481 organizations. Because I include every identifiable protest, the analysis does not single out any one type of organization. Instead, I compare the protest behavior of different types of organizations and find interesting systematic differences.

Finally, I use information about specific organizations to identify their party alliance characteristics and conduct quantitative analysis of the impact of party alliance on protest, both when the ally was in and out of power. In singling out this aspect of the political context, I fall short of specifying the full range of factors that shape the political opportunity structure (POS), defined as "consistent – but not necessarily formal, permanent or national – dimensions of the political environment which either encourage or discourage people from using collective action." (Tarrow, 1994: 18) Originally attributed to Eisinger (1973), the current usage reflects the definition of Sidney Tarrow (1983, 1989a). Tarrow (1989a: 34–35) singles out four general aspects of the POS: (1) the "extent to which formal political institutions are open or closed to participation by groups on the margins of the polity"; (2) the "stability or instability of political alignments ... [including] changes in the parties' electoral strength"; (3) the "presence or absence of influential allies"; and (4) "political conflicts within and among elites."

However, POS "threatens to become an all-encompassing fudge factor for all the conditions and circumstances that form the context for collective action. Used to explain so much, it may ultimately explain nothing at all" (Gamson and Meyer, 1996: 275). Only by isolating specific aspects of the POS and engaging in explicitly comparative work can we begin to uncover their relative causal significance.[1]

Parties are a key component of the political opportunity structure. They can provide individual organizations with symbolic and material resources and offer access to policy-making bodies. They may attempt to co-opt, repress, or demobilize movements and thus affect the costs of protest. Yet parties have been under-studied as they relate to protest and strategic decision making by social organizations. The literature on parties tends to focus on formal behavior, like campaigns and legislative action, while the literature on popular movements tends to focus on informal and unconventional activity. As a result, the intersection between these two worlds is too seldom explored despite the reality – increasingly acknowledged – that "there is only a fuzzy and permeable boundary between institutionalized and non-institutionalized politics" (Goldstone, 2003: 2). Many organizations use both conventional institutional channels and unconventional and noninstitutional tactics to achieve their goals. My central question is what factors incline them toward one tactic versus another.

This book makes three major claims, all provisional but highly suggestive:

1. The internal structures and political culture of social movement organizations significantly shape protest behavior, and constrain the ability of organizations to respond rapidly to changes in political opportunity. Protest can be a key part of organizational maintenance and survival. Because of these organizational motivations, the election of one's partisan ally does not necessarily reduce protest.

2. Nevertheless, continuity is not immobility. Organizations do respond to changes in the political context, even if these factors are not the most important ones driving protest behavior. In particular, governmental cycles matter. In the first year of a new

---

[1] I was inspired to try this approach by McAdam, who suggests that researchers, "recognize that a number of factors and processes facilitate mobilization and resolve to try to define and operationalize them so as to maintain their analytic distinctiveness. Only by doing so can we ever hope to determine their relative importance to the emergence and development of collective action" (McAdam, 1996: 26).

government, organizations have particularly strong incentives to protest in order to establish their priority order in the policy agenda. Allies, in fact, may be seen as particularly soft targets, more likely to respond positively to protest than opponents.

3. Not all organizations respond in the same way to changing political opportunities. We need to know their resources, political culture, and level of institutionalization to understand how different kinds of organizations are likely to react.

The findings of this study have important practical as well as theoretical implications. Protest can bring down governments, result in major policy change, or handicap the economy by scaring investors. Protest can clarify the meaning of a broad electoral mandate by supplying specific issue items about which people feel most strongly, or place on the political agenda the demands of intense minorities. More generally, the analysis of protest behavior over time can address broader theoretical questions about the limits of strategic flexibility in social organizations.

THEORETICAL FRAMEWORK

The complexity of protest makes it difficult to study effectively. The number of variables and levels of analysis that can affect protest generates many possible combinations. Consistent findings based on individual cases or even small samples can therefore be elusive. The problem is complicated by the difficulty of obtaining reliable information about protest – often, only a semilegal activity. And finally, this project focuses on the intersection of three large literatures: the literature on political parties/party systems, on protest/contentious political action, and on social movements in general. With some stellar exceptions (e.g., Burstein, 1985; Tarrow, 1989b; 1994; Costain, 1992; Jenkins and Klandermans, 1995; Andrews 1997; 2001; McAdam and Su, 2002), these literatures often fail to talk to one another; as one author notes, "neither the relationship between movements and parties nor their joint impact on policy has been studied very much. Disciplinary boundaries are partly to blame: sociologists primarily concerned with social movements pay little attention to political parties, and political scientists studying parties seldom devote much effort to examining movements" (Burstein et al., 1995: 289). The fragmentation of scholarship as well as the complexity of protest has generated a fairly messy and contradictory set of findings about the underlying causes of variation in protest behavior.

Resource Mobilization and Identity

The first set of hypotheses comes from sociological traditions that view movement tactics as reflecting its set of resources, both material and nonmaterial. Most basically, "the greater the resources of groups, the more they will employ 'insider tactics' (e.g., lobbying, litigating); the fewer the resources commanded by such groups the more they will use 'outsider' tactics (e.g., demonstrating)" (McCarthy et al., 1996: 305). Protest is the weapon of resource-poor groups that lack regular access to government officials and have few other methods for influencing policy (see also Piven and Cloward, 1977; Walker, 1991). Many scholars of social movements interpret protest as a sign of movement health. The decline of protest signals a transition from social movement status to mere (boring) institutions. Indeed, the very conceptualization of social movements as,

outsiders … [who] seek to represent a constituency not previously mobilized to participate in politics … create[s] an ironic problem for those who analyze movement outcomes. Both [Tilly and Gamson] suggest that once a movement begins to succeed – by mobilizing its constituency or gaining formal representation – it ceases to be a movement, even if its goals, membership, and tactics do not change. (Burstein et al., 1995: 277)

Thus, "a true movement organization must continue to emphasize movement over organization or risk losing the initiative to more institutionalized groups" (Tarrow, 1989b: 274). Even a temporary reduction of protest at the behest of a party ally might permanently discredit the movement, reduce its future mobilizational capacity, and eventually result in its extinction, a sociological version of the "use it or lose it" rule.

Specific tactics may also follow from the organizational form and resource configuration of a movement. When unions decide to protest, for instance, they are more likely to strike than to block a street because their primary leverage comes from their ability to disrupt the workplace. However, this was not always the case. In Tilly's fascinating discussion of the "invention of the strike," he mentions increasing concentration of workers in large shops as well as residential segregation and changing views of the role of workers as among those factors affecting the propensity to adopt strikes as a form of collective action (1978: 159–166). More generally, he notes, "unquestionably, the type of organization of interest...affects the *type* of collective action of which a contender is capable; in many circumstances it affects the quantity of collective action as well" (Tilly, 1978: 58–59).

Beyond the initial linkage between resources and types of action, organizations "learn" how to perform specific tactics. They get good at that tactic. When a new cause of discontent arises, they fall back on what they know how to do. Thus, protest repertoires become fairly sticky characteristics of movement organizations. Previous mobilization also leaves lasting traces. Compared to equally poor and powerless groups, organizations that have successfully mobilized once are more likely to act collectively again, to claim new rights, or to defend against new threats (Tilly, 1978: 75–76).

Finally, mobilization may become intertwined with identity. New social movement theory places great emphasis on identity (and solidarity based on a common identity) as an important nonmaterial resource sustaining collective action. Even though most new social movement theory refers to identity in terms of established social categories such as women or ethnic groups, identity is at least in part a social construction resulting from mobilization itself. Thus, protest repertoire may overlap with protest culture and group identity. Essentially, "The answer to 'who are we?' need not be a quality or a noun; 'We are people who do these sorts of things in this particular way' can be equally compelling" (Clemens, 1996: 211).

It may be difficult for such groups to stop protesting without jeopardizing that sense of common identity. For example, some Salvadoran unions born in the context of a civil war had trouble adapting to peace: "although labor leaders recognized that these old institutions had served their purpose and should be discarded or radically altered, to date they have not been able to create new labor forces that can meet the challenges of participating in a democratizing postwar society" (Fitzsimmons and Anner, 1999: 117). From this point of view, protest tactics are not infinitely flexible. Thus, one would expect considerable continuity over time in levels, tactics, and targets of protest regardless of fluctuations in external conditions.

> Hypothesis 1: The propensity to protest reflects endur- ing organizational and sociological characteristics of movements themselves, including type of resources and internal structures.
>
> Hypothesis 2: The propensity to protest reflects previ- ous experience with protest, which builds resources/ skills and shapes movement identity.

Political Opportunity Structures and the Impact of Parties

Much of the early literature on protest saw it as a symptom of a dysfunctional political system, for which political parties were the cure. In particular, parties with deep roots in civil society, allied to mass organizations, tended to inhibit protest and stabilize political systems. One of the first formulations came from scholars working within the modernization theory paradigm. The structural–functionalist view (e.g., Almond, 1960; Smelser, 1963) described the role of parties as reconciling the interests of many groups through the creation of a program that aggregated and prioritized demands. By successfully channeling demands through institutional channels and providing access to policy making, parties offered a viable alternative to protest. While the absence of protest might have many causes (such as the difficulty of organizing collective action or the costs of repression), the *presence* of protest indicated the failure of formal political structures to perform these aggregative and expressive functions. The very def- inition of protest often incorporates this notion, that protest is "used by people who lack regular access to institutions" (Tarrow, 1994: 2).

Huntington (1968) further highlighted parties as the solution to the social dislocations created by modernization in the developing world. Essentially, Huntington saw violence and instability as the result of a gap between rapid socioeconomic modernization and slow political modernization. The challenge was to construct political institutions that could absorb the rising participation produced by modernization. Huntington assigned this role principally to parties. Thus, "violence, rioting and other forms of political instability are more likely to occur in political systems without strong parties than in systems with them" (Huntington, 1968: 398, 409).

This hypothesis has been challenged by later work; nevertheless, much of the contemporary literature on democratic consolidation implicitly or explicitly makes very similar arguments about the effects of a well-institutionalized and socially rooted party system on protest and democracy-threatening disorder: that such parties "help groups express their interests while allowing governments to govern. ... [Institutionalized parties] channel political demands and can dampen political conflicts" (Mainwaring and Scully, 1995a: 23). Hence, "institutionalizing a party system is important to the process of democratic consolidation" (Mainwaring and Scully, 1995a: 1).

Parties have the most significant impact on protest if they command the loyalties and influence the decision making of organizations in civil society. Parties seek alliances with such organizations primarily for electoral support. Thus, systems with well-developed linkages between parties and organized interests should also have high levels of party loyalty and lower electoral volatility. In new democracies, the creation of linkages between existing organizations and emerging political parties can bolster the process of partisan identity formation – extending existing loyalties to new political institutions and stabilizing patterns of electoral competition. As a result, "the strength of the affective attachment to the party of members and supporters ... is likely to be strongest where the political party is identified with a broader social movement" (Randall and Svåsand, 2001: 88).

If strong party ties inhibit protest, the converse may also be true: weakly rooted parties encourage and/or permit it. Studies of post-1990s Venezuela, for example, link rising protest to a "vacuum of effective channels of communication between society and State that has been produced as a result of the de-legitimation and de-institutionalization of the establishment parties." (López Maya, 2002: 2) This theory parallels the arguments made by scholars of politics in the advanced industrial democracies who explain declining participation in electoral politics as being correlated with "the shift in overall political involvement toward ... unconventional forms of participation, such as petitions, protests and demonstrations" (Dalton, McAllister, and Wattenberg, 2000: 61).

**Hypothesis 3: Independent organizations are more likely
to protest than organizations allied to political parties.**

Nevertheless, an important subset of the literature on parties points
to the role that parties may play in generating protest. Indeed, the
creation and maintenance of "socially rooted parties" suited to inhibit
protest in general may require party support for protest at times, in
order to gain the trust and support of protesting organizations. As
Williams notes in the case of India (2001: 618), the "core task of
'crafting well-organized parties' emerges as a potentially disruptive
activity." If these arguments are correct, then hypothesis 3 will be
falsified.

The key to the *positive* association between parties and protest lies
in their organizational networks. In pursuing electoral support, parties seek connections to social groups, offering their own resources
and organizational networks as incentives. Particularly among social
groups that face strong barriers to collective action, like the poor,
parties may be the principal agents of organization. For example,
Schneider (1995: 156) notes the key role played by activists from the
Communist Party in organizing Chile's urban slums after the 1973
coup forced the party underground. As a result, "the neighborhoods
that were most active during the 1983–1986 protest cycle were those
most closely linked, historically, to the Chilean Communist Party."
The Chilean case is far from unique. All over Latin America, Left-
leaning parties endured periods of repression under the military dic-
tatorships of the 1970s and shifted their organizing efforts from
electoral to nonelectoral arenas (e.g., Dietz, 1998; Oxhorn, 1995). The
popular organizations they helped create played a key role in struggles
to redemocratize.

Another cause of party-led protest is competition with organizations seeking to mobilize a similar base. Tarrow's work finds clear
evidence of the importance of parties in generating cycles of protest.
Indeed, "a protest cycle begins with conventional patterns of conflict
within existing organizations and institutions" and then expands
through a competitive dynamic to include new groups, new demands,
and new tactics (Tarrow, 1989b: 8). In the early stages, parties and
their associated groups account for most protest; the weight of unorganized citizens and new movement organizations outside parties only

increases later. Thus, "the function of organization ... was not to smother and routinize protest but to reproduce it and make it a more effective weapon"[2] (Tarrow, 1989b: 222).

However, the tendency for party alliance to encourage protest may depend on whether or not the party is in power. Parties may be especially prone to encourage protest when they are not its target – that is, when they are in the opposition and seeking to mobilize a constituency to win the next election (Kriesi, 1995; Wallace and Jenkins, 1995). Similarly, the presence of party allies in the government should make it possible for organizations to achieve their substantive goals without incurring the costs of protest. Rational actors should not protest unless they think it makes a difference in the likelihood of achieving their goals. If they can achieve their goals without protest, through partisan access to government, they should avoid incurring the costs of protest (Finkel and Muller, 1998). Kriesi (1995), for example, suggests that Left electoral victory should most affect movements allied to the Left party. They no longer have their ally's support for protest, *and* they no longer need to protest to get what they want. Similarly, Robertson's recent work on labor unions (2004: 270) argues that "when allied parties are in power, alliances tend to have a moderating effect on the level of mobilization. The contrary tendency is observed when allied parties are in opposition. Consequently, where parties and unions are closely linked, the partisan political conjuncture is crucial in explaining the level and nature of labor mobilization."

Hirschman sums up these incentives as the calculations of exit, voice, and loyalty. Hirschman posits exit and voice as alternative ways for members of an organization to inform management about performance failures. Members exercise the exit option when they leave the organization (or stop buying the firm's products). Voice is defined as "any attempt at all to change, rather than to escape from, an objectionable state of affairs ... through various types of actions and protests, including those that are meant to mobilize public opinion" (Hirschman, 1970: 30).

---

[2] Similarly, Rucht's (1998: 42) analysis of postwar Germany finds that political parties played a growing role in the sponsorship of protest, which he notes "cannot be attributed to 'movement parties' such as ... the Greens."

Exit and voice are not equally available in all circumstances. Voice is a messier and potentially more costly option "because it can be graduated, all the way from a faint grumbling to violent protest" (Hirschman, 1970: 16), Hirschman views voice as a residual option, used "whenever the exit option is unavailable." Since citizens cannot literally exit the control of the state, the realm of politics is inevitably the realm of voice. Nevertheless, exit does play a role in protest calculations. For one thing, the limits on exit apply more to states than to organizations within states such as voluntary associations or political parties. Leaders must remember that if they ask members to engage in costly activities, especially if they do not achieve results, members can exit, falling into inactivity or joining competing organizations. What determines whether members will accept the costs of protest?

In general, four factors play a role: the benefits of protest, the likelihood of successful protest, the costs of protest, and, Hirschman's final concept, loyalty. These factors point toward a scenario in which the expected utility of protest declines when an organization is allied to the party in power. The likelihood of success increases, as one's partner is more likely to listen, but if benefits can be obtained from the government without incurring the costs of protest, then less costly versions of voice (the "faint grumbling" to contacts in the government) should be preferred.

In addition, to the extent that organizations feel loyalty to a party ally, they may be inclined to cut it some slack. Voice can alert the government to one's demands, but "it must then give management, old or new, some time to respond to the pressures that have been brought to bear" (Hirschman, 1970: 33). Otherwise, "discontented customers or members could become so harassing that their protests would at some point hinder rather than help whatever efforts at recovery are undertaken" (Hirschman, 1970: 31). Loyalty functions to delay excessive voice just as it acts to delay exit. Loyalty may also affect organization leaders more than members. Hirschman notes that, in some cases, members care about the deterioration of an organization even after they leave, either because its deterioration has consequences that continue to affect them or because they believe that their departure contributed to its deterioration, as for example when they are particularly influential members. To the extent that the leaders of popular organizations see their personal futures tied up in the fate of the PT or PRD, then, they should be less willing to damage the party's electoral prospects by protesting against its policies.

Nevertheless, this picture of parties and movements working in tandem conceals underlying contradictions. For one thing, the *need* for protest may decline when one's ally is in power, but if the prospect of success affects calculations about whether to protest, an ally might be a better target than an opponent. Being in the opposition "reduces the possibility for the movement to have any effect on government policy" (Klandermans, Roefs, and Olivier, 1998: 174). Moreover, the election of an ally may "encourage unrepresented groups to protest in the belief that the costs of insurgency have been lowered – as when a sympathetic political party comes to power and makes clear that it will not support repression" (Tarrow, 1989a: 36).

Second, parties have many allies whose interests and demands they must balance. Hence, it is not necessarily true that organizations can expect to achieve their goals as a matter of course without putting pressure on their party ally to be first in line. Especially if the organization thinks that protest against the ally is likely to succeed, protest might even increase against allies. Hypothesis 4 thus proposes two possible contradictory scenarios, both dependent on whether a party ally is in power.

> **Hypothesis 4: Organizations will decrease protest against a party ally in power. OR, Organizations will increase protest against a party ally in power.**

Finally, the potential benefits of protest may vary according to a regular schedule that creates "windows of opportunity." Examples of such windows of opportunity include the prospect of an upcoming election, the annual discussion of the budget, or the expiration of a work contract. Kingdon's (1995) work on agendas and public policy in the United States suggests that "the first year of a new administration is clearly the prime time for preoccupation with the subject of change ... people all over town hold their breath in anticipation, waiting to see what the new administration's priorities will be." For an organization, letting this moment slip by without attempting to influence the administration's priorities can be costly. Because of the "scarcity of open windows ... participants ... compete for limited

TABLE 1.1. *Main Independent Variables*

Resource Mobilization/ Organizational Resources	Hypothesis
Type of resources	1
Institutionalization	1
Leadership competition	1
Identity	
Past history of protest	2
Positive view of protest	2
Independent of parties	3
POS	
Allied to party in power	4
Electoral cycle effects	5
Economic grievance	

space on agendas and queue up for their turn" (Kingdon, 1995: 154, 204). Thus, there may be particular moments when a general desire not to hurt your party ally is outweighed by the prospect of a time-limited window of opportunity.

> **Hypothesis 5: The propensity to protest varies systematically over the course of an administration.**

A Summary of Variables

These hypotheses generate a series of independent variables, which succeeding chapters will explain and operationalize more fully. Each is linked loosely to a major school of thought and more clearly to a hypothesis. The alert reader will note the addition of "leadership competition" as a variable; though connected to the idea that internal structures matter, this particular variable derives primarily from the work of Murillo (2001) and Burgess (2004) on labor unions, which I discuss further in Chapter 4. I also include economic grievance here as a traditional control variable (see Table 1.1).

RESEARCH DESIGN

I test these hypotheses in the context of two developing-country cases – Mexico and Brazil – in the hope of expanding the analysis of protest beyond the advanced industrial democracies. Mexico and Brazil both belong in the group of Third Wave democracies, a category that has expanded dramatically since the late 1970s. Most of the Latin American transitions to democracy took place during the 1980s, as did many of the Asian transitions (e.g., South Korea and Taiwan). Democratic transitions in Eastern Europe and the former Soviet Union followed in the late 1980s and early 1990s. A more tentative but still significant wave of democratization reached Africa in the mid-1990s. Brazil is among the older Third Wave democracies. It can boast of more than twenty years of formal democracy and two alternations in power at the national level. Mexico is one of the newer Third Wave democracies. Although its transition was unusually drawn out and has been dated as early as 1994, most analysts date its conclusion to 2000, the year of the first alternation in power at the national level.

Nevertheless, the quality of democracy in Mexico and Brazil – as in many Third Wave democracies – remains questionable. Brazil spent most of the 1990s as a "Partly Free" country. Mexico, despite its advances, remained on the verge of the "Partly Free" category in 2005, with a ranking of 2.5.[3] Though it improved to a "2" in 2006, its contested 2006 presidential election and subsequent confrontational protests renewed concerns about the commitment to democracy of at least some major political actors, principally on the Left. Moreover, as in many of the new democracies, public support for democracy and democratic values has remained soft in Mexico and Brazil and may be vulnerable to performance failures. In 1997, just 57.5 percent of Brazilians and 52.9 percent of Mexicans expressed unequivocal support for democracy according to Latinobarometer surveys, below the Latin American average of 65 percent and well below comparable rankings of "democratic legitimacy" in Western Europe (Montero, Gunther, and Torcal, 1997: 8; Canache, 2002: 67, 69). Further, 12 percent of Mexicans and nearly 20 percent of Brazilians felt that it would be good to have a "strong leader who does not have to bother with parliament and elections" (Canache,

---

[3] Countries with a score of 1–2.5 are classified as "Free" according to Freedom House. Countries with a score between 3 and 5 are classified as "Partly Free." Countries with a score between 5.5 and 7 are classified as "Not Free." This represents a change as of 2003; previously, scores between 1 and 3 were classified as Free.

2002: 67, 69). By 2000, support for democracy had fallen below 40 percent in Brazil and below 50 percent in Mexico (Encarnación, 2003: 182, from Latinobarometer polls).

The choice of Mexico and Brazil also maximizes variation in society–party linkages. The main Mexican Left party, the Party of the Democratic Revolution (Partido de la Revolución Democrática, or PRD), has relatively few ties to unions or social movements outside of a few regions. The old ruling party, the Institutional Revolutionary Party (Partido Revolucionario Institucional, or PRI), captured these organizations in the 1930s and has controlled them ever since. In Brazil, most parties are weak with few ties to civil society. The exception, however, is interesting: the Leftist PT was created by unions and social movements and maintains some of the strongest formal ties to organized society of any Leftist party in Latin America. Thus, these two countries allow us to separate, at least to some extent, the impact of Leftist ideology from the impact of party alliance. The PT and PRD share many ideological premises but few alliance characteristics. In Mexico, an organizationally disconnected Left competed against an organizationally embedded centrist party (at the time of my study, pro-neoliberal). In Brazil, an organizationally disconnected set of centrist and conservative parties competed against an organizationally embedded Left.

However, the data requirements for testing these hypotheses are substantial: reasonably complete and reliable data on protests (and the absence of protests), by organization name, and with information about the partisan alliances of specific organizations. Thus, instead of attempting an analysis of protest on the national level, I focused on urban politics in two major cities, Mexico City and São Paulo, each the center of multiple media outlets that report on protest. I collected data on protests in each city over the course of two Leftist and two non-Leftist governments. In addition, I sampled protest patterns for four years in the Brazilian capital, Brasilia, to make sure that any differences between São Paulo and Mexico City could not be attributed simply to the fact that the former is not the capital city. In all, I cover ten administrations, five Leftist and five non-Leftist governments.

STRUCTURE OF THE BOOK

The quantitative portion of the book analyzes this protest dataset. By recording events according to individual sponsors, I was able to conduct statistical tests of the relationship between protest rates, organizational characteristics, and several aspects of the POS. Chapter 2 sets the stage for this analysis by describing the cities where data were gathered, the methods used to code events, and aggregate patterns of protest. Chapter 3 presents the statistical analysis of this data. Chapters 4 and 5 present two case studies of municipal employee unions in São Paulo (Chapter 4) and Mexico City (Chapter 5). Using interviews, internal union documents, and supplementary quantitative analysis of union protest, I trace the process by which decisions to protest were made and then discuss the reasons given by the union leaders who make such tactical choices. Chapters 6 and 7 extend the case study analysis to urban popular movements and draw conclusions about differences between the protest behavior of unions and urban popular movements. Chapter 8 places my findings in context of other cases and presents my overall conclusions.

2

Setting the Stage

Research Design, Case Selection, and Methods

This chapter establishes the empirical and historical context in which protest data were collected and describes the methods used to collect it. It also provides a first-order analysis of aggregate patterns of protest. Preliminary findings suggest that organization type, party alliance, and electoral cycles all matter for protest strategies.

MUNICIPAL GOVERNMENTS AND PROTEST

In order to test the theoretical hypotheses proposed in Chapter 1, the data must meet several criteria: (1) cover an adequate number and variety of organizations (to measure the impact of organizational type); (2) include a variety of organizational alliances, as well as organizations not allied to political parties; (3) cover periods of at least one alternation in power (to measure the impact of party allies in and out of power); and (4) cover these organizations across a sufficient span of time to determine whether behavior changes according to cyclical patterns (to measure whether electoral, budgetary, or administrative cycles matter).

The choice to focus on municipal governments addresses these criteria admirably. The particular municipal governments I examine administered large urban areas. I do not mean to suggest that rural protest is unimportant; indeed, movements like the Landless Movement (MST) in Brazil and the *zapatistas* in Mexico have had a significant impact on their respective nations' politics. Nevertheless, large urban areas tend to produce a wider variety of organization types and party alliance choices, permitting maximum variation on two key independent variables. These areas also offer the pragmatic advantage of multiple local media covering protest. Media sources closest to the location of protests are more likely to cover protest patterns reliably over time.

Municipal governments are also significantly more likely than national governments to have experienced multiple periods of alternation in power, and in particular to have experienced rule by Left parties. Before Left parties began to win power at the national level in Latin America, they prepared the way by capturing important municipal and state-level governments. In a context where Left parties had to overcome the legacy of prolonged periods of repression and illegality during military rule or other authoritarian governments, these local government experiences provided important tests of their credibility. On the one hand, Left parties were challenged to prove that they would follow the rules and accept the constraints of the democratic process despite their previous rejection of electoral democracy as a bourgeois trap. They had to dispel popular images of the Left as violent, disorderly, and dangerous – images that mass protests tend to confirm. On the other hand, they could not simply accept the status quo. The status quo in Latin America means high levels of inequality, poverty, unemployment, discrimination, and powerlessness for their core constituents. Betrayed repeatedly, these constituents distrusted politics and politicians. The willingness of Leftist leaders to risk their lives directing protests against authoritarian governments was the source of much of their moral authority and trust among such alienated audiences.

Left parties in government therefore found themselves in a difficult position with respect to how to handle protest. Continued mobilization by Left-allied organizations might jeopardize the willingness of conservative opponents to allow the Left to participate in the political process and negatively affect the Left's reputation for governmental effectiveness. But ending mobilization might distance leaders from their popular base. More broadly, "it was the most obvious risk of the leftist strategy that in order to gain respectability and legitimacy, it would have to go too far in compromising its agenda for change, which in the end would make it indistinguishable from other political forces."[1]

Leftist parties could most safely learn to handle this balance between following and breaking the rules in local government, where the stakes were reduced. Most significantly, local governments do not have to manage macroeconomic policy and therefore run a lower risk of conflict with the fundamental interests of national and international economic elites. Elites could accept local Left victories (however grudgingly), while the expectations of Left voters were reduced to more manageable levels by the limited capacity of local government.

As a consequence, it is at the local level where we find the best opportunity to conduct systematic comparisons of how organizations react to different parties in power. Indeed, the local level may provide a better window than the national level. Some organizations do focus on national policy (regime change, labor law, or trade), but many if not most popular organizations are concerned with issues of primarily local significance, like the extension of water service to a poor neighborhood or working conditions in a local factory. Left victories at the national level may not affect the mobilization strategies of these organizations because their demands are directed at a different level of government. In my datasets – which include two national capitals – protests directed at the federal or state government outnumbered protests directed at the local government in only one case (Mexico City), and even here, the balance is quite close: protests targeting local government accounted for 37.7 percent of all protests versus 43.5 percent targeting the federal government.

However, in collecting data, I made an effort to include all protests, not just those targeting the local government. In the first place, whether or not a given protest targets the local government, it may test the capacity of local government. Citizens often care more about the traffic disruptions caused by protest than about whose fault the protest is. Where the protest involves allies of the local party in power, it may raise questions about the government's ability to manage its allies. In the second place, if movements are reluctant to target their

---

[1] In this quote, Schönwälder (2002: 116) is referring specifically to the risks of the demobilization strategy pursued by Alfonso Barrantes as the new Leftist mayor of Lima.

own allies but have other reasons to continue mobilization, target switching – changing targets to a level of government where one's ally is *not* in power – could provide a solution. Thus, I counted all protests taking place, regardless of target.

DATA COLLECTION

The basic method is event coding of newspaper reports. A more complete account of my methodology can be found in the Appendix. However, a general discussion of the approach will be useful to the reader in understanding the genesis and limitations of the information presented.

Event data based on newspaper reports have some problematic characteristics. For one thing, media agendas do not match the scholar's need for accurate, unbiased, and complete records. Protests that fit the news cycle have a better chance of coverage than events that take place at an inconvenient time, for example. Some kinds of protest attract more attention than others, particularly large, violent, or visually provocative protests. And newspapers may have a political bias that affects the events they report and how they report them. Media preferences may thus introduce bias into the database. For this reason, some scholars (e.g., Oliver and Maney, 2000) suggest that government records of protest permits and police records of marches provide more accurate statistics. However, in authoritarian governments or transitional democracies such as Brazil and Mexico, government statistics cannot be obtained, are recorded irregularly over time, and/ or are falsified. Protesting groups may avoid registering for permits out of fear of repression, and police forces are notoriously corrupt.

In part for such pragmatic reasons, using newspapers has become a common way to study protest (e.g., Tilly, Tilly, and Tilly, 1975; Tarrow, 1989b). Koopmans argues that newspapers,

> have distinct advantages over these sources [such as police reports, and movement archives]. They report a large number of news events on a regular day-to-day basis, and because they are in competition with each other and need to maintain their credibility as reliable news sources, they – or at least those "quality" papers with an educated readership – are obliged to cover important events with some degree of accuracy. (1999: 3)

Finally, media attention is not an accidental byproduct of movement attempts to influence government. Rather, movements deliberately try to attract media attention as a central tactical goal, in order to enlist public opinion in their favor. Newspapers may favor covering larger, more disruptive events, but savvy movements are aware of this and do their best to design protests that meet the requirements for media attention, either by increasing their size, using disruptive violence, or making the protest picture-worthy.[2] Movements that succeed in this objective arguably constitute a more accurate sample of important and influential movements than the universe of those who register a permit with the police. My use of local newspapers, rather than newspapers based in other cities or international media, should minimize the risk of biasing the sample too strongly in the direction of the most disruptive protests.

To limit the potential effects of political bias, I used two newspapers for each city, chosen for overall quality, coverage of local events, and distinct editorial perspectives.[3] I used every newspaper day rather than a sample.[4] To identify a protest, I looked for events that were: (1) public, (2) collective (i.e., not disgruntled individuals), (3) intentional, (4) disruptive, and (5) targeted.[5] The target could be another movement, a school board, or a private business as well as the

---

[2] For example, to gain the roving eye of photographers, organizations often use public nudity, dress up in costumes, or give away products (like chicken or fruit) to attract a crowd.

[3] In Mexico City, I used *La Jornada*, *Reforma* (from its foundation in 1994 through 2003), and El Financiero (from 1992 through 1994). In São Paulo, I used O Estado de São Paulo and Folha de São Paulo. In Brasilia, I used Correio Brasiliense and Jornal de Brasilia. Overlap was greatest in Brazil (30 percent of events were reported by both papers in São Paulo and Brasilia) and lower in Mexico (20 percent of events were reported by both papers). Most of the difference reflects the unusual attention of *La Jornada* to protest in Mexico City. It reported over 70 percent of all events recorded in the Mexico dataset. No other paper reported more than 60 percent.

[4] Sampling is recommended by Oliver and Maney (2000) and Rucht, Koopmans, and Neidhardt (1999). However, I felt that it is difficult to apply where the distribution of protest over time is unknown (i.e., no previous studies have been done). Moreover, in both Mexico and Brazil, labor protests peak around the time of contract negotiations – set at the federal level for all unions. Each union has an annual contract negotiation date different from the others. Thus, the distribution is unlikely to be regular over time and a random sample might well underestimate the extent of union protest.

[5] My definition is consistent with definitions in the literature: for example, "a collective public action by a non-governmental actor who expresses criticism or dissent and articulates a societal or political demand" (Rucht and Neidhardt, 1999: 68).

government, but the protest had to single out some entity as being responsible for taking action. The criteria of intentionality did not eliminate spontaneous actions but did restrict events to those where the protesters intended to protest. And finally, disruptiveness indicates an attempt to alter some aspect of normal operations (traffic, production, service delivery, etc.).[6] This criterion eliminated petitions as a category – a useful result in the end since newspapers do an especially bad job of reporting petitions. Last but not least, I excluded electoral rallies even though critiques of government often came up. Elections occur on a regular basis and parties have little choice about whether to hold them, no matter who is in power. Including these events would therefore exaggerate the role of political parties in protest and fluctuate more with the electoral calendar than with the strategic factors in which I am interested.

After identifying events, I coded each event according to the targets, sponsors, location, tactics, and demands (see the Appendix for a sample coding sheet). Following Rucht and Neidhardt (1999), I allowed up to two targets, two tactics, three sponsor types, and three demands per event.[7] However, the vast majority of all recorded events had only one type in each coded category.[8]

THE EMPIRICAL CONTEXT: MEXICO, SÃO PAULO, AND BRASILIA

Given the large number of potentially important differences in institutional and economic context that can affect protest, I center my

---

[6] This criterion also has an intellectual pedigree: Tarrow (among others) notes that "The main resource of protesters is ... their determination to disrupt the lives of others and the routines of institutions" (1989a: 3).

[7] Rucht and Neidhardt (1999: 68) base their decision on the logic that "an event has a beginning and an end. We regard as an event only a distinct action undertaken by the same group of actors for the same specific purpose over a continuous period of time." A single protest event that involves both a march and a street blockage should not be counted as two events since it is the same group of actors, the same time, the same location, and for the same purpose. Rather, it is preferable to code two tactics per event.

[8] The average number of tactics, targets, sponsor types, and demands was 1.1 for all three cities across all protests. Because only one coder was involved, the usual intercoder reliability statistics cannot be generated.

statistical comparisons on change within each city over time, to hold constant as many variables as possible. Nevertheless, I tried to select cities that were broadly comparable. While I could do little to control for idiosyncratic characteristics like mayoral personality, I compensated for these effects by selecting cities with at least two experiences of Left government, São Paulo and Mexico City. Brasilia was added for reasons that will shortly become clear. In only one of these cases – São Paulo in 2003 – did the governing local party enjoy the support of a president from the same party.

Socioeconomic Structures

Like many developing countries, Brazil and Mexico produced a "primate city." A common result of industrialization in capital-scarce countries, primate cities concentrate disproportionately large shares of a developing nation's population, industry, and universities. Mexico City and São Paulo are prototypes of this phenomenon. Each is among the largest cities in the world, with eight million to ten million people in the city proper, and fifteen million to sixteen million in the metropolitan areas. They concentrate 16.3 percent (Mexico City) and 9.8 percent (São Paulo) of the total national population in their respective metropolitan areas.[9] By way of comparison, the metropolitan area of New York City holds only about 7 percent of U.S. population (Goldsmith, 1994: 21).

Just as importantly, they are industrial and financial giants with relatively wealthy, well-served, and well-educated populations. Mexico City accounts for about 21 percent of national industrial production and 24 percent of services, especially banks. One enterprising author calculated that in the late 1990s, Mexico City consumed roughly, "20 percent of the electric energy, 95 percent of books and records, 80 percent of the paper, 60 percent of the milk, 60 percent of the fruit,

---

[9] Estimates of population vary by source, but most estimates dating to the mid-1990s fall within this range. For metropolitan estimates, see Gilbert (1996: 2); for national population and city population estimates, see Wilkie (2002: 147, 167–168). In both Mexico City and São Paulo, the metropolitan area grew faster than the city itself in the 1990s, with the result that some estimates from 2000 put the metropolitan area population at over 20 million in each case (Myers, 2002: 9).

more than 50 percent of the cheese, and 30 percent of the meat ... [as well as] 40 percent of the buses and half of the taxis in the country" (Álvarez Enríquez, 1998: 45). And of course, Mexico City is the national capital. Purportedly the oldest continuously inhabited capital in the Americas, Mexico City retains even today some of the mystique embodied in the Aztec term for the area, "the navel of the world."

In Brazil, the political capital is located hundreds of miles from anywhere, in the central sierra city of Brasilia. In other respects, São Paulo holds the same dominating position with respect to national politics that Mexico City does. As of the 1990s, the metropolitan region of São Paulo accounted for almost 30 percent of Brazil's gross national product – three times its percentage of national population (Santos, 1996: 224). São Paulo is simultaneously Brazil's major industrial and financial center. The city itself lost many industrial jobs in the 1990s due to economic crisis and the relocation of industrial plants to peripheral areas around São Paulo. Nevertheless, almost a third of its economically active population worked in manufacturing, more than in any other Brazilian city (Santos, 1996: 224). São Paulo's financial district on Avenida Paulista is a major hub not only for Brazil but also for much of the Southern Cone. By the late 1980s, 33 percent of Brazilian banks and 18 of the 23 foreign banks operating in Brazil had their headquarters in São Paulo (Santos, 1996: 227). Thus, despite the transfer of the political capital to Brasilia, São Paulo is

the *de facto* center of Brazil. It is here that everything of national import in Brazil is to be found, except for the formal attributes of national political power. ... As such, São Paulo parallels Mexico City and ... the other capital cities of Latin America in that it is the center of the country not just in economic and demographic terms but in cultural and educational ones too. (Graham and Jacobi, 2002: 298)

Mexico City and São Paulo share another, less comfortable characteristic: devastating extremes in incomes and standards of living. The very qualities that made these cities stand out in economic terms also made them attractive to poor migrants looking for jobs, better schools, and public services. Ironically, initial waves of migration from stagnant rural areas were deliberately induced by interventionist states that concentrated investment and infrastructure in a few key locations in order to create poles of economic development.[10] The policy worked too well. Migrants came so quickly that they overwhelmed the capacity of local service networks and housing markets. Poverty, underemployment, growth of the informal economy, precarious housing, poor health and nutrition, and rising crime rates therefore accompanied city growth.

These problems persist into the twenty-first century even though the rate of migration to both São Paulo and Mexico City has slowed to a trickle. Neither Brazil nor Mexico has managed to create sufficient jobs to employ their millions of poor and unskilled laborers. In fact, the economic crises that racked both countries in the 1980s and 1990s tended to increase poverty. Both countries responded with similar economic policies: deals with the IMF that led to cuts in state budgets; state withdrawal from economic investment; the end of subsidies, price controls, and regulation; antiinflationary policies; and a global shift toward free trade. These structural and economic similarities should contribute to the emergence of similar social movements. Differences between Mexico City and São Paulo might then be more readily attributed to political differences between them, including the nature of movement-party alliances.

Institutional Structures

The basic institutional structures of local government in Brazil and Mexico also share important similarities. Local governments possess legal autonomy under a formally federal system, have an executive-centered balance of power, use proportional representation to fill seats on city councils, and have multiparty systems, though the Brazilian party system is considerably more fragmented.[11] One potentially significant effect of legislative fragmentation is that while the mayor of Mexico City has never governed without a legislative majority of his

[10] As Cornelius (1978: 9) notes, "During the 1950s and most of the 1960s, the conventional wisdom held that the concentration of people, private enterprises, and public investments in one or two large metropolitan areas in each country was essential to achieving higher rates of economic development." See also Portes and Walton (1976: 28).

[11] On average, 5 parties win seats in the Mexico City Asamblea, compared to 11 parties in São Paulo and 7.5 parties in Brasilia.

TABLE 2.1. *Legislative Seats in Municipal Legislatures*

Local Administration	Parties with Seats	Percentage of Seats Held by Largest Party	Mayor Able to Form Legislative Majority
Mexico City 1992–1994 (PRI)	6	60.6	Yes
Mexico City 1995–1997 (PRI)	5	57.6	Yes
Mexico City 1998–2000 (PRD)	5	57.6	Yes
Mexico City 2000–2003 (PRD)	4	56.1	Yes
São Paulo 1989–1992 (PT)	12	28.0	No
São Paulo 1993–1996 (PPB)	9	25.5	Yes
São Paulo 1997–2000 (PPB)	10	34.5	Yes
São Paulo 2001–2003 (PT)	13	32.7	Yes
Brasilia 1995–1996 (PT)[a]	7	37.5	No
Brasilia 2001–2002 (PMDB)	8	25.0	Yes

[a] The PT, the party of the mayor, was not the largest party in this legislature. In all other cases, the mayor's party did have the largest block of seats in the local legislature.

Sources: "Camara decide bloquear projetos de Erundina" 1990: C5; "Vereadores eleitos" 1996: A5; Becerra Chavez 2001: 25–26; www.asambleadf.gov.mx (Mexico City Legislative Assembly/Asamblea Legislativa); www.cl.df.gov.br (Brasilia Legislative Chamber/Câmara Legislativa); www.camara.sp.gov.br (São Paulo Legislative Chamber/ Câmara Legislativa).

own party, the mayors of São Paulo and Brasilia have never governed *with* such a majority. However, in only two cases did these Brazilian mayors fail to construct a stable legislative majority, primarily via the distribution of pork and government positions as an incentive for legislative cooperation (see Table 2.1).

However, three differences distinguish these cities from one another and make them less-than-perfect matches: (1) the delayed democratization of Mexico City; (2) the different constitutional status of the two federal districts (Mexico City and Brasilia) vis-à-vis São Paulo; and (3) the financial resources available to each city.

Like many Latin American capital cities, Brasilia and Mexico City had a federal district mayor appointed by the national president until quite recently – 1989 in the case of Brasilia and 1997 in the case of Mexico City – at which point popular election of both mayor and city council occurred. However, only in Mexico City does data collection include part of the nondemocratic period. The need to compare Leftist to non-Leftist local governments drove the decision to include the 1992–1997 PRI local administrations despite the fact that they had neither an elected mayor nor a city council with significant legislative powers.[12] The Left (PRD) won the first two post-1997 mayoral elections, so the pretransition PRI governments were the only possible comparison.

Nevertheless, the comparison to PRI governments is especially meaningful in part because of their nonelected status. In Mexico, the PRI had far deeper ties with organized civil society than the independent Left, through a system of legal and financial controls that subordinated unions and popular organizations to decisions by party and government leaders. PRI controls – particularly of unions – gave civilian leaders of Mexico the tools to avoid the kind of social unrest that led to military coups in most of the rest of Latin America. It is thus peculiarly fitting that the capacity of the independent Left to manage protest should be compared to that of the champion of social management: the PRI, in all its undemocratic glory.

Still, Mexico City's PRI Regents did not have the same status as subsequent popularly elected ones. The position and political future of a Regent depended more on his ability to please the president – often by shutting down protest – than his ability to satisfy popular demands. Furthermore, his status as a presidential appointee may have led organizations to see him as part of the president's entourage rather than as a target of protest in his own right. These factors may influence the size and direction of some trends in protest after the PRD's 1997 victory.

A second major difference affects the comparison between São Paulo and Mexico City: Mexico City is a national capital, and

---

[12] Mexico City did have an elected city council, known as the Assembly of Representatives, beginning in 1988. However, its powers were limited to consultation. In 1994, the PRI expanded the powers of the city council and, in 1995, authorized popular election of the mayor. See Davis (2002) and Álvarez Enríquez (1998).

São Paulo is not. Because of this difference, I found myself forced to alter the original two-city design, after a first field season in São Paulo, to include Brazil's national capital. The problem is not the percentage of protests directed at the federal government; I can easily remove these from the sample. Rather, the issue is the addition of an extra layer of governmental authority in São Paulo: the governor and state assembly. As Nickson notes (1995: 121–122),

the respective competencies of different tiers of government are notoriously ill-defined [in Brazil], even by the standards of Latin America, and the prevalence of concurrent powers among federal, state, and local government remains a significant feature of Brazilian local government ... the outcome of this complex legal arrangement is that there is almost no service uniformly offered by all municipalities, and very few in which the state may not be an alternate provider or regulator.

Thus, the mayor of São Paulo shares responsibility with the state governor for the provision of many public services demanded by local popular movements, including public transportation, education, and health care. In the case of education, for example, the municipal government runs the vast majority of preschools and day-care centers, 32 percent of primary education, and less than 1 percent of middle schools. State government responsibilities follow an inverse trend, from 81 percent of middle school education and 52 percent of primary school education to less than 1 percent of early childhood education.[13] In addition, teachers and health care workers are split among state- and municipal-level services rather than having a unified union, a factor that may affect prospects for collective action. The practical consequence, I would argue, may be to reduce mobilization.

In contrast, the two national capitals have a federal district structure that unites the powers of a governor with those of a mayor. They are much more attractive targets for protest. Where mayors and governors in São Paulo can shift responsibility for unmet demands to one another, the mayor/governor of the federal district is the lone authority.

---

[13] Private schools account for 15–20 percent of all of these categories except preschools, where they account for 25 percent of students. Figures from *Diario Oficial do Municipio de São Paulo* (2002: 428).

One of the consequences of this difference in legal status has to do with the mayor's ability to alter the risk of repression. In contrast to both Mexico City and Brasilia, São Paulo's mayor does not control police forces except for a small metropolitan guard limited to security for public buildings. Instead, the state government controls the military and civil police.[14] Even in Brasilia and Mexico City, however, mayors share responsibility for policing protest with federal authorities. Protest in the national capital is simply too potentially dangerous for national governments to leave the responsibility entirely to local government. Thus, in all three cases, changes in the potential costs of repression probably do not drive shifts in protest strategies.

The third significant institutional difference divides Brazilian cities from Mexico City. In general, Brazilian cities have more financial resources and legal autonomy than Mexico City. In Brazil, the period of Portuguese colonialism (and the extraordinarily difficult topography of Brazil) left a legacy of "relatively greater municipal autonomy ... [that] still distinguishes the Brazilian local government system from its counterparts elsewhere in Latin America" (Nickson, 1995: 118).

More immediately, the Brazilian transition – unlike the Mexican transition – involved a complete rewriting of the national constitution. The 1988 Brazilian constitution effectively shifted power from the federal level to state and local governments. In practice, state governments benefited more from the subsequent division of resources and authority than municipal governments. Nevertheless, local government's share of total state spending rose from 11 percent in 1980 to 18 percent in 1990, higher than in any other Latin American nation except Colombia (Nickson, 1995: 52).

By way of comparison, Mexican municipalities controlled only 3 percent of total revenue (Nickson, 1995: 44). Limited revenues handicap the efforts of all mayors to develop alternative spending priorities.

---

[14] The Brazilian constitution divides responsibility for public order between the civil police (responsible for investigation of crime) and the military police (responsible for making arrests and policing the streets). Brazil's constitutional designers intended to limit the kind of political intelligence gathering that had in the past fueled human rights abuses by the military government. Although the two police forces are formally run by state governments, most governors have relatively little influence over the internal management and operations of either force.

There simply is not much available as discretionary funds after salaries and operating expenses are paid. Unlike Brazilian cities, Mexico City does not have its own health care system, primary education network, or housing fund. To the extent that these problems make demands more difficult to resolve, frustration and protest may increase, although its weakness could also make the Mexico City government a less attractive target.

Alternation in Power

These aspects of the institutional context changed slowly if at all over the period of data collection. In contrast, the party in power changed at least once in each city.

In Mexico City, three different PRI Regents governed from 1992 to 1997. The first of these, Manuel Camacho (1992–1994), represented a more liberal wing of the ruling party and had good connections with many urban popular movements by virtue of his previous position as head of the federal Ministry of Urban Development during negotiations to rebuild housing destroyed by the 1985 Mexico City earthquake. His successors Manuel Aguilera (1994–1995) and Oscar Espinosa (1995–1997) lacked these connections to popular movements, but they still had the benefit of PRI-controlled unions. All three were appointed by neoliberal presidents of Mexico.

When reforms in 1996 introduced direct election of Mexico City's mayor, the two-time presidential candidate of the PRD, Cuauhtémoc Cárdenas, decided to run. Buoyed by popular outrage at the ongoing economic crisis of 1995–1996, Cárdenas won handily. After two years in office, he resigned to run a third time for president, leaving as interim mayor Rosario Robles, the first female mayor of Mexico City. In 2000, the PRD's candidate easily won election. Andrés Manuel López Obrador governed Mexico City until 2005, when he too would step down to run for president.[15]

In Brazil, the high rate of party switching by politicians (except for PT members) makes party labels less relevant than political factions. In São Paulo, the 1993–1996 and 1997–2000 administrations came

---

[15] The term of the mayor was initially only three years (1997–2000), but increased to six years – the term of a Mexican governor – in 2000.

from the same conservative political clique, led by local businessman and politician Paulo Maluf. Maluf won the mayoral election of 1992 and took power in 1993. It was his second term as mayor. The first time, he governed as the appointed mayor of the promilitary party ARENA (the Aliança Renovadora Nacional), under the military government that lasted from 1964 to 1985. Maluf's local connections and approval of his administration made it possible for his hand-picked protégé Celso Pitta to get elected as his successor.

The PT candidates, in contrast, came from different political factions. The first PT mayor, Luiza Erundina, came from the radical wing of the São Paulo PT. Her background as a nongovernmental organization (NGO) adviser to urban popular movements gave her a sympathetic view of protest and close connections to many protesting organizations. She was one of the first PT mayors elected to head a large city. The second PT mayor was elected in 2000 amid a wave of popular disgust with the corrupt and incompetent Pitta administration. Marta Suplicy was an attractive, middle-class, self-described "sexologist" with her own television talk show (think Dr. Ruth). Her position as the wife of a prominent *petista* gave her ties to the moderate, proinstitutional faction of the party.

Unfortunately, time constraints prevented collection of an equivalent set of data for Brasilia (from 1995 to 2002). Instead, I sampled two years (1995–1996) from the city's only Leftist government (Cristovam Buarque) and two years (2001–2002) from the administration of Joaquim Roriz. Maluf and Roriz shared both a conservative ideology and control of a clientelistic machine (in Roriz's case, under the imprimatur of the PMDB, the Partido do Movimento Democrático Brasileiro). By fortunate coincidence, the political situation in Brasilia neatly mirrors that of São Paulo: the Left governed in Brasilia while the Right governed in São Paulo, and vice versa. To the extent that local party control matters more than national political context, trends should diverge in the two cities.

The result is a total of ten cases, which are summarized in Table 2.2. The selection of cases nicely varies the key economic and political conditions. The Left does not always "go first," and does not always take over in periods of economic crisis. Data on patterns of protest covers fifteen years in São Paulo, twelve years in Mexico City, and four years in Brasilia.

TABLE 2.2. *Municipal Administrations and Economic Conditions*

	São Paulo			
	PT: 1989–1992 (Erundina)	PPB: 1993–1996 (Maluf)	PPB: 1997–2000 (Pitta)	PT: 2001–2003 (Suplicy)
GDP growth	−0.3%	4.5%	2%	1.5%
Inflation	1,441%	1,021.5%	5.5%	7.4%
	Brasilia			
	PT: 1995–1996 (Buarque)			PMDB: 2001–2002 (Roriz)
GDP growth	3.5%			1.5%
Inflation	41%			7.4%
	Mexico			
	PRI: 1992–1994 (Camacho, Aguilera)	PRI: 1995–1997 (Espinosa)	PRD: 1998–2000 (Cárdenas, Robles)	PRD: 2000–2003 (López Obrador)
GDP growth	3.3%	2%	5.3%	2.4%
Inflation	11%	30%	14%	5.5%

PATTERNS OF PROTEST

The data I collected provide a fairly complete picture of protest in these three cities during the years covered (see Table 2.3). In all, I recorded 4,501 events in Mexico City, 2,485 in São Paulo, and 851 in Brasilia. This breaks down to an average of 375 per year in Mexico City, 213 per year in Brasilia, and 166 per year in São Paulo. Average attendance at events in Mexico City was 7,600, compared to 6,427 in São Paulo and 1,535 in Brasilia.[16] Such a substantial and consistent difference in protest volume is highly suggestive. Although we cannot know for sure without more cases, it is certainly interesting to note that the country with the strongest voluntary party-organizational

---

[16] I am skeptical of attendance figures. Figures frequently varied 200 to 300 percent from one newspaper source to the other, even though other aspects of the reports were highly consistent. There is also an unusually high level of missing information on attendance, as newspapers often failed even to guess at it. For these reasons, I do not use attendance alone as a dependent variable in my statistical analysis. However, averages over time should be worth slightly more because they involve more data points.

TABLE 2.3. *Aggregate Levels and Characteristics of Protest*

	Mexico City	São Paulo	Brasilia
Total events	4,501	2,485	851
Average number of protests/year	375	165	213
Average participation in events	7,600	6,427	1,535
Total named groups	961	501	246
Average number of groups/event	1.46	1.03	1.26
Events involving unions	26.7%	39.9%	45.3%
Events involving urban popular movements	22.5%	15.1%	15.7%
Events involving transport workers	6.4%	19%	9.4%
Events involving aggressive tactics	34.9%	44.5%	42.3%
Events targeting local government	37.7%	38.8%	56.5%

alliances has a lower volume of protest across virtually all organization types. Even though *shifts* in protest strategies do not reflect the strength of party-organization alliances, as the other chapters will show, the overall *volume* of protest may.

A second finding is that protest propensity is not distributed evenly across different types of organizations. Some kinds of organizations account for much more protest than others. In all three cities, unions account for the largest share of protests, ranging from 27 percent of protests in Mexico City to 45 percent of protests in São Paulo. If we add in protests by unionized transportation workers, police, and vendors, the figure rises to 42 percent of protests in Mexico City and 64 percent of protests in São Paulo. Despite the attention given to urban popular movements by the literature on popular mobilization in Latin America, they do not account for the lion's share of protest. Instead, traditional class-based organizations dominate. These patterns also contrast with much of the literature on contentious politics in Europe and the United States, which focuses more on postmodern issues and causes, like environmental politics or women's rights. While environmental problems in Mexico City and São Paulo are certainly severe, they do not seem to motivate most protest. To the extent that environmental issues capture the attention of social organizations, they operate more within institutional channels.

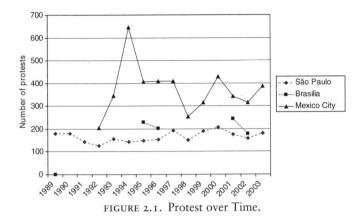

FIGURE 2.1. Protest over Time.

Third, there is no consistent evidence of cyclical patterns in protest over time. In Mexico, protests peak in presidential election years (1994 and 2000). But in Brazil, protests seem to fall slightly in most presidential election years (1990, 1994, 1998, and 2002). Protest rates appear less variable in Brazil, but small increases in protest seem more likely during the first year of a new local government than during any election year (see Figure 2.1).

Finally, Leftist governments in Mexico City and São Paulo faced fewer protests, but these protests were larger and more aggressive. In all statistical tests, the unit of observation is one organization-year. Organizations enter the database the first time they protest. Each year thereafter, another observation is entered for each organization, reflecting the number of protests it held in that year, including zero if it did not protest. Most organizations in most years get zeros. Because of the violation of independence assumptions and the strongly skewed distribution of the dependent variable, I used negative binomial regression.[17] The results differ for each of the three cities. In São Paulo, Left electoral victory has no significant effect on total protests but significantly reduces protests targeting the local government. In Mexico City, Left victory significantly reduces both total protests and protests aimed at the local government.

---

[17] See Long and Freese (2003) for an explanation of the conditions for using negative binomial analysis.

Ironically, the size of the effect is larger for Mexico City than for São Paulo. Instead of stronger party-union-movement ties giving Brazil's PT greater influence over their allies, Mexico's loosely organized PRD proved *better* able to shift movements away from protest. This outcome seems all the more surprising when one considers that the alternative to the PT was not another center-Left party (for whom PT movements might have felt some sympathy) but a reactionary local politician with ties to the previous military government. Nevertheless, PT governments did not get much lower levels of protest than their conservative rivals. And in Brasilia, Left victory significantly *increased* protest against the local government.

Moreover, protests were consistently larger under Leftist administrations. In Mexico, median attendance at protests was 250 under PRD administrations compared to 200 under the PRI.[18] In São Paulo, the median attendance at protests was 450 under PT administrations versus 350 under the *malufista* administrations. And in Brasilia, median attendance at protests under the PT was 275 compared to 250 under the conservative administration of Roriz. Despite the limited ability of mayors to protect demonstrators from repression, especially in São Paulo, there seems to be a modestly positive effect of Left victory on the size of protests.

Protests were also generally more aggressive against the Left. Protests are separated into two general categories – relatively aggressive (strikes, street blockages, and building occupations) and relatively unaggressive (marches, demonstrations, hunger strikes). The percentage of events that were aggressive is recorded for each organization-year. When all targets are included, Left power is significantly associated with aggressiveness in only one case (São Paulo). However, when the focus narrows to include only events with local government as the target, Leftist governments are significantly and positively associated with aggressiveness in all three cities.

One possible cause of this relationship is a perception that Leftist local governments are less likely to quash aggressive protests than conservative governments. Although mayors cannot prevent police

---

[18] I report medians here because they are less likely to be distorted by one or two very large marches, such as May Day marches, and thus are more reflective of the real average size of protests.

responses to protest (the risk does not drop to zero), they can call for aid, even in São Paulo where the mayor has no administrative authority over the police. The risk of police action may not fall under a Leftist government, but it could rise under a conservative one, resulting in a cost gap.

CONCLUSIONS

Chapter 1 proposed a series of independent variables that might affect protest rates, including type of organizational resources, alliance to political parties (versus independence), electoral cycles, and alliance to the party in power. Analysis of aggregate patterns of protest provides preliminary evidence that some types of organization in the dataset protest more frequently than others. Protesting organizations in Brazil and Mexico are much more likely to be class-based organizations like unions than neighborhood or identity or issue-based organizations.

The importance of cyclical effects – and their nature – is not clearly demonstrated in these aggregate data. Mexico seems to have a presidential election year effect, but Brazil does not. Brazil seems to have slightly higher protest levels right after a new administration takes office, but Mexico does not. And the significance of these effects remains uncertain.

Similarly, the effects of Left victory on protest are curiously mixed. Leftist governments were the target of *less* protest in Mexico City and São Paulo, but *more* protest in Brasilia. Furthermore, Leftist governments were likely to be the target of larger and more aggressive protests even if the number of protests fell. Protesting organizations do not tone it down in the expectation of a sympathetic response; instead, they shout louder and push harder, perhaps believing that a Leftist government will not push back. The effects of party alliance are not measured directly in this chapter, but if Leftist parties are likely to have more organizational allies than conservative ones, then party alliance may have much more complex effects on protest strategies than a simple model of sparing friends and attacking opponents would suggest.

Chapter 3 follows up on these initial findings in a multivariate model, including variables for cyclical effects, additional organizational characteristics, and party alliance.

3

The Limits of Loyalty

The man who adapts his course of action to the nature of the times will succeed, and likewise ... the man who sets his course of action out of tune with the times will come to grief.

– Machiavelli

Character is destiny.

– Heraclitus

This chapter compares the effects of various aspects of organizational character and identity with the effects of changes in the political opportunity structure on the protest strategies of a wide variety of organizations. The results suggest that the characteristics of organizations themselves, particularly type of organization, age, and history of protest, explain more of the variation in protest patterns than changes in the political opportunity structure. Party alliances matter, significantly and consistently, but seem to tap into enduring political orientations toward the state and toward protest itself rather than causing significant changes depending on the party in power.

Nevertheless, POS is not irrelevant. Organizations are especially likely to protest in the first year of a new administration – whether friend or foe – probably in order to capture the attention of the incoming government. They do not systematically spare their party allies. Although the sign for alliance to the party in power is negative in two of the three cities (indicating less protest), the variable fails to reach statistical significance.

MEASURING PARTY ALLIANCE

What does it mean to say that an organization is "allied" to a given political party? This question raises particularly difficult problems in the context of developing nations. Mass parties of the type described by Duverger (1954) – parties of members – have always been relatively rare in the developing world. In Europe, mass parties mobilized a working-class base. The weak position of labor in newly industrializing countries may make unions a less attractive electoral base; parties simply cannot win elections with the support of labor alone. Some party–union alliances emerged in Latin America, including the Mexican PRI. However, in many of these cases, union affiliation with the party was constructed from above. Rather than leading to strong working-class identification with the party, such ties existed primarily at the level of elites.

Moreover, repeated democratic crises in Latin America frequently aimed at repressing labor. Parties built on unions, like the Peronists in Argentina, sometimes found themselves proscribed from political participation and targeted for investigation as national security threats. From 1964 until the early 1980s, union-based parties were outlawed in Brazil. In Mexico, the combative unions incorporated into the PRI in the 1930s subsided relatively quickly into passive tools of the ruling authoritarian party. Independent Leftist parties like the Mexican Communist Party could not legally participate in elections until 1979. Even then, the PRI made every effort to ensure that newly registered Leftist parties did not develop deep ties to popular organizations – especially unions – through a combination of carrots and sticks offered to organizations for remaining independent or affiliating themselves with the PRI.

By the time democracy began to spread throughout the region in the 1980s, changes in global capitalism had begun to undermine unions not only in Latin America, but also in the European social democracies that created the prototype of the mass party. Competitive tendencies did not lead toward the spread of the mass party form as Duverger once expected; rather, mass parties began to reduce their dependence on unions in order to increase their economic policy flexibility and to attract support from non-union sectors. These trends made alliances between popular organizations and parties everywhere weaker and more contingent. My research question, in part, asks whether such weak alliances have continuing effects on mobilization.

However, the more immediate problem is how to determine when an alliance exists, given that alliances in general are more tenuous. I established five criteria for party alliance: (1) the organization runs candidates (or attempts to run candidates) under the party label;[1] (2) the organization publicly endorses and campaigns for the party's candidates; (3) the organization contributes to or receives financial assistance from the party; (4) the organization's leaders and members participate in party leadership (double militance); and (5) the organization is legally affiliated with the party. Since party alliance takes different forms, I allowed any four of these criteria to constitute alliance. In Brazil and Mexico, the typical alliance pattern for the Left included the first four criteria; in the case of the PRI, it also included the fifth. However, while legal affiliation did not usually occur, there was often a public declaration of affiliation by the organization or recognition of a special relationship to a particular party at specific points in time. As a result, I could determine when organizations changed their alliance status over the period of data collection and record this change in status.

Using a combination of interviews with organization members, examination of newspapers and organizational documents, and consultation with local experts, I had little difficulty in classifying the party alliances of the more active groups in the sample. The problem is that the missing information – groups that I was unable to classify by party alliance – is systematically biased to exclude smaller and less active groups. Many newspaper accounts of protests did not name the group involved, making it impossible to identify its party alliance. This category constituted from 19.5 percent of events in Brasilia to 25.7 percent of events in Mexico City. In addition, it was difficult to identify the alliance characteristics of groups that protested relatively little and therefore were less well-known.

Fortunately, a small number of groups account for the lion's share of protest. In each city, over half of all named groups protested only

---

[1] Smaller organizations have less success in getting coveted candidacies. In order to prevent biasing my criteria against small organizations, I included the attempt to get a candidacy as a criterion. In practice, the focus on local politics tended to lower this threshold: even fairly small organizations managed to get a candidate on party lists from time to time.

once during the entire sample, while the top 5 percent of groups accounted for almost 40 percent of protest in Mexico City, 29 percent of protest in Brasilia, and 27 percent of protest in São Paulo. The top 10 percent of groups accounted for between 40 and 55 percent of protests in every case. Virtually all of these groups were identified by alliance type. As a result, over 70 percent of protests with named sponsors have party alliance data attached.[2] Nevertheless, the statistical models presented here reflect primarily relationships at one end of the distribution of potential protesters: the protest-specialists, who demonstrate the most variation in protest activity.

Party Alliance and Protest

The majority of groups with known alliance characteristics were independent in all three cities. However, they account for less than a majority of total protests. For example, independent organizations in Mexico City account for 64.3 percent of groups with known affiliation, but only 49 percent of protests (by groups with a known affiliation). Conversely, groups affiliated with *any* political party protested more frequently than their share: even the supposedly docile PRI organizations, which account for 19 percent of groups with a known affiliation, led 21.2 percent of protests. But the PRD is the real star. Only 12.7 percent of all groups were affiliated with the PRD at any point, but they accounted for 27.1 percent of protests.

The advantage of the Left is even more lopsided in Brazil. Although similar percentages of groups were independent (57.7 percent of known alliance groups in São Paulo and 53.1 percent in Brasilia), groups affiliated with a party other than the PT accounted for 11 percent of groups in Brasilia and just 8.6 percent of groups in São Paulo. Again, independent groups protested less often than one would expect if protest rates were the same among all alliance types, while the Left protested much more. In São Paulo, PT-affiliated organizations constituted 33 percent of groups with known alliance characteristics, but 66 percent of protests were by these groups.[3]

---

[2] See the Appendix for further discussion of this point, including comparison of the behavior of nonnamed and nonidentified groups vis-à-vis identified ones.

[3] In Brasilia, PT-affiliated organizations constituted 36 percent of all groups with known alliance characteristics, but 74 percent of protests were by these groups.

The evidence is less clear with respect to whether organizations with party alliances spare their allies when they win power. On the one hand, PRD-allied organizations protested more than PRI-allied organizations in every year before 1998 – the year the PRD took office in Mexico City – but less than PRI-allied organizations in every year afterward, with the exceptions of 1994 and 2000 (presidential election years) when they were virtually tied. This is exactly what we would anticipate if organizations spare their party allies and target their foes. On the other hand, we see only modest evidence of such behavior in Brazil: average protest rates by PT groups against PT administrations in São Paulo were lower than against the *malufista* administrations (though just barely), but in Brasilia, PT-allied groups protested *more* frequently against the local PT government than against the PMDB government of Roriz.

In tactical terms, protest portfolios evolved in similar ways over time regardless of the party in power. Hypothetically, movements should shift to less aggressive (and costly) tactics against their ally in government and increase their aggressiveness against political rivals, who presumably would need more convincing to give in to demands. Thus, "in-groups" should have portfolios weighted toward softer tactics, such as demonstrations, and "out-groups" should have portfolios weighted toward harder tactics, such as street blockages. In fact, groups are either consistently more aggressive or consistently less aggressive in their tactics. Trends toward more aggressive tactics developed in tandem among groups with quite different party alliances.

Street blockades and building occupations are perhaps the most telling category, since strike capacity largely reflects whether a party had any union allies. Street blockades also are especially unpopular because they cause traffic disruptions that result in inconvenience and economic losses across a broad spectrum of the population. In a 2001 Mexico City survey, 91 percent of residents opposed all protests that blocked streets regardless of the motive ("Aceptan marchas reguladas," 2001: 4B); 85 percent in a separate poll thought that marches on major thoroughfares should be banned (Ramirez and Romero, 2001: 36). The majority (63 percent) reported that marches had affected them personally ("Aceptan marchas reguladas," 2001: 4B). In São Paulo, disapproval of street blocking is slightly lower. Nevertheless, a 2000 poll found that 69 percent of the population opposed street blockages and 75 percent opposed building invasions, compared to 40 percent that opposed strikes in the education sector.[4] Nevertheless, street blockades became more popular over time among all groups.

OPERATIONALIZATION OF VARIABLES

Chapter 2 looked at the impact of organizational type and Left party victory on aggregate protest patterns. This chapter adds several additional variables, including party alliance. However, to understand whether these associations have any significance, we must measure them against the effects of other factors. A review of key independent variables will help set the stage for this statistical analysis.

One of the POS variables has now been introduced: in-group. In-group is a dummy variable, which takes on a value of one when a group is allied to the party in power and zero if it is either allied to a rival party or independent of party affiliation.[5] If organizations spare their allies in power, in-group should be significant and negative. If they see their ally as a soft target and have other reasons for protesting, they may protest more against their ally than against other party governments (hypothesis 4); in this case, in-group would be significant and positive.[6]

I include two additional dummy variables to capture the effects of electoral cycles. The political opportunities faced by movements – and

---

[4] A higher percentage, 52 percent, opposed strikes in the health sector (Biehler Mateos, 2000: A10).

[5] I tried various specifications of this variable. In one version, in-group is compared only to party allies out of power, and independent is incorporated as a separate variable. In another, all types of party alliance are coded from zero to two, with zero as alliance to the party in power, one as independent, and two as allied to an opposition party. None of these versions produced results any different from those discussed here. Since only those with special access and loyalty should have motives to change their behavior when their ally is in power, I present this version as the most direct reflection of the theoretical expectation.

[6] I initially included "Left party in power" as a second POS variable, on the hypothesis that Left parties might be seen as more sympathetic targets by groups of all political alliances. However, Left party victory and in-group are correlated at statistically significant levels. Therefore, statistical models used only one of these variables at a time. This chapter will present models using in-group because it is more directly related to the theoretical hypotheses.

the costs of protest – may not be constant over the term of a specific government. The first variable is "honeymoon effect," coded as one for the first year of a new administration and zero for all other years. Movements might be inclined to reduce their protest during a government's first year in office. The second variable is "election effect," coded as one for a local election year and zero for all other years. Movements may want to increase their protest in electoral years in order to demonstrate their importance as potential electoral partners as parties draw up their candidate lists and electoral platforms.

In both cases, organizational reactions to electoral cycles might depend on who is in power at the time. For example, they reduce protest if their ally is in power in order to minimize the electoral embarrassment that protests could cause and increase protests if an opponent is in power for the opposite reason. Similarly, organizations might step up protests in the first year of an opposition government to warn them against attacking entrenched privileges and give honeymoons only to their allies. Thus, I also include interaction effects with in-group for these two variables.

So far, only one kind of organizational characteristic has been introduced: organizational type. According to resource mobilization theories, the capacity to protest depends in part on the ability to draw on resources like networks of solidarity, money, skills, numbers, or position to disrupt key political institutions. Different types of organizations are unevenly endowed with these resources, as are different individual organizations of the same type. Many aspects of resources are difficult to measure quantitatively. Nevertheless, organizational type captures at least some aspects of resource distribution in that some organizations benefit from more legal protection, regulation, and/or subsidies from the state; this is particularly true for unions in both Brazil and Mexico. To see whether there are systematic patterns of protest based on organization type, I included dummy variables for the most common types of organization (unions, neighborhood associations, transportation workers, students, and vendors). In addition, I included a dummy variable for two organizations that had unusually high protest rates: the Consejo General de Huelga (General Strike Council, or CGH) responsible for a year-long wave of protests aimed at the National Autonomous University (UNAM) in Mexico City, and the volatile Union of Bus Drivers and Conductors in

São Paulo (abbreviated here as MOCO, for its Portuguese initials; the official name of the organization is the Sindicato de Motoristas e Cobradores).

A second factor commonly discussed is the concept of organizational life cycle (e.g., Michels, 1962; Gamson, 1975; Panebianco, 1988). According to this argument, organizations get more conservative over time, gradually relying less on protest. Unfortunately, it proved impossible to identify the actual foundation dates of many organizations. As a proxy for literal age, I used the number of years since the organization first entered the database. In essence, this variable captures some effects of aging: the time elapsed since an initial mobilization.[7]

Third, to look at the possibility that a history of protest shapes subsequent organizational behavior I added a measure of lagged protest (protests in the previous year).[8] The most direct reading of this measure is that protest lag tells us to what extent high levels of protest are clustered closely in time. A movement in the midst of a wave of protest may have a higher propensity to protest than a movement that is not. More generally, the protest-lag variable tells us something about organizational reliance on protest and perhaps also about organizational culture.

An additional measure of organizational culture is the type of party alliance. The party alliance variable reflects both strategic resources and cultural attitudes toward protest and confrontation, though I am choosing here to portray it as primarily cultural. The choice to participate in politics at all requires a certain kind of framing analysis inside an organization, which sees the organization's goals as subject to public policy intervention. Many organizations (sports clubs, etc.) do not pass this threshold. The choice to ally with a specific political

---

[7] In using this proxy, I am picking up some random error because the first possible "age" is the start of my data collection. Thus, organizations affiliated with the PRD might have the same "age" as PRI organizations founded long before the start of the data collection. The fact that the order of administration type is different in each city helps ensure that even if this effect occurs in one case, it should not be systematically biased across the three cities. In addition, the characteristics of Brazil's transition to democracy produce *real* similar ages across a variety of organization types. Thus, if the impact of this variable is similar all three cases, we can conclude that we are picking up a real effect.

[8] Lagging the variable by *more* than one year did not affect the results.

party – or, conversely, to remain independent – reflects the political identity and ideology of an organization. Hypothesis 4 proposed two possible types of association: either that alliance with the Left is associated with higher rates of protest, or that independence is associated with higher rates of protest. Dummy variables for Left party alliance as well as independence are included in the analysis, leaving the comparison category alliance with other parties.[9] My classification of party alliance type as a measure of culture foreshadows my results in subsequent chapters and my final understanding of what these variables actually tap into.

Finally, I tried out several economic variables as controls, on the grounds that economic crises give people new reasons to protest and may affect the time and resources they have to engage in such protests. After several iterations, inflation (logged) worked better than alternative specifications and therefore is presented in Tables 3.1 through 3.4.[10]

Summary of Main Independent Variables

In Table 3.1, the left-hand column is taken directly from Chapter 1, the list of key variables, even though not all of these variables can be tested quantitatively.

---

[9] This comparison is most meaningful for Mexico because there were relatively few instances of other party affiliation in Brazil compared to independents. When independence is used as the omitted category, the results for the PT affiliation variable remain significant and positive, and coefficients increase. However, it is worth noting that these variables are constituted as separate variables. PT alliance is one for PT and zero contrasted with non-PT *and* independence; independence is contrasted with PT and other parties. These Left and independent variables therefore do have some original value despite the paucity of other party-allied organizations.

[10] Using lagged economic variables (e.g., inflation from the previous year) or other economic measures (e.g., GDP growth rate) did not change the outcomes. Using more than one economic variable in the models was problematic from a statistical point of view. In reality, there were only fifteen possible pairs of inflation and GDP growth rates in São Paulo; for example, each value of inflation for a given year was always paired with the same value of GDP growth, over and over for each organization that protested in that year. Thus, these were not independent correlations and presented multicollinearity problems. Interestingly, Remmer's (1991) analysis also finds that inflation had a more significant negative impact on votes for incumbent parties in Latin America than short-term variations in GDP and exchange rate depreciation.

TABLE 3.1. *Operationalization of Key Variables: Quantitative Models*

Variables	Operationalization
Organizational Resources	
Type of resources	Union
	Urban popular movement
	Street vendor
	Transportation union
	Controls for outliers (CGH and MOCO)
Institutionalization	Age
Leadership competition	Not tested
Identity	
Past history of protest	Lagged protest
Positive view of protest	Left party ally
Independent of parties	Independence
POS	
Allied to party in power	In-group
Electoral cycle effects	Honeymoon year
	Election year
	Interaction, in-group with honeymoon year
	Interaction, in-group with election year
Economic Grievance	Inflation rate (logged)

RESULTS

The results suggest that organizational characteristics and identity outperform political opportunity structures as explanations of protest level and aggressiveness. Since alternation in power took place only at the local level, the model presented here includes only protests directed at the local government (see Table 3.2). Models including all protests are consistent with these effects, but some variables lose significance, and most coefficients are lower. Unstandardized coefficients are reported, and for significant variables, the percentage increase or decrease in the expected protest count given a unit increase in the independent variable is given.

Left party alliance has a significant positive effect in all cases regardless of which party is in power. The results are very robust, even when other variables and outliers are dropped. The effects of alliance

TABLE 3.2. *Number of Protests: Local Government Target*

	Mexico City	São Paulo	Brasilia[a]
Organizational Resources			
Union	.72***(106.3%)	.61***(83.8)	.30
Neighborhood association	.41**(51.2%)	−.17	.71* (103.1%)
Transportation	.59**(80.7%)	.23	(dropped)
Student	−.001	(dropped)	−1.1
Vendor	.31	(dropped)	(dropped)
MOCO (union of bus drivers)	n.a.	1.9***(567.7%)	n.a.
Age	−.16***(−14.5%)	−.08***(−8.1%)	−.28*** (−24.2%)
Identity			
Left party ally	.48**(61%)	.51**(67.1%)	1.13*** (209.8%)
Independent	−.33**(−28%)	−.27	−.59
Protests in previous year	.30***(35.4%)	.20***(22.3%)	n.a.[b]
POS			
Allied to party in power	−.44	−.03	−.75
Honeymoon year	.38**(45.6%)	.78***(117.1%)	.36
Election year	.17	−.09	n.a.[b]
Interaction: Honeymoon year and allied to party in power	−.36	−.46	.41
Interaction: Election year and allied to party in power	.78**(118.9%)	−.20	n.a.
Economic Grievance			
Inflation (natural log)	−.04	−.02	.19
Pseudo R^2	.12***	.14***	.15***

***significant at .01   **significant at .05   *significant at .1

[a] None of the Brasilia years had elections.

[b] Inclusion of this variable for Brasilia eliminates roughly half of the cases from the sample, given that I had discontinuous data. Only 1996 and 2002 protests had information from the previous year; the rest had missing data on this variable. I therefore omitted it from the model presented here. When it is included, however, age and Leftist party ally remain significant in the same direction and alliance to party in power reaches statistical significance.

with the Left range from an increase of 61 percent in the expected protest count (Mexico City) to an increase of 209.8 percent in the expected protest count (Brasilia); the effect of PT alliance in São Paulo is closer to that of Mexico City (67.1). Independence from parties has a significant negative effect in Mexico City and is negative though not significant in the other two cities. Thus, in contrast to what some of the literature on social movements has suggested, autonomy from political parties did not improve the ability of organizations to sustain mobilization. Instead, organizations associated with political parties (not just Left-leaning parties) protested more frequently than independent organizations.

Age also consistently reduced protests, though some of this effect must be due to organizational extinction rather than moderation over time.[11] In contrast, lagged protest has a strongly positive effect. Organizations that protested a lot in one year continued to protest in the next year. In São Paulo, for example, one additional protest in the previous year leads to a 22.3 percent greater expected protest rate in the current year. For Mexico City, the projected increase is 35.4 percent. Since protest cycles over a specific issue rarely last more than a month or two, protest in the previous year should be causally unconnected to protest in the current year. It is worth noting that the effects actually last much longer than one year: four of the top ten protesting groups in the first data year are also on the top ten list for the last data year in São Paulo, Brasilia, and Mexico City, though ten to fifteen years passed in the interim. Thus, the impact of this variable probably does not result from autocorrelation, but from real differences in attitudes toward mobilization over time.

Finally, unions consistently account for more protest than other categories of organizations.[12] This makes some intuitive sense. Legal

---

[11] One of the robustness tests I performed involved omitting from the sample all groups that had not protested for varying lengths of time. Below a certain point (six years for Mexico City and eleven years for São Paulo), age has no significant effect on protest rate. The loss of significance could result in part from smaller sample size, but age loses significance long before any of the other variables do.

[12] In addition to the categories listed in the tables, omitted types of organizations included parties, environmental groups, religious groups, human rights organizations, ethnic organizations, peasant organizations, business organizations, and "other." For the purposes of the statistical analysis, I folded police/army protests into the main union category since they involved work-related issues almost

protection and financing of unions in Mexico and Brazil help them overcome some of the collective action problems that beset other kinds of organizations. Unions face regularly scheduled and legally mandated opportunities for protest, in the form of contract expiration dates set by law. Protests by a given union tend to peak in the month when their contract is due to expire. Omission of organizational type leaves more of the predictive effects to be picked up by party alliance, increasing its significance but lowering the overall explanatory value.

In contrast, variables associated with POS have much less explanatory power. Alliance to the party in power is negatively associated with protest in all three cities, but it falls short of statistical significance.[13] Neither the PT nor the PRD was able to change the protest strategies of its allies. Cyclical effects are more important. However, protests do not *decrease* in so-called honeymoon years; instead, protests *increase* significantly in the first year of a new government, by 117.1 percent in São Paulo and 45.6 percent in Mexico City.[14] Rather than giving new governments a grace period, organizations respond by immediately mobilizing. The incentives for protest affected opponents, independents, and allies of the new government alike: there is no significant interaction effect between honeymoon and alliance to the party in power. The effect is not as robust as one would like, but its consistency across the three cases is striking.[15]

None of these models does a very good job of explaining variation in protest rates. The pseudo-R^2 of the model ranges from .12 to .15,

exclusively. Most of these types of organization accounted for too few protests for valid statistical findings and were therefore dropped from the calculation.

[13] Barely, in the case of Mexico City (p = .11) and Brasilia (p = .12). Alternative specifications, including a variable capturing interaction effects between the Left party in power and the Leftist ally also failed to reach significance. Only when the Leftist government was included in the model did in-group reach statistical significance, in Mexico City and São Paulo. Evidently, Left-allied in-groups are just a little bit nicer to their allies than groups allied to other political parties are to their own allies. For Mexico, this means that PRI-allied organizations are less inclined to spare the PRI than PRD organizations are inclined to spare the PRD. Chapters 4 and 5 will address this pattern more directly.

[14] In Brasilia, the effect is not significant, though this may have something to do with the small number of years observed.

[15] The coefficient for honeymoon year is higher when Leftist administration years are omitted from the models; running the models with only Leftist administrations, in fact, reduces the significance of the variable below .1 in Mexico City, though it is still positive.

suggesting that barely 12 to 15 percent of variation in protest rates can be explained by the joint combination of organizational characteristics, identity, and political opportunity. This is not entirely surprising, given the relatively crude measures used and the high degree of random noise in protest rates overall; as the next chapters will discuss, sometimes organizations protest just because their competitors do. Still, it is worth noting that in all three cases, the models are statistically significant at the .01 level.

Moreover, the goal of this book is not to explain *all* causes of decisions to protest but to analyze whether changes in protest strategies follow systematic and predictable patterns, based on the characteristics of organizations and their strategic environment. The answer, clearly, is that they do. Party alliance has significant and robustly consistent effects on the propensity of individual organizations to protest. Other organizational characteristics, like age and organization type, also have consistently significant effects. Finally, political cycles matter: honeymoon years are difficult for new administrations. But an organization's relationship to the party in power has no significant effect on protest rates.

DISRUPTIVE PROTEST

Up to this point, I have treated all protests as equivalent: a demonstration by twenty-five neighborhood residents against the demolition of a public gymnasium and a demonstration by 500,000 city workers each count as one event. Yet, for many reasons, we might care more about highly disruptive events.

How can we measure "disruption"? Several components come into play, including the duration of the protest, the number of participants, the violence associated with the event, the aggressiveness of the tactics, and the subjective "threat": a building occupation by heavily armed, striking police officers is likely to seem more threatening than a building occupation by accountants who want their boss fired.

The solution is to construct an index, but there are important methodological challenges. First, some factors are hard to quantify. Should a strike count for two points and a building occupation for one – or does it depend on *who* is striking? Second, units are not commensurable. In particular, tactics are binary variables (zero or one) while participation may be measured in the hundreds of thousands. Third, the reliability of some measures is better than others. Most importantly, the reported number of participants in a protest is notoriously unreliable, with huge variation in estimates for the same event. Similarly, duration is not consistently reported. Most newspapers do a better job of reporting the start of an event (like a sit-in) than reporting exactly when it ended. Duration may also mean different things depending on the kind of event. A hunger strike of twenty-five days is impressive and may capture increasing attention. A strike of twenty-five days is far more common but unless accompanied by other events (like marches) it tends to fade from public awareness unless a major public service is involved. Fourth, different components do not necessarily go together. Violent events may involve fewer people than peaceful demonstrations, at least in part because of the greater costs and risks of such aggressive action. And finally, evaluation of disruptiveness is complicated by the fact that my database is organized in terms of organization/years, not individual events.

In the end, I constructed my index around three dimensions: (1) clustering of protest, (2) participation, and (3) aggressiveness. The cluster variable takes a value of one if the organization has one episode of more than four protests in four weeks (not necessarily calendar months), two if there are two such episodes in the course of a year, and so forth. The measure of clustering ranges from zero to eleven in Mexico City, zero to four in São Paulo, and zero to three in Brasilia.

Participation is based on estimates of average attendance at the organization's protests during the year. However, I convert raw attendance data into quartiles. If a group's average attendance fell in the bottom quartile of all groups (indicating particularly small protests), it received a score of zero, in the second quartile one, in the third quartile two, and in the top quartile three. Standardizing attendance figures in this way helps to minimize the potential bias introduced by inaccurate attendance estimates and makes the measure more commensurable with the cluster component.[16] Moreover, the

---

[16] For example, the measure of clustering, or waves may range from zero to eleven in Mexico City but the mean is only .10: most groups in most years have no clusters at all. Clearly, adding even a logged score of participation would give this component too much weight. In any case, clustering is arguably a better measure of the intensity of activity than participation in a single large rally.

measure captures an important theoretical dimension of participation: that a "large and impressive" demonstration in one context may look rather small and insignificant in another. A demonstration attracting a hundred people may be quite important where few people dare to protest in public.

Finally, I counted the number of events per group per year that involved at least one aggressive tactic (strike, street blockage, or building takeover). Groups with none got a zero; groups with one aggressive event got a one; groups with between two and five aggressive events got a two; groups with between five and ten aggressive events got a three; and groups with more than ten aggressive events got a four.[17] I use this measure rather than whether there was violence during an event because violence often depends as much on police responses as on the intent of demonstrators. My goal, in contrast, is to understand *intent*, why groups choose to engage in more disruptive tactics. Intent is better captured by looking at tactics, but tactics are not unrelated to the potential for violence. There is a greater risk of violence when groups select a tactic that implies confrontation with police (such as street blockages and building takeovers) or that involves significant costs to demonstrators and their target (such as strikes).

My disruption index sums these three scores together. For Mexico City, the value of the index ranges from zero to sixteen, with an average score of 2.2. For São Paulo, the value of disruption ranges from zero to ten, with an average score of 2.2. For Brasilia, the value of disruption ranges from zero to nine, with an average score of 2.4.

The distribution of "disruption" is if anything more skewed than the protest number, so I repeated the negative binomial procedure. The results suggest that disruptiveness is primarily a function of organizational characteristics. Unions protested more frequently; they also were more disruptive. The average disruption score of unions (including transportation unions) is much bigger than for non-unions (3.0 versus 1.9 in Brasilia, and 2.9 versus 1.7 in São Paulo). The difference is smaller in Mexico City (2.5 versus 2.1), which probably reflects the more passive character of PRI unions, but is still in the same direction. In Mexico City and Brasilia – but not São Paulo – neighborhood

---

[17] As with the participation component, the goal of scoring the variable in this way is to make each component of roughly equal value.

associations are significantly more disruptive than other groups, at least when the sample is limited to protests that target the local government.

Alliance with a left party is significantly, consistently, and positively associated with disruptiveness against all targets. The number of protests in the previous year is also significantly and positively associated with disruptiveness. The impact of age in these models reverses direction: where age is associated with fewer protests over time in the general models, it is positively associated with disruptiveness of protest, and significant in two of the cities (see Table 3.3). While time usually results in diminishing protest rates (and organizational extinction), surviving organizations are in general more capable of disruptive protest than very new organizations.

In contrast, political context seems to have little or no effect on the disruptiveness of protest. Honeymoon year never reaches significance; neither does election year. Alliance to the party in power makes no significant difference in São Paulo or Mexico City, and is *positively* and significantly associated with disruptiveness in Brasilia. Table 3.3 reports the model analyzing disruptiveness against all targets, but political context is not significant in models looking only at protests targeting the local government either.

CONCLUSIONS

The central lesson of this chapter is that both overall propensity to protest and the aggressiveness of tactics are strongly associated with organizational characteristics and only weakly responsive to changes in the political opportunity structure. Movements do not systematically spare their party allies; in fact, during the first year of any new administration they protest more rather than granting it a honeymoon. Organizations allied with Left-leaning parties protest more no matter who is in power. Movements with a history of protest will continue to protest. And unions seem more capable of sustaining protest – especially disruptive protest – over time. Table 3.4 summarizes these findings. Significant results are in bold type.

These findings leave us with several puzzling questions. Why are unions more disruptive than other kinds of organizations, especially

TABLE 3.3. *Level of Disruption: All Targets*

	Mexico City	São Paulo	Brasilia
Organizational Resources			
Union	.19***(20.9%)	.38***(45.7%)	.42***(52.7%)
Neighborhood association	.01	.21*(23.2%)	.30
Transportation	.03	.20	.55*(73.6%)
Student	.14	(dropped)	.17
Vendor	−.13		
MOCO (São Paulo bus drivers)			
CGH (Mexico City university students, 1999 strike)	.03	.70***(102%)	Not applicable
Age	.01	.02**(1.8%)	.11***(11.2%)
Identity			
Left party ally	.15**(16.5%)	.22*(24.4%)	.42*(51.7%)
Independent	−.004	−.06	.07
Protests in previous year[a]	.03***(3.2%)	.02***(2.2%)	(omitted)
POS			
Allied to party in power	−.15	−.05	.41*(50.9%)
Honeymoon year	.02	−.03	.002
Election year	.01	−.01	Not applicable
Interaction: Honeymoon year and allied to party in power	.11	−.04	−.15
Interaction: Election year and allied to party in power	.17	−.09	Not applicable
Economic Grievance			
Inflation (natural log)	.08**(8.9%)	.03*(2.7%)	.10
Pseudo R^2	.08***	.10***	.14***

***significant at .01   **significant at .05   *significant at .1

[a] Inclusion of this variable for Brasilia eliminates roughly half of the cases from the sample, given that I had discontinuous data. Only 1996 and 2002 protests had information from the previous year; the rest had missing data on this variable. I therefore omitted it from the model presented here. When it is included, only age remains significant, in the same direction.

TABLE 3.4. *Summary of Results: Quantitative Models of Protest Rates*

Variables	Operationalization	Results
Organizational Resources		
Type of resources	Union	**Increases protest**
	Urban popular movement	**Increases protest in Mexico City and Brasilia**
	Street vendor	Insignificant
	Transportation union	Mixed results
	Controls for outliers (MOCO)	**Increases protest**[a]
Institutionalization	Age	**Decreases protest**
Leadership competition	Not tested	
Identity		
Past history of protest	Lagged protest	**Increases protest**
Positive view of protest	Left party ally	**Increases protest**
Independent of parties	Independence	Insignificant, though negative
POS		
Allied to party in power	In-group	Insignificant, though negative
Electoral cycle effects	Honeymoon year	**Increases protest**
	Election year	Insignificant
	Interaction, in-group with honeymoon year	Insignificant
	Interaction, in-group with election year	Increases protest in Mexico City only
Economic grievance	Inflation rate (logged)	Insignificant

[a] If MOCO is omitted, its impact is picked up by the transportation union variable. The same thing happens to the "student" variable when the CGH (Mexico City's 1999 university student strikers) is omitted from models of protests against all targets. No other variables change in significance.

given general expectations that globalization has reduced the capacity of unions to defend labor interests? Why don't organizations give a new administration time to demonstrate its intentions before protesting against it? What is the matter with Leftists? And most fundamentally, why is protest apparently so impervious to changes in the POS? Are organizations simply not rational, protesting just to protest?

Three possible explanations come to mind. First, protest repertoires may reflect relatively sticky cultural attitudes. Certain organizational frames, and perhaps especially those that developed under authoritarian conditions, may interpret protest as cleaner than negotiations. Protest once proved the courage and independence of movement leaders from authoritarian rulers; negotiation, in contrast, was a suspicious activity indicating possible cooptation. Protest may reflect views of the state that do not change when the people in the government change. In his discussion of organizational survival and niches, Michael Hannan (2005: 59–60) finds that, "changing an organization's core features, those tied to its identity, entails a heightened risk of failure and mortality ... changes in core features likely cause problems because they violate expectations of relevant audiences (inside and outside the organization)." Thus, once an organization has become dependent on a specific frame for recruiting members and demonstrating leadership competence, it may be difficult to switch frames and declare negotiations acceptable – even with party allies.

Second, protest may have less direct but no less rational purposes than simply getting the government to respond to a specific demand. The public visibility of protest makes it a signaling mechanism useful for internal organizational maintenance as well as for making demands on government. Leaders may use protest to demonstrate their relative strength to rivals within their own organization, or to prove that their organization has more guts than rival organizations competing for the same members. Members can use their participation in protests to demonstrate superior loyalty to leaders who must allocate scarce resources among the membership. Protest as an emotionally moving experience helps popular organizations create and renew the solidarity ties that are a key resource in overcoming collective action problems. To restate a point made in the introduction, the original hypothesis held that if the benefits expected from protest can be obtained from the local government without incurring the costs of protest, then less costly versions of voice should be preferred. But this argument suggests that the benefits of protest are not limited to the resources obtained from government. Instead, they extend to functions of organizational maintenance and leadership competition. Because these benefits derive from the act of protest itself, they cannot be obtained without incurring the costs of protest. As Tarrow (1989a: 22) has remarked, "Regarding collective action as a resource of social movements implies a corollary: that collective action does not necessarily cease when people's grievances are satisfied."

Similarly, protest during honeymoon years may serve more as a signaling mechanism than as a direct expression of grievance. New governments when they come into office have only a general sense of their goals. Organizations make it their business to supply the new government with a list of specific policy priorities. As Kingdon (1995: 204) puts it, "when a [policy] window opens, problems and policies flock to it." But "the scarcity of open windows constrains participants. They compete for limited space on agendas and queue up for their turn." By protesting publicly, organizations can signal to the new government that they are especially strong/important/intensely determined and therefore worthy of taking priority over competing organizations in the new administration's list of "things to do."

Finally, from a rational choice point of view, cost–benefit calculations for in-groups versus out-groups may not result in starkly different expected benefits of protest. Costs go up against enemies, and the probability of success declines. As Banfield puts it, "the effort an interested party makes to put its case before the decision-maker will be in proportion *to the advantage to be gained from a favorable outcome multiplied by the probability of influencing the decision.*"[18] Allies have a predisposition to respond to protest and are likely to impose lower costs.

However, the difference between the ally's program and the organization's own is also smaller. The friendly government already wants to do what you want it to do – whether you protest or not. Thus, the gain from successful protesting is smaller than when an unfriendly government is in power and there is a big difference between that program and yours. A successful protest could deliver big benefits compared to what would happen if the organization did nothing. But the likelihood that an opponent will listen even to aggressive protest is lower than if the organization were dealing with a friend. Thus, the *expected* benefit of protest remains about the same because the probability of success and the policy gap move in opposite directions.[19]

---

[18] Cited in Albert O. Hirschman, *Exit, Voice, and Loyalty: Responses to Decline in Firms, Organizations, and States*, (Cambridge, MA: Harvard University Press, 1970): 39, from Edward C. Banfield, *Political Influence* (New York: Free Press, 1961): 333.

[19] I am grateful to Stuart Kasdin for making this suggestion.

These explanations are plausible and could all be true. However, in order to answer the questions left by the statistical analysis a different approach is required. Chapters 4–7 develop case studies of two types of organization: unions and neighborhood associations. Based on interviews, personal observation, and organizational life histories, I find evidence of all three processes at work. Organizations do not mindlessly pursue protest at any cost, but protest does become part of organizational culture and identity. Organizations that rely more on protest have internal institutional reasons for doing so. And organizations do respond rationally to changes in political opportunity.

4

A Union Born Out of Struggles

The Union of Municipal Public Servants of São Paulo

Among the most difficult roles for Leftist governments to assume is that of employer, particularly when they must juggle this role against the demands of affiliated unions of public employees. In the opposition, Left-leaning parties can feel free to champion the claims of public employees for higher wages, better benefits, and job security. In power, satisfying these demands may conflict with budget constraints and with competing demands for public services. The tension between defending labor and "governing for everyone," between the representation of one's own base and the requirements of good government, has put many a Leftist mayor between a rock and a hard place. Moreover, unions may expect more from Leftist governments than from conservative governments, compounding the potential for conflict. As a result, "the phenomenon [of conflict with municipal unions] is present in almost all experiences [of Left government in Latin America], despite the different characteristics of the unions."[1]

The next two chapters examine one arena where we can observe these conflicting expectations closely: municipal employee unions in Mexico City and São Paulo. What makes the comparison particularly compelling is the fact that while municipal employee unions are affiliated with the Left (PT) in São Paulo and Brasilia, they are affiliated with the Left's political rival, the PRI, in Mexico City. If party alliance

---

[1] Stolowicz (1999: 190). See also the discussion of the Barrantes administration in Lima in Schönwälder (2002: 129).

drives behavior, we should see contrasting reactions to Left electoral victory. Much of the existing literature argues that:

> Other things being equal, union leaders are more willing to restrain their militancy when their allied parties are in the government and increase it when their allies are in the opposition. That is, unions may need strikes to probe governments they distrust, but not their allies in power. Strategic politicians, in turn ... prefer to reward the loyalty of allied unions rather than to give in to unions who have no attachment to the governing party and fewer incentives for restraint. (Murillo, 2001: 15)

These constraints should be most evident in the case of Mexico, where the union's party ally – the PRI – developed effective mechanisms to punish union leaders for disloyalty or reward them for faithful restraint.

As anticipated, the PRI municipal union protested significantly more against the Left (PRD) than it did against PRI governments. However, despite a relationship to the PT that verges on the incestuous, the São Paulo municipal employee union also protested more against its own ally than against opposition administrations. In both countries, then, the Left found itself the preferred target of protest regardless of the party affiliation of the municipal employee union. Figure 4.1 summarizes these findings by administration. In São Paulo, municipal employees protested nearly twice as often against PT governments compared to the conservative *malufista* governments.[2] In Brasilia, municipal employees protested thirty-one times a year on average when the PT was in power, versus twenty-four times a year when it was not. And in Mexico City, municipal employees protested almost three times as often when the PRD was in power. The biggest difference turns up in Mexico City, suggesting that the tendency to protest against Leftist governments is magnified when the municipal employee union sees the Left party as a political enemy. Nevertheless, the behavior of Brazilian unions contradicts what would appear to be their political interests.

---

[2] That is, the SINPEEM, representing local public school teachers, and the SINDSEP, representing all other municipal employees.

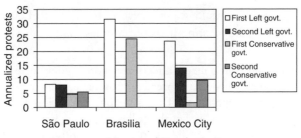

FIGURE 4.1. Municipal Employee Protests.

Even more interestingly, municipal employee protests occurred primarily in the first two years of PT administrations, accounting for most of the difference in average rates. High rates of protest against the PT did not reflect growing desperation by unions who initially trusted their ally and only turned to protest when trust produced no results. Rather, the unions came out swinging shortly after inauguration day.

The first section of this chapter establishes the framework of discussion and the variables. The second section puts São Paulo's municipal employee union within a broader context of public-sector unionism in Brazil. The third section analyzes the case of the SINDSEP (Sindicato dos Servidores Publicos Municipais de São Paulo – the Union of Municipal Public Servants of São Paulo). Chapter 5 will then contrast the SINDSEP with Mexico City's municipal employee union and introduce a pair of quantitative models of protest that isolate unions from non-unions.

Overall, I conclude that for these unions, protest is more important for internal leadership competition than for organizational survival. Organizational culture – shaped by the political context in which unions emerged – also affects the propensity to protest. In Brazil, organizational culture led unions to engage in more confrontational behavior, whereas in Mexico confrontation was mostly sponsored by internal dissenters from the unions' prevailing culture of cooperation with the PRI. Unions responded to changes in the POS – but their perception of opportunity did not necessarily lead them to spare their political allies. Instead, it led them to increase protests when they expected a positive response. As it turns out, that meant unions protested more when the Left party won, regardless of whether or not they were allied with it. The Left was seen as more sympathetic, less likely to repress labor, and more likely to respond positively to mobilization than the local alternatives.

OPERATIONALIZING THE VARIABLES

In these chapters, I use a more qualitative approach to begin to address the questions raised in Chapter 3 regarding the effects of organizational culture, the causes of union aggressiveness, and the significance of "honeymoon year" protests. This approach also clarifies in many respects why organizations may appear not to react to changes in POS. In particular, the use of internal organizational records and interviews reveals how organizational leaders perceive "political opportunity" and how they understand the constraints imposed upon them by alliance with a political party. Qualitative analysis also allows me to explore the impact of additional organizational characteristics, including the role of protest in organizational maintenance, the importance of ideological frames for the construction of movement identity, the consequences of where organizations get material resources, and the effect of different mechanisms for internal leadership selection. This last factor emerges from two recent studies of union resistance to market-oriented reforms, by Victoria Murillo (2001) and Katrina Burgess (2004).

Murillo's complex and compelling argument attributes variation in levels of labor mobilization against a party ally to two key conditions: leadership competition and union competition.[3] Leadership competition refers either to "competition between rivals associated with different political parties ... [or] competition for leadership among rivals associated with diverse factions of the same party." The risk of being replaced as their union's representative motivates union leaders to increase militancy: "if they believe that rival leaders are taking advantage of their restraint vis-à-vis market reforms ... militancy is not irrational. Nor is it a bargaining strategy. ... It is a leadership tactic for political survival."[4] Union competition refers to "the rivalry

---

[3] See also Robertson (2004) for an empirical confirmation of the effects of competition on mobilization by labor unions, based on cases from Eastern Europe.

[4] Murillo (2001: 15–16). One precursor for this argument can be found in J. Samuel Valenzuela's discussion (1992: 75) of types of unionism. The contestatory type, in which "political and ideological divisions lead to a process of competition between

among unions for the representation of workers in the same sector."
Union competition mostly affects whether governments decide to
concede to union demands: "governments should be less likely to
make concessions to competing unions because they are weaker than
monopolistic unions" (Murillo, 2001: 16–17). Thus, when union
leaders must worry about being replaced by partisan rivals in internal
elections, they will tend toward mobilization – either effective extrac-
tion of concessions if unions do not compete, or ineffective resistance
if they do. In the absence of leadership competition, unions should
cooperate with party allies even if these allies ask them to accept
market reforms, unless they fear their members will defect to rival
unions. However, their resistance will be futile.

Murillo's argument makes two assumptions. First, she assumes
that labor-based parties are trying to engage in market reforms. Under
these conditions, "partisan loyalties can become contradictory to
constituencies' demands, thereby affecting leadership survival and the
incentives of labor leaders in their interaction with governments"
(Murillo, 2001: 15). Clearly, local labor-based parties do not engage
in macroeconomic policy making, but a larger context of market
reforms still results in budgetary constraints that affect their freedom
of maneuver in labor negotiations. In a context of plenty, labor parties
can afford to meet the demands of their union allies. In a context of
scarcity, interests will conflict.

Second, union leaders who mobilize because of leadership competition (they "fear losing their positions") must assume that members
will punish them for restraint and reward militancy. But why should
members necessarily reward militancy? True, the impact of neoliberal
reforms on wages and living standards is likely to make workers
unhappy. Still, Murillo implicitly assumes that workers perceive
militance as *functional* in terms of resisting neoliberal reforms. My
argument implies that workers may support militance, even when
they do not think that neoliberal reforms can be effectively resisted,
because of organizational repertoires, culture, and framing.

the different tendencies for the allegiance of union militants ... generates union
leaderships which are highly responsive and attentive to rank-and-file aspirations and
easily leads to an escalation of union demands." However, "unions in this type of
labour movement are normally quite weak. This is partly a consequence of the very
divisions that lead to the competition in the first place."

Katrina Burgess (2004) adds another important factor: institutional structures within the party ally. If the party permits internal dissent and elects its leadership autonomously, it may support labor's efforts to resist painful reforms rather than support copartisans in the government, thereby rescuing leaders from having to choose between loyalty to union members and loyalty to the party. If parties are less internally democratic, then union leaders must decide which group has more power to punish them: workers or party leaders.

Leadership competition is therefore added to the list of variables from Chapter 3. Some of these variables are only examined qualitatively, through the case studies, while others are also tested quantitatively.

PUTTING THE SINDSEP IN CONTEXT: PUBLIC-SECTOR UNIONISM IN BRAZIL

Public-Sector Unionism in a Neoliberal Age

There are strong theoretical and empirical reasons to believe that analysis of public employee unions can tell us a lot about how changes in the POS affect the prospects for protest. Most importantly, public employees are more directly affected by which party is in power than any private-sector union. The government is their employer. Its attitude toward wage increases, labor rights, pension plans, and so forth, affects their immediate prospects. Employees of a private company may also be affected by government attitudes, but the impact is indirect, by way of its economic policies. Public employee unions should therefore experience larger shifts in costs and benefits when the government changes hands.

Second, public-sector unions have specific advantages that facilitate collective action. As a result of these advantages, public-sector unions are more likely to have the *capacity* to protest if they choose than private-sector unions or non-union organizations. Public employees face a single employer – the state – rather than a fragmented set of private actors. This can create incentives for cooperation across regions and even occupational categories, incentives often missing in the private sector. Public employees are uniquely positioned to disrupt state activities and compel government response. Public employee unions also tend to have a high proportion of educated, middle-class professionals who can provide leadership and resources for collective action.

Finally, neoliberal reforms affect state employees especially adversely. While some manufacturing sectors may benefit from the opening up of exports, neoliberal constraints on state expenditures directly impact the state employee's pocketbook. Privatization of state-owned companies may result in lost jobs, wage increases are often postponed, benefits are cut, and pensions are privatized. In Mexico, state bureaucrats experienced the largest salary erosion of any occupational sector between 1991 and 1997 (Rendón and Salas, 2000: 74–75). In Brazil, federal employees went without a raise for six years, resulting in a 75 percent decline in their real wages between 1995 and 2001 – *after* the stabilization of the Brazilian currency (Filipini, 2001: 9).

At the same time, the state's ability to restrain demands by public employee unions may significantly affect both political stability and economic performance. For Garrett (1998: 26), economic viability under globalization depends quite critically on the organizational characteristics of labor unions. Markets can constrain wage increases in the private sector without any formal coordination. Workers may accept wage restraints in order to maintain international competitiveness and thus reduce their risk of job loss. Public-sector unions face different incentives. Public-sector workers are protected by the privileged position of the state as a monopolistic provider of public goods. Global pressure on wages does not make the state "uncompetitive," forcing wages down. Nevertheless, "wage push in the public sector ... will lower the competitiveness of the exposed [private] sector" (Garrett, 1998: 41). The combination of strong left-wing parties and encompassing trade union movements permits the state to restrain wages in the public sector without provoking strikes and protest. As a result, the "political, economic, and social stability characteristics of social democratic corporatism – coupled with the high productivity of labor – provide an attractive home for investors in the uncertain and volatile international economy" (Garrett, 1998: 130).

In developing countries, the constraints may be less internal (social democratic corporatism) than external (IMF packages), but the effect on investor expectations is the same: where states fail to exercise fiscal restraint, investors may withdraw their money. Since payroll constitutes a significant percentage of total state spending, labor demands create a serious dilemma. The government can either accept labor demands at the cost of undermining fiscal stability or accept the risk of strikes and protests that could damage investor confidence. The best solution for the state is to have unions that voluntarily accept wage constraints.

Under what conditions will unions of public employees accept such economic sacrifices? Most countries fall short of the combination that Garrett's argument singles out as the most promising: high levels of union organization and integration with parties. But can party loyalties substitute in some ways for broader peak organizations, restraining demands by at least those sectors of public employees that are organized and integrated with parties? Or are public employee unions likely to accept sacrifices only when their enemies present them with an unacceptably high risk of repression and/or a low probability of success?

Public-Sector Union Organization in Brazil

Brazil has a relatively high rate of unionization, with public-sector unions particularly prominent despite the effects of privatization and neoliberal reform. With approximately 44 percent of nonagricultural employment unionized, Brazil is more densely unionized than eleven of eighteen European countries for which statistics are available.[5] Though Brazil carried out an extensive privatization program in the 1980s and 1990s, public employees continued to account for approximately 13 percent of Brazilian nonagricultural employment as of 2000 (Wilkie, Aleman, and Ortega, 2002: 407). Of all registered unions, 17.2 percent represented public-sector employees in 2001 – more than industry or commerce (Mouteira, 2003: B15). Public-sector unions also protested more often than private-sector unions, and their strikes lasted longer, resulting in thirteen times as many lost workdays as industrial strikes (Martins Rodrigues, 1990: 52).

Despite the potential appeal of unions as an electoral base, Brazilian unions never became effectively tied to parties during the rise of mass politics. Collier and Collier label Brazil as an example of state incorporation, where "the state sought primarily to impose new methods of

[5] www.ilo.org; see also Norris (2002: 174–175).

control," without making a major effort to mobilize unions as a base of support (Collier and Collier, 1991: 16). Indeed, "union–party links were prohibited, and pre-existing political currents in the labor movement were repressed" (Collier and Collier, 1991: 163). Compared to Mexico, state incorporation would involve fewer benefits for labor and a less favorable political position.

However, precisely because "the incorporation experiences had not left a legacy of deeply ingrained political ties between the union movement and a multi-class party ... in the aftermath of state incorporation, workers' political affiliations were less well-defined, and in that specific sense the labor movement had a greater degree of political independence" (Collier and Collier, 1991: 355). Initially, the politicization of the working class resulted in polarization, which led to the 1964 military coup and the repression of parties, like the Communist Party, that had attempted to mobilize unions. Nascent union–party links were severed.

Thus, when Brazil began moving back toward democracy, no party had successfully secured the loyalty of unions. Those unions that managed to break free of state controls had unusual liberty to construct their own system of alliances. In an extraordinary reversal of the usual order of events in Latin America, the independent union movement in Brazil avoided alliance with all existing parties and created its own, the Workers' Party (PT), in 1982. Union leaders were not the only sponsors of the PT – popular movements, Catholic Ecclesial Base Communities, intellectuals, and older Left parties also played a role – but it was clear that "the PT was founded largely at the initiative of labor leaders, who continued to dominate its leadership and remained the key spokespersons for the party" (Keck, 1992: 167).

Significantly, the PT did not legally incorporate unions, since labor law in 1982 still prohibited union–party affiliations. Nevertheless, unions developed an unusually close and trusting relationship with the Workers' Party through informal linkages. Most early PT leaders came out of the union movement, including the PT's first national president, Luis Inácio (Lula) da Silva. Union leaders also did the bulk of the organizational work needed to secure official PT registration, including Olívio Dutra (the bankers' union), Devanir Ribeiro and Djalma Bom (the metalworkers' union), and Jacó Bittar (the oil workers' union). Lula, Dutra, and Bittar were the president, vice-president, and secretary-general, respectively, of the provisional PT leadership elected in 1980 (Keck, 1992). Seven of the fourteen members of the first national executive of the PT had a background in union leadership, all in unions affiliated with the United Workers' Central (Central Único dos Trabalhadores, or CUT), formed by independent unions in 1983.[6]

Over 40 percent of the early members of the PT participated in a union at the time of their party affiliation.[7] Later on, recruitment to the CUT went hand-in-hand with recruitment to the PT. For example, at the Third Congress of the CUT, in 1988, 90.9 percent of delegates preferred the PT even though most of the delegates (67 percent) had been recruited into the CUT less than seven years earlier – after the foundation of both the PT and the CUT.[8]

A significantly more diverse set of party preferences is evident among delegates to the first Congress (in 1991) of the CUT's main rival, the union confederation Força Sindical (Union Power). No party got more than 20 percent of delegate preferences. The largest group – 19.8 percent – indicated *no* party preference.[9] Força Sindical maintains no loyalty to any specific party. Although its leaders may affiliate with parties to get a candidacy for a specific election, they join different parties in different locations and change parties from one election to the next.[10]

---

[6] I could not find records on one of the members of the first national executive committee of the PT: Helio Doyle. However, he has a background as a journalist. He later worked for the non-PT government of Roriz. Thus, I do not count him as a CUT member. List of members found in Partido dos Trabalhadores (1998: 95, 116).

[7] An additional 27.3 percent declined to answer, while 32.1 percent declared that they did not belong to a union (César, 2002: 226).

[8] Of the delegates, 37 percent had participated in union activism for less than three years and an additional 30.8 percent had participated for less than seven years (Martins Rodrigues, 1990: 79–80).

[9] 16.9 percent favored the PMDB, 16.6 percent the PDT, 13.5 percent the PSDB, and 17.7 percent preferred the PT itself (Martins Rodrigues and Moreira Cardoso, 1993: 116). Among the national leadership, the PT did far worse: only 3.3 percent of the national directorate preferred the PT. However, preferences were split fairly widely, with four parties getting at least 10 percent of preferences, and "none of the above" garnering 16.4 percent (Martins Rodrigues and Moreira Cardoso, 1993: 119).

[10] For example, the president of Força Sindical, Paulo Pereira da Silva, belonged to the Partido Democrático Trabalhista (PDT) from 1983 to 1993, quit, went through a couple of other political parties, and came back to the PDT in 2003, along with 2,000 of his closest friends (Força Sindical, 2003).

Association between PT and CUT activism is even more marked in the case of public employee unions. Public employees did not acquire the right to register unions until after the transition from military rule and the approval of a new constitution in 1988. Public employees could only form "associations," which mostly provided social services to workers. Nevertheless, some of these associations were among the first to join the wave of independent union strikes started by metal-workers in São Paulo in the late 1970s. In 1978, a strike by public school teachers in the state of São Paulo mobilized nearly 80 percent of the state's 180,000 teachers over a period of several weeks. This movement was followed by strikes of teachers in Paraná, Brasilia, Rio de Janeiro, Rio Grande do Sul, and Minas Gerais.

The early mobilization of these associations led to their partici-pation in the formation of the CUT and the PT. Initially – largely due to their ambiguous legal status – public-sector unions were a distinct minority. In the first CUT Congress, held in 1983, just 7.2 percent of the participating organizations represented public employees (Mazzei Nogueira, 1999: 60). In the 1997 CUT Congress, 55 percent of CUT delegates came from public-sector unions, compared to 29 percent representing the private sector and 14 percent representing rural workers (Jard da Silva, 2001: 133). Virtually all public employee unions joined the CUT, whereas Força Sindical represents private-sector unions almost exclusively.[11]

Despite this close association, we find routinely high levels of conflict between PT municipal governments and their allied municipal employee unions. In 1989, the PT elected thirty-six mayors across Brazil. By 1992, twelve of these mayors had left the PT because of factional disputes; of the remaining twenty-four mayors only twelve won reelection, at least in part as a result of internal conflicts, often with municipal employees (Baiocchi, 2003b: 18). The case of Luiza Erundina in São Paulo is classic:

Among Erundina's most serious difficulties were clashes with municipal unions over the issue of wages. The municipal unions, controlled by *petistas* and affiliated with the . . . CUT, from the start demanded raises to meet rising

---

[11] At its founding congress, less than 5 percent of Força delegates worked in the public sector. See Martins Rodrigues and Moreira Cardoso (1993: 27, 51) and Martins Rodrigues (1990: 15, 42).

inflation rates...municipal employees called their first strike in August 1989, despite the raises given by Erundina's administration at the beginning of the year. (Baiocchi, 2003b: 19)

Barely eight months leeway had been granted to the PT mayor since her inauguration. Clashes with municipal unions also lay behind the collapse of the PT administration in Campinas and the resignation of mayor Jacó Bittar, a key PT founder, from the PT. Conflicts with municipal employees "paralyzed the administration three times before the mayor announced he was quitting the party" (Baiocchi, 2003b: 21).

Similarly, Cristovam Buarque, the PT mayor of Brasilia, faced more strikes by municipal workers than his conservative counterpart, Joaquim Roriz, despite the fact that Buarque had a union background, despite the political affiliation of the major employee unions with the PT, despite his inclusion of the leaders of local employee unions in his administration,[12] and despite his efforts to preserve municipal jobs and avoid pay cuts. By 1996, "Brasilia was spending 80 percent of its liquid assets on public sector workers' wages and other benefits ... compared to around 67 percent at the start of Buarque's term." Nevertheless, voters in Brasilia ranked Buarque worst on his management of public employees, probably as a result of the high level of strike activity. Buarque lost his bid for reelection. Thus, "the Achilles heel of the [Buarque] administration turned out to be the conflicting claims of reducing public spending and meeting the claims of public sector workers" (Macauley and Burton, 2003: 148–149).

In these examples, we can see the trigger of conflicts in the diverging expectations of union leaders on the one hand and PT government officials on the other. In the opposition, union leaders became accustomed to full support from the PT. In government, as Jacó Bittar objected, "I am a trade unionist but I cannot behave like one in the mayor's office ... giving in to all the demands made by public employees." The constituency of a mayor includes not only unions but also the "disadvantaged, the unorganized and the voiceless, whose interests [the party] promises to prioritize" (Macauley and Burton, 2003: 135–136). Add to this the roadblocks erected by elite and conservative

---

[12] For example, one-third of the executive board of the Brasilia Teachers Union (SINPRO) held a position in the Buarque government in 1995. And yet, SINPRO went on strike six times in 1995 ("Sinpro é disputado por partidos," 1995: 15).

opposition and you have a recipe for dramatic confrontations. As another PT mayor warned, "Petista mayors have to prepare themselves because, without a doubt, they will face many more strikes than other mayors will."[13]

Yet why have unions not assimilated these lessons, particularly given the negative consequences for continued PT governance in many cities? Municipal employees in São Paulo protested nearly as frequently against the 2001–2003 PT government of Marta Suplicy as they did against the 1989–1992 PT government of Luiza Erundina.

THE SINDSEP

The municipal employees' union in São Paulo enjoys a legal monopoly over representation of the city's 168,000 workers according to the Brazilian legal principle of *unicidade*. *Unicidade* gives unions a legal monopoly over an occupational category within a given territory. However, Brazilian unions do not enjoy the privilege of a closed shop or a separation exclusion clause that would require employers to fire workers who refuse to join the union. This creates pressure on union leaders to actively recruit members. Moreover, because *unicidade* combines two criteria for monopoly of representation (occupational category and territory), workers can theoretically join multiple associations, introducing a further form of competition for members. For example, an accountant in São Paulo might qualify to join an accountants' union or the union of municipal employees. Thus, the Union of Municipal Public Servants of São Paulo (SINDSEP), "represents, juridically, all 168 thousand public municipal employees in São Paulo," but "not all are affiliated" (SINDSEP, 1995: 7). In fact, SINDSEP claimed only 22,000 active members as of 2002.

PT leaders have relatively little ability to punish "disloyal" union leaders. The Brazilian unions that created the PT did not want to feel dependent on any party for a voice in the policy arena, even their own. Most of the democratic opposition in the early 1980s believed that the best chance of a successful democratic transition lay in uniting all opponents of the military regime in a centrist opposition party, but

---

[13] This mayor governed in the second set of PT administrations (1993–1996) (Baiocchi, 2003b: 23).

Lula insisted that unions needed a party untainted by compromise with the Brazilian conservative elites. As he put it in typically vivid fashion, "after talking with all the congressmen, I went home thinking the following: I was a fool. ... How could we expect that the allies of our bosses could make laws in the interests of the working class? ... [We needed] to create a political instrument."[14] They intended the PT to act for labor in the unique arenas of legislative and electoral politics, and from these positions to block state repression of the labor movement. Nevertheless, unions remained skeptical of the value of electoral politics as a method of promoting workers' interests. A union central uniting all of the independent unions would also be necessary. Thus, the PT was founded in 1982 and the CUT in 1983.

Particularly during its formative years, the PT was more dependent on the CUT than the other way around. The party's public image, as well as its ability to survive early electoral disappointments, reflected its identification with independent unionism. The PT gave the CUT a place in legislative politics as well as in the administrations of a growing number of PT mayors and governors.[15] But the CUT could – and did – speak for itself. The effects of the CUT's independence and feelings of ownership of the party counteracted its incentives to restrain protest when the PT got into power. Party leaders have few legal or institutional means to punish union leaders for disloyalty because the unions set it up that way to protect union autonomy.

In contrast, union members did have institutional means of holding their leaders accountable. The implementation of internally democratic rules within the CUT resulted from deliberate rejection of previous forms of union leadership. Union leaders have to face regular internal elections. Within the SINDSEP, leadership consists of an elected directorate with a triumvirate of president, vice president, and secretary general at the top and a varying number of functional and

---

[14] This conversation took place in 1978, after the first wave of strikes, when Lula went to Brasília to protest a new antiunion law forbidding certain "essential" workers from striking. Lula first proposed the idea of a Workers' Party in December 1978 to a small group of union leaders, who formed a seven-man committee to lead the "pro-PT Movement" (Harnecker, 1994: 48, 57).

[15] At one point, 30 percent of PT state deputies were linked to trade unions – as much as the PRI at the height of union strength. In 1979, 31 percent of PRI congressional representatives came from PRI unions. By 1997, only 17 percent did (Shidlo, 1998: 85; Bensusán and Alcalde, 2000: 170).

sectoral heads of department in charge of organizing workers by occupational type.[16] The directorate is elected on the basis of factional lists, called *chapas*. Elections are held every four years, timed to coincide with the inauguration of a new municipal administration. Usually, two or three *chapas* compete in SINDSEP elections, although a unified CUT *chapa* is typically created via prior internal negotiations. The informal norm in these negotiations is proportional representation of the CUT/PT factions, which account for approximately 80 percent of SINDSEP leaders (interview with Leandro Valquer Leite de Oliveira, president of SINDSEP, August 2003). Significantly, when a dispute exists over the relative strength of a faction within the CUT *chapa*, one of the ways of solving the dispute involves protest: counting the number of people a factional leader can bring to a public demonstration or assembly.[17]

Despite the top-down nature of these internal negotiations, leadership turnover is substantial. Only eight of the twenty-seven members of the 2002–2005 SINDSEP directorate appeared in the list of directors in 1991. Moreover, non-CUT and non-PT members – many of them from rival Leftist parties, like the Communist Party of Brazil (PCdoB) – serve openly in top union posts. In 2002, for example, the dominant PT faction held 77 percent of the directorships in SINDSEP, but members of Unity and Struggle (close to the Brazilian Communist Party, PCB) and the Classist Union Current (close to the PCdoB) were also represented, as was a Trotskyist tendency (interview with Leandro Valquer Leite de Oliveira, August 2003). Most of these parties consider themselves more radical than the dominant CUT, limiting potential

---

[16] In 2002, for example, these included a *Secretaria* of press relations, political formation, legal affairs, interunion policy, social policy and events, administrative workers, women workers, education workers, workers in the autarchies, health workers, operational workers, health policy (benefits), and workers in SAS, SEME, SMC, and SMMA (municipal administrative departments). In addition, there were ten regional coordinators responsible for maintaining local offices for member services and recruitment in São Paulo's sprawling territory.

[17] I actually witnessed this solution during similar negotiations in a meeting of urban popular movements. Smaller factions were given a minimum of representation, resulting in slight overrepresentation. Larger factions fought bitterly over their share of the pie. The three largest factions decided to leave some of the seats on the delegation "unallocated," to be divided up according to which group could bring the largest number of people to an assembly where the final slate of delegates would be decided.

tendencies toward moderation. The norm of including political minorities guarantees internal leadership diversity and continued discussion of mobilization even in a context of PT/CUT control.

At the national level, the largest faction within the CUT – Articulação Sindical – had less than half (49 percent) of the delegates to the Fourth CUT Congress. Articulação had enough delegates to control the new leadership in concert with several small factions, but two opposition factions collectively represented 32 percent of the delegates (Jácome Rodrigues, 1994: 51). Disputes among factions within the CUT are endemic and sometimes alarmingly intense. Di Tella notes that

The factionalism in CUT is much more accentuated than in the PT, because here it is not only the internal divisions within the PT that confront each other, but they must also compete with other leftist parties, like the Socialist Party and the maoist Communist Party. … Typically the PT congresses are peaceful, albeit tense, while the meetings of CUT sometimes end in violence. (1995: 42)

Union leaders mentioned competitive pressures in interviews as a reason for continuing protest. Restraint was also associated with losing ground to rival unions. As one union leader argued, "because of the contradiction of having in the [Erundina] government, for example, government *compañeros* who previously were at the head of strikes, we didn't advance more, *creating an opening for Força Sindical*"[18] (emphasis added).

In much the same way, the PT-affiliated Teachers' Union of Brasilia (SINPRO) reacted to internal opposition by stepping up mobilization. In its mid-1995 leadership election, opposition came principally from a non-PT slate that accused the *petistas* of "being at the service of the Government [of PT Mayor Cristovam Buarque]" ("Sinpro é disputado por partidos," 1995: 15). Pro-PT union leaders reacted by giving interviews arguing that "we helped elect Governor Buarque,

---

[18] Interview with Claudete Alves, fourth president of the SINDSEP (1996–1999), published in *SINDSEP 1987–1997: 10 anos de Lutas*, 1997: 25. In my own interviews, another SINDSEP leader, from the pre-school teachers' sector, talked about increasing competition with other education unions for members, as well as three major *petista* tendencies within the union. She dated increasing divisions within the union to the point when the reclassification of pre-school teachers as education workers made them eligible to join other unions of teachers (Interview BD3, São Paulo, September 2003).

but we will not spare him criticism," and "we are not in a position of servitude" ("Apoio ao GDF divide eleição para o Sinpro," 1995). Two months after narrowly holding onto control of SINPRO, its PT leaders threatened a major strike against the municipal government, despite warnings by Buarque that he would not pay strikers. Protests by SINPRO doubled in 1996 over 1995.

However, competitive pressures do not force union leaders into unrestrained protest. Union leaders recognize that their actions can undermine governments with which they identify ideologically. Thus, in the case of Erundina, the SINDSEP claimed that "The Government ... was protected from a stronger critique by the organized popular movements because the workers knew that any criticism would be used by the reactionary right against the Government" (SINDSEP, 1991: 16). Mobilization by the SINDSEP declined drastically in 1991 and 1992, an immediate preelectoral period.

Moreover, protest does not always work. Leaders know that strikes can be risky for them personally: "if you use that instrument badly, you will be discredited" (interview with Leandro Valquer Leite de Oliveira, August 2003). Thus, rather than mobilizing, the SINDSEP in 2002 argued for negotiation in tandem with other local unions:

"it is important not to fight [the PT administration] in isolation. Of the 29 entities of public employees that make up the Sinp,[19] only part can be considered *cutista* [CUT members]. If we remain isolated in this process, we will lose politically. ... [I]t is risky ... for us to remain outside of the table of negotiations with the Mayor's Office." (SINDSEP, 2002b: 26)

In such a context, the attitudes of members toward protest matter. How will members respond to negotiation? How will they respond to protest? The political culture developed in the CUT and the PT distinctly favors protest and mobilization over negotiation. Brazil's "new unionism" emerged in a context of mobilization against employers and the state:

the existence of an authoritarian political system ... that condemned the union movement to a situation of marginality ... [was] quite favorable to the

---

[19] Initiated in 2002, the System of Permanent Negotiation (Sinp) is a forum where the unions and associations of municipal employees discuss issues with the municipal administration outside of their regular contract revision date (*database*) and prepare joint negotiations across categories to equalize salaries and benefits.

development of a confrontational unionism, founded in the conceptions of class struggle, in the idea of an irreversible conflict between capital and labor, in which the terms "understanding," "cooperation," and "participation," sounded like treason to the working class. The CUT was the expression of this conjunctural moment. (Martins Rodrigues and Moreira Cardoso, 1993: 156)

Força Sindical, in contrast, "emerges under the 1988 Constitution, in a period of broad formal democracy ... in a moment of recession, of unemployment, in conditions fairly unfavorable for a confrontational unionism." Moreover, "with the market for unions already occupied by the CUT, on one hand, and by the Central Geral do Trabalho (General Work Central, or CGT) on the other, what was left for the new central was the banner of modernity, to be contrasted to *cutista* socialism and the corporatism of the CGT" (Martins Rodrigues and Moreira Cardoso, 1993: 157–158). Thus, "the ambition of Força Sindical is to be the union central of the post-socialist era, capable of defending the interests of the workers here and now ... without utopian proposals" (Martins Rodrigues and Moreira Cardoso, 1993: 21).[20]

Most Força Sindical leaders and activists came out of official corporatist unions (CGT, et al.), rather than from the combative "Authentic Unionism" that gave birth to the CUT (Martins Rodrigues and Moreira Cardoso, 1993: 80–81). They tended to view the CUT as "sterile radicalism, [and] inconsistent partisanship" (Martins Rodrigues and Moreira Cardoso, 1993: 21). Eighty-nine percent of delegates to the founding congress of Força Sindical agreed that "the strike is an important instrument of struggle, but it must only be used as a last resort when negotiations fail" (Martins Rodrigues and Moreira Cardoso, 1993: 92).

The CUT, in contrast, viewed demobilization with suspicion. In 2001, the São Paulo CUT published an Educational Workbook (Caderno de Formação), intended for union activists and entitled *Union Action in the Local Context*. Several articles deal with the relationship between CUT unions and PT administrations. The basic problem they underline is that

the more the influence of left forces grows in public administration, especially municipal, the greater the potential for conflict between public employee unions and those administrations. This is because in a context of 'globalization' and

---

[20] See also the biography of Força Sindical founder Antônio Medeiros (Gianotti, 1994).

imposition of neoliberal policies, pressures grow for rigorous fiscal controls, with disastrous consequences for services and public employees. (Ladosky and Véras, 2001: 83)

The document acknowledges that PT electoral victories create new avenues of access for the CUT. It recognizes that the causes of conflict between public employee unions and PT administrations are as much external (globalization) as internal (betrayal by PT mayors). It also recognizes that the effects of these conflicts "can be disastrous ... as much for the popular administrations and their projects ... as in the field of the CUT (with losses of unions in an area that becomes ever more strategic)" (Ladosky and Véras, 2001: 83).

Nevertheless, "with every advance in institutional access, the pressure for institutional behavior increases ... [with the risk of] substituting negotiations for mobilization, restricting with this the level of direct participation and politicization of the union bases" (Véras, 2001: 178). Union members cannot directly participate in negotiations, only in mobilization. Thus, institutionalization is equated with elitization of the CUT, while protest implies participation and the development of class consciousness. This attitude conflicts with more pragmatic evaluations of the CUT's tactical options.

The SINDSEP's view of protest is presented in its "autobiography," a history written by union activists and published in a special tenth anniversary edition of the SINDSEP journal. Entitled "A Union Born out of Struggles," this history identifies the SINDSEP as a "combative union," and links its foundation to the "principal struggles of the Brazilian workers against the bosses and also against the military dictatorship" (SINDSEP, 1997: 6, 8). Even prior to the union's official formation, municipal employees staged major strikes (then illegal) in 1979, 1983, 1985, and 1987. Ten years later, the 1995 SINDSEP congress continued to argue that "the strike is the principal weapon of the worker in defense of his rights" – not a "last resort" to be used only when negotiations fail, as Força Sindical would have it (SINDSEP, 1995: 10).

This mobilizational political culture is shared by most of the groups that formed the PT. The very enterprise of creating a Workers' Party rather than supporting a unified opposition party against the military tended to attract activists with more radical Leftist perspectives, fewer ties to military-era institutions, and less willingness to compromise principle in the service of pragmatism. Union leaders in particular, "carried into the PT a mixture of orientations that combined a *movimentista* character ... an *anti-state* character, present in the search for autonomy and in the constant distrust of politicians and institutions; and a *participatory* character, resulting from the form of organization of the unions" (Gonçalves Couto, 1995: 63).

Positive orientations toward protest are coupled with suspicion of the state and its potentially corrupting effects. There is, as Keck relates, "a profoundly anti-statist element in the PT's self definition as a democratic socialist mass party" (1992: 247). PT preferences for direct participation and the empowerment of civil society have led to some of its most appealing political experiments, including the construction of Participatory Budgeting councils in a variety of PT-governed cities (e.g., Abers, 2000; Baiocchi, 2003b). But preferences for direct participation also correlate to rejection of nonparticipatory processes, including representative democracy as practiced in legislatures and administrative efficiency as practiced by PT executives. The dilemma for PT mayors (and presidents) is to reconcile the party's historic identity as "a party that was, and cannot renounce being, a party of struggle," with its position as "a party of government."[21]

Gonçalves Couto's analysis of the Erundina administration makes much of this contrast between "movement party ... oriented toward the passing on of demands of the organized (or unorganized) sectors that it seeks to represent," and "governing party," defined by the "preoccupation with formulating and implementing policies ... [and] aggregating demands, being therefore responsible ... to the whole of the governed" (Gonçalves Couto, 1995: 88). As long as it remained in the opposition, "the PT was able to maintain the logic of a movement-oriented party and a revolutionary party without grave problems, and even to some advantage. To maintain such a posture allowed the party to appear as the most 'authentic,' the purest, the only one really committed to popular causes." When it won power, however,

"those *petistas* who assumed positions of responsibility within the government found themselves suddenly ... becoming the agents that first, within the

---

[21] Tarso Genro, one of the party's founders and two-time mayor of Porto Alegre, made these remarks in a 1997 conference (Genro, 1997: 15–16).

system, had to respond to those demands that they used to express and many others as well, and second, to see to the preservation and efficient functioning of the administrative mechanism. Even more, [they] had to negotiate, above all within the legislature, in order to approve legislative initiatives that would permit them to implement their policies. (Gonçalves Couto, 1995: 89–90)

Newly elected PT officials frequently step down from party posts in order to further this separation of roles. Thus, conflicts between PT governments and the municipal party leadership occur nearly as often as conflicts with labor unions. In São Paulo, municipal party leaders sided openly with the SINDSEP and against Erundina. As Burgess notes, "if the party is able (and willing) to oppose its own government and join labor in resisting the reforms, labor leaders will no longer have to choose between loyalty to the party and loyalty to workers. Instead, they can oppose the reforms with the party's blessing" (2004: 6). The availability of PT allies in favor of mobilization – even against PT governments – made union decisions to protest much less wrenching.

Election also transformed party leaders into politicians. Not even Lula was considered safe from the seductive temptations of power. By mid-2004, "Lula: Traitor" placards had begun to appear at union rallies. CUT-affiliated unions broke into the Congress, while reforms to the public employee pension plan were being discussed, smashing the glass doors. And João Pedro Stedile, leader of the PT-aligned Movement of Landless Workers (MST) gleefully endorsed calls for a "red April" – stepping up land invasions in order to put pressure on Lula for immediate and radical land reform.

Similar effects can be observed in the two PT administrations of São Paulo. SINDSEP leaders describe the Erundina administration as a "path toward collision." The SINDSEP's history of those years attributes conflicts primarily to the fact that "many leaders and milit- ants of the union assumed important positions in the Government. Perhaps that is the key to the mystery . . . these leaders and militants . . . began to 'disqualify the demands of the union'." As a result,

on the one hand, the SINDSEP accuses the Mayor's Office of not seeing the strategic importance of public employees for the Administration and for society. And, on the other, the Mayor's Office accuses the Union of making outrageous demands and of not seeing the strategic importance of a popular democratic government faced with terrible financial difficulties and bitter opposition from [conservative political factions]. (SINDSEP, 2002b: 9–10)

Bear in mind, these were all PT members. After two bitter terms excluded from municipal power, the union campaigned hard for Marta Suplicy in 2000. Yet when she won, the union's initial instinct was to demonstrate. Their view of these events – and their relationship to protest – is worth quoting at some length:

Many attacked the leadership of the Union for this political position [campaigning for Suplicy]. "They accused us of being harnessed to the Administration," said [SINDSEP president] Claudete [Alves] resentfully. But how can anyone be "harnessed" to someone when even before that someone had taken office as Mayor the Union was already in the streets organizing and mobilizing workers for a strike and demonstrations, followed by a vigil at the City Council building? It is because autonomy from the State and governments are principles defended by the CUT, and which the SINDSEP follows religiously. This is the fundamental question. "As they say, the government should govern and the union should unionize!" jokes Claudete. (SINDSEP, 2002b: 10)

At the time she made these remarks, Claudete Alves was a member of the government herself, having won a seat in the city council as a PT candidate. Still, she supported protest, justifying it less in terms of benefits than as visible proof of the union's independence. Hence its timing, before the administration had even taken office, before it could be expected to deliver anything. Internal union histories explain strikes against Erundina similarly: "many strikes took place immediately in the first months of [Erundina's] government, which demonstrated the independence of SINDSEP in relationship to the mayor" (SINDSEP, 1997: 10).

Union leaders also expressed concern that sparing a PT administration could harm organizational unity. For example, one leader in 2003 discussed the union's reaction to the perpetual problem of subcontracting. In the view of union leaders, subcontracting allowed the municipal government to "get around labor law," by putting subcontracted workers in a different legal position than regular salaried workers. Salary increases applying to regular workers do not extend to subcontracted workers. Subcontracted workers are not eligible for benefits obtained by regular workers through union struggle. "This will break the unity of the municipal worker," she explained. Thus, when the non-PT government of Maluf attempted to institute subcontracting for municipal health clinics, the union mobilized to stop him. They called on workers not to participate in the new cooperatives being given contracts by the municipal government. And after two years, they succeeded in making the program unviable. When Marta Suplicy came to power, she transformed these clinics into autarchies (like parastatal enterprises), not directly administered by the municipal government. But the problem of subcontracted workers remained. Marta "stopped halfway." Thus, continued protest was justified. For this leader, the union and the PT government "can have a relationship but keep fighting" (interview BD4, with SINDSEP leader, August 2003).

Public expectations that unions should remain independent form part of cultural values and attitudes and therefore enter into leaders' calculations. As one union leader noted, "people will take it out on us if they think we are *pelegos* [acting to limit union activism on behalf of the government]" (interview BD1, with SINDSEP leader, September 2003). The visibility of protest makes it particularly well-suited as a means to demonstrate independence from the government to people (especially but not exclusively workers) with whom union leaders have only limited avenues of communication. But the belief that protest in and of itself is good also tends to reinforce continued protest.

There can be little doubt that a mobilizational culture exists within the PT and many CUT unions. Party and union leaders use protest to appeal to their base. The question is whether these conditions – internal competition, lack of party ability or will to punish disloyal union leaders, and a political culture favorable to protest – suffice to explain the PT unions' extraordinary behavior in protesting *more* against PT governments than against conservative administrations. If anything, the victory of a non-PT mayor should release union leaders from their loyalty dilemma and free them to indulge their desire to protest even more extravagantly.

The requirements of organizational maintenance do not appear to explain this puzzle. Solidarity and identity might well be helpful for a *party*, for whom [ideology] is the principal source of collective incentives. It maintains the identity of the organization for party members, especially militants, for whom these types of incentives are virtually their only form of reward. (Gonçalves Couto, 1995: 142)

However, such resources appear far less necessary to the organizational survival of unions. Brazilian unions receive substantial financing from the state, in the form of a union tax collected from workers' paychecks. The money permits unions to offer selective incentives for participation, including medical services, dental treatment, and legal aid for members.

Instead, two factors related to shifts in political opportunity tipped unions toward greater protest against the PT than conservative opponents. First of all, the need to demonstrate independence only emerges when the PT gets elected, creating potential confusion about the relationship between the union and the PT government. This confusion is worst right after the election, generating pressure to mobilize immediately rather than take a wait-and-see attitude.

Second, the probability of *successful* protest increases when a PT administration takes power. Brazilian union leaders are quite aware that constant mobilization that produces no results would endanger their positions just as much as no mobilization at all. Thus, reported one union leader, he would not call a strike unless "it's really going to work ... [not] just for amusement."[22] In both São Paulo and Brasília, the union's partisan opposition was extremely conservative, aligned with promilitary parties prior to the transition and inclined to repress dissent. The probability of success of any action declined dramatically.

In addition, strikes and demonstrations were at least partly intended to put union demands at the top of the new government's policy agenda. The PT, after all, has *many* popular allies, all making demands. The local government cannot possibly satisfy them simultaneously on limited resources. Protest thus reflects movement efforts to prove that they deserve first priority. From this point of view, protests early in an administration make more sense than protests later on. If leaders satisfy pent-up demands accumulated under a previous conservative

---

[22] The word used, *brincadeira*, can also mean a bluff. Interview with Leandro Valquer Leite de Oliveira, August 2003.

administration, they can bolster their prestige and leadership within the movement. More pragmatically, waiting could mean that the movement's demands are suspended by the subsequent election of a non-PT government. What's the lesson? Get what you can as soon as you can.

The example of Erundina tends to confirm the existence of rational calculations at the root of protest timing. According to SINDSEP, "workers believed that with the inauguration of Erundina all of their problems would be resolved." Erundina was a municipal employee (a social worker), active in popular and union organization. During the 1985 municipal employee strike against mayor Mario Covas, Erundina – a local city council member at that time – intervened on behalf of union organizers to get them released from detention.[23] Many union leaders supported Erundina's selection as the PT candidate over the majority faction's candidate. Yet despite their belief in her, they began to protest against her government before she even took office. The union later came to distrust Erundina, but the initial motivation for protest was not lack of trust.

In fact, Erundina brought some of her troubles on herself. As a candidate for the PT nomination, Erundina did not have the support of moderate party factions, being distinguished instead by a "participatory discourse with revolutionary overtones ... [that] made nervous those PT leaders interested in attracting sectors of the middle class toward the party." For her, "the government ought, frequently, to mobilize the population," largely to stimulate the growth of popular movements (Gonçalves Couto, 1995: 104). Erundina won the election by a razor-thin plurality.[24] She did not have a legislative majority in the city council. Yet she refused to enter into the traditional deal-making with other parties, involving the exchange of administrative posts for legislative support. Instead, she argued that "we can establish a new working relationship with the municipal Legislature, where popular pressure can force temporary alliances for the projects presented by the Executive or the PT bench" (Gonçalves Couto, 1995: 202). Among the policy initiatives on the PT agenda were such controversial

---

[23] Interview with Alice Vicente, third president of the SINDSEP (1993–1996), published in SINDSEP (1997: 22).

[24] After this election, new electoral rules provided for a run-off between the top two candidates in executive races.

ideas as higher property taxes, an end to expensive spending on roads and infrastructure in middle-class neighborhoods, and a reorientation of municipal budgets to housing programs for the poor. Far from giving movements a vacation from the need to protest, "it was believed that mobilizational capacity would increase with the arrival of the party to the Executive. Thus, the municipal [PT] leadership put pressure on its government to act in the sense of mobilizing the population and reinforcing popular movements, criticizing it when it did not do so" (Gonçalves Couto, 1995: 204).

When Erundina found through bitter experience that popular pressure did not in fact force non-PT legislators to support her initiatives, she gradually moved toward negotiating with opposition councilmen. The PT, however, did not. It increasingly sided with unions and popular movements against her administration. Moreover, Mayor Erundina continued to permit union meetings during working hours and in government buildings. Workers were allowed to leave work to attend demonstrations. The effect of these rules pushed protest by lowering the costs of attending. As one veteran of those strikes remarked, "I still do not know today if people went to the demonstrations and strikes because they got time off from work or because of class consciousness."[25] Finally, even after relations had soured, union leaders continued to argue that "we do not believe that Luiza Erundina will want to carry the political burden of beating up workers."[26]

In short, the municipal employees' union had every reason to expect that Mayor Erundina would respond positively to mobilization. Even after two years of confrontation and growing bitterness, the union's official position remained that "in this administration, in contrast to the ones that preceded it, we have better chances to advance in organization and conquests for municipal workers" (SINDSEP, 1991: 17). Thus, SINDSEP mobilization against Erundina not only helped the union demonstrate its independence but also seemed likely to produce results, even – or perhaps especially – in the first months of her administration, before she changed her mind about the benefits of

---

[25] Interview with Claudete Alves, fourth president of the SINDSEP (1996–1999), published in SINDSEP (1997: 25).

[26] Quoting a member of the CUT-linked Sindicato dos Trabalhadores da Economia Informal (a union of street vendors), in 1992 (Villas-Bôas, 1996: 27).

protest and before the financial constraints on her government became apparent. The union did not mobilize in the last two years of her administration at the same rate.

Moreover, while protest rates do not seem to follow economic conditions, union leaders take them into account when deciding *how* to protest. For example, the SINDSEP continued to protest at roughly the same rate in 2002 as it did in 1989, but far fewer actions involved strikes. The president of SINDSEP, Leandro Valquer Leite de Oliveira, questioned the viability and usefulness of strikes because the severity of unemployment had made workers more risk averse about strikes that might result in lost wages or even lost jobs.[27] As a result, union leaders shifted from strikes to demonstrations: "it used to be easier to get the workers to strike," noted one SINDSEP leader. Today, she added, fear of getting fired is so great that "even though everyone shouts, they pull back when it comes right down to it." For this reason, the union held more demonstrations that "take the place of strikes" (interview BD3 with SINDSEP leader, São Paulo, August 2003).

CONCLUSIONS

I draw four main conclusions from this analysis of the SINDSEP. First, organizational culture matters. Union identity is bound up in historically positive orientations toward protest and suspicion of negotiation. As a result, union leaders worry that demobilization will cost them support. When they consider strikes too costly, they substitute other forms of protest but do not demobilize entirely.

Second, where the organization itself favors protest as a tactic, leadership competition enhances incentives to protest. Union leaders used protest to measure their relative strength against internal rivals and to bolster their credibility among members. Their exposure to internal elections encouraged them to be concerned about their reputation with members. Moreover, internal democracy within the PT tended to give them more freedom to protest even against PT governments. PT leaders who wanted the support of union members, especially

---

[27] In some cases, unions successfully demand that their employer repay any wages lost during the strike, but the longer the strike continues, the more likely it is that only a portion of wages – or none – will be repaid. Quote from interview in SINDSEP (2002b: 26).

those outside the governing PT faction were inclined to support the union.

Third, despite the lack of statistical significance for POS variables, union leaders are in fact keenly aware of shifting political opportunities. They weigh the costs of protesting against their ally and the costs of silence. Particularly in a context of leadership competition, protest often seems attractive. The increased likelihood of protest success under PT governments also appeals to ambitious leaders. Successful protest enhances their prestige. They get to deliver benefits, in a way that demonstrates both their independence from the government and their commitment to fight for workers.

Finally, the significance of protest in honeymoon years appears twofold. First, union leaders used protest to signal their autonomy from the party they just fought to put into power – years prior to that party having to face reelection. Second, union leaders saw the election of an ally as an opportunity to redress accumulated grievances. It must be noted that in São Paulo, PT governments always took over from non-PT governments in the time frame studied; they were never reelected. The agenda-setting function of protest at the start of a new administration remains consistent with this framing of union motivations, though most union leaders did not put it in these terms.

Chapter 5 continues the analysis by contrasting the case of the SINDSEP with that of the Mexico City employee union.

5

Partisan Loyalty and Corporatist Control

The Unified Union of Workers of the Government of the Federal District

Where the SINDSEP was "born out of struggles" against an authoritarian regime, Mexico City's municipal employee union was a pillar of support for Mexico's authoritarian regime for over sixty years. Its passive organizational culture, hierarchical internal structures, and limited leadership competition would all distinguish it from its Brazilian counterpart. This chapter explores the consequences of these differences for protest behavior. Although in general these characteristics made the union's leaders less capable of sustaining protest when they attempted to do so, the union's inability to process internal conflicts through democratic competition also produced a high proportion of protests associated with internal dissent. A final section analyzes union behavior more broadly, using process-tracing over time and additional quantitative analysis.

PUTTING THE SUTGDF IN CONTEXT: PUBLIC-SECTOR UNIONISM IN MEXICO

Public-Sector Unionism: Brazil and Mexico Compared

Public-sector unionism in Mexico shares important similarities with Brazil. Mexico has a similar rate of unionization (43 percent of nonagricultural employment versus 44 percent in Brazil).[1] Public employees

---

[1] www.ilo.org; see also Norris (2002: 174–175). Unionization rates vis-à-vis the economically active population are considerably lower: 11.6 percent in Mexico as of 1997. See Aguilar García (2001: 112).

account for approximately 14 percent of Mexican nonagricultural employment as of 2000; the same percentage as in Brazil (Wilkie, Aleman, and Ortega, 2002: 407). By 1999, roughly half of all union-ized workers in Mexico were public employees.[2] My own data recorded more public-sector unions than private-sector unions in every case.[3] Public-sector unions also had higher rates of protest. In Mexico City, for example, public-sector unions averaged 13.2 protests per year compared to 3 protests for private-sector unions. In Brazil the disparity is less, but it still ranges from a ratio of 1.5 times as many protests by public-sector unions in São Paulo to 1.8 times as many protests in Brasilia. Thus, state employee unions are among the largest and most combative unions in both countries.

Despite these similarities, unions developed along distinct political trajectories in Mexico and Brazil. Where Brazilian unions developed in conjunction with a wave of mobilization against an authoritarian regime, Mexican unions were politically neutralized by the terms of their relationship to the ruling hegemonic party. They remained largely unavailable for alliance with the independent Left even after the PRI–union alliance began to deteriorate.

Labor Organization in Mexico

Unionism in Mexico has embodied a paradoxical combination of strength and weakness since the creation of the party–union alliance by President Lázaro Cárdenas in the 1930s. On the one hand, Cárdenas encouraged the formation of labor unions, organized them into peak associations, stimulated and rewarded mobilization, and made unions a cornerstone of the postrevolutionary hegemonic party. On the other

---

[2] These figures refer only to federal jurisdiction workers registered with the government under Heading A (private sector) and Heading B (public sector). It excludes workers subject to local jurisdiction (a minority of all workers) as well as workers with temporary or part-time contracts who do not qualify for the health and pension benefits available through government registration. See Bensusán and Alcalde (2000: 176). Similar results can be found in Águilar García (2001: 134–135) and Zapata (1995: 147).

[3] In Mexico City, I found 101 public-sector unions and 100 private-sector unions. In São Paulo, I found 86 public-sector unions and 77 private-sector unions. And in Brasilia, I found 67 public-sector unions versus 31 private-sector unions.

hand, he separated peasants, urban/industrial workers, and state workers' unions into competing sectors within the PRI in order to limit their influence. The Federation of Public Service Workers' Unions (FSTSE), for example, was founded, "in order to ensure that federal government employees would be represented by a union separate from the Mexican Workers' Confederation (CTM)," which grouped together most of the unionized industrial workers in the private sector (Middlebrook, 1995: 91). By 1978, the FSTSE included less than 1 percent of all unions in Mexico but 37.3 percent of union members (Middlebrook, 1995: 152). However, its power was balanced by the equally giant CTM confederation and by separate PRI-affiliated unions representing workers in the major state-owned companies, including railroad workers, electrical workers, nuclear energy workers, telephone workers, airline workers, and – most important – petroleum workers. Significantly, Cárdenas put the FSTSE into the "popular sector" of the PRI and the CTM into the "labor sector." In this way, the system created competition between private and public unions, giving the state some autonomy in managing salary negotiations and quotas of power within the PRI.

PRI unions enjoyed state protection of their monopolies, closed-shop privileges, guaranteed seats on state boards that set the minimum wage and settle labor disputes, a quota of PRI candidacies for Congress, and state subsidies of their operating budgets. In return, they accepted labor discipline, limits on leadership selection, and responsibility for mobilizing electoral support for the PRI. Thus, despite high unionization rates, most observers discounted Mexican unions as independent actors. Instead, they became famous for their "sounds of silence" in the face of eroding wages and living standards (Middlebrook, 1989: 195). By the 1980s, unions had ceased to be effective watchdogs of workers' rights.

Mexico's labor movement represented a classic example of corporatism. Labor relations are

corporative to the degree that there is (1) state structuring of groups that produces a system of officially sanctioned, noncompetitive, compulsory interest associations; (2) state subsidy of these groups; and (3) state-imposed constraints on demand-making, leadership, and internal governance ... in contrast to the pattern of interest politics based on autonomous, competing groups, in the case of corporatism the state encourages the formation of a limited number of officially recognized, non-competing, state-supervised groups. (Collier and Collier, 1991: 51)

The establishment of corporatism in Mexico involved "broad electoral mobilization of labor support, a major effort to link unions to the party, and ... a parallel incorporation of the peasantry" (Collier and Collier, 1991: 165). These political and institutional ties bolstered the legitimacy of the postrevolutionary government, helped the state manage economic conflict and promote growth, prevented large-scale unrest, and thus lessened the temptation for elites to support military coups. Most critically for this analysis, it tied virtually all unions to a specific party alliance and prevented independent Left parties from developing a labor base.

Dissident movements, many of them within public-sector unions, challenged this system of control from the beginning. The most important democratic union movements in the 1970s emerged within public employee unions that had a highly skilled base, like electrical workers, nuclear energy workers, telephone workers, and teachers.

By the late 1990s, a growing number of unions had severed their ties to the PRI altogether. In 1986, only 67 unions were not affiliated to the PRI-dominated Workers' Congress (Congreso del Trabajo, or CT); by 2000, 469 unions were not affiliated to the CT (Aguilar García, 2001: 380). Still, most unions remained formally affiliated to the PRI even as the benefits of PRI affiliation eroded. The CTM alone had as many members in 2000 as all of the autonomous unions combined (Aguilar García, 2001: 379). Independent unionism in Mexico remained mostly limited to a few public- and service-sector unions.[4] Industrial unions, for various reasons, failed to break away from CTM and PRI control.[5]

---

[4] Members of the main independent confederation, the UNT, include the union of telephone workers, bank workers, airline pilots, stewardesses, some university workers, and public social security system workers. All began as public employee unions, though some were subsequently privatized. Two auto workers' unions (Dina and VW) as well as a steel-workers union (the Union of Workers in Iron and Steel) also joined the UNT. However, nearly 70 percent of UNT members belong to the remaining public employee union, the National Union of Social Security Workers. See Bensusán and Alcalde (2000: 173).

[5] Among other factors, the development of a *maquiladora*-style industrial economy, with strong export links dominated by foreign companies, has led to the fragmentation of industrial unions. Indeed, within the *maquiladora* sector, the predominant form of

And not until 1999 did Supreme Court rulings allow all public employees to join union centrals other than the FSTSE.

The privatization of the state's railroad, telephone, and airline companies in the early 1990s contributed to the decision of these unions to abandon their political affiliations to the PRI and join a nonpartisan union central, the National Workers' Union (Unión Nacional de Trabajadores, or UNT) in 1997. The FSTSE remained intact until December of 2003, when conflict over the reelection of the confederation's PRI leader Joel Ayala led to a major split and the departure of seventeen of the FSTSE's sixty-one unions. The departing unions included two of the FSTSE's largest affiliates: the teachers' union and the Mexico City municipal employee union (SUTGDF). In one fell swoop the FSTSE lost 80 percent of its membership.[6]

However, these newly independent unions did not rush to affiliate with the PRD. As Carr notes (1991: 126), "suspicion of political parties is hardly surprising given the unfortunate precedent set by the relationship between the PRI and its union affiliates." The fact that many PRD leaders built their careers as PRI politicians compounded union distrust. The PRD's principal founder was the son of the man who created the PRI union structure in the first place. Cuauhtémoc Cárdenas both benefited from association with his father's attention to popular interests and suffered from suspicion that alliance with his new party would end up trapping unions again.

unionism is so-called white unionism, in which unions that exist only on paper are given legal rights to represent *maquila* workers and sign contracts with employers. The neoliberal PRI governments considered *maquila* workers primarily as enticements to foreign investors, not as electoral resources, and therefore they were not incorporated within the PRI. The PRI's core unions (the CTM and other industrial unions) developed during the period of import substitution industrialization and represent some of the sectors least advantaged by free trade. They have few alternatives to continued PRI loyalty for getting remaining benefits and have mostly remained loyal.

[6] Besides the teachers and the SUTGDF, departing unions included the Mexico City subway workers, air traffic controllers, and federal unions of workers in the ministries of Agrarian Reform, Social Development, Agriculture Fishing and Livestock, Statistical Research (INEGI), and Communication and Transportation (Martínez, 2003: 8). Accounts of the same event in the rival newspaper *Reforma* (Salazar and Reyes, 2003: A1, A4, A5) cite a figure of twenty-one unions departing, but *Reforma*'s list includes several dissident fractions of unions that officially remained within the FSTSE.

THE SUTGDF

During the period under study, Mexico City municipal workers were organized in a single PRI-affiliated union, the Unified Union of Workers of the Government of the Federal District (Sindicato Único de los Trabajadores del Gobierno del Distrito Federal, or SUTGDF), founded by Lázaro Cárdenas in 1936. In 1995, the SUTGDF claimed over 110,000 members, making it second only to the national teachers' union as the largest public-sector union in Mexico. The services provided by SUTGDF workers – water, garbage collection, sewage, health care, and so on – make it possible for the giant capital city to function on a daily basis. Mexico City's public employees are ideally placed to disrupt vital services if they choose.

Internally, the SUTGDF is a complex organization with thirty-nine different sections representing employees of different functional units within the Federal District government.[7] These sections organize vastly different groups of workers, from the 18,000 unskilled garbage collectors of Section One to the 600 educated administrators of Section Thirty-Nine's Information Directorate (Fernández Allende, 1995: 18). The health care workers in the two medical sections (Twelve and Thirteen) have very different class positions and education than water or sewage workers.

The SUTGDF has historically been characterized by nonexistent internal democracy, very secure leaders, dependence of the leadership on external validation by the government, and no competition with other unions for members. The central leadership of the SUTGDF was "elected" at an annual General Congress held in April and attended by three delegates from each section. Formally, the Secretary of Labor had the ability to certify the validity of these elections and disqualify elected leaders should the result not be to the liking of the national PRI. Informally, the Regent (mayor) of Mexico City chose the Secretary General of the union, who was duly elected at the Congress. Other

---

[7] The internal diversity of the union made it extremely difficult to sample its leadership. I interviewed ten members of the section leadership of the union, from eight union sections. Four of these sections had a reputation as PRI unconditionals and four had developed a more independent stance. I consider these interviews as illustrative of the diversity of union leaders' views rather than as a representative sample. All interviews took place between September 2000 and November 2000, in Mexico City.

positions were apportioned to the various factions and sections within the SUTGDF by means of informal quotas and an expectation of rapid rotation (terms of office typically lasted three years).

In terms of the explanatory variables, the SUTGDF should rank among the least likely to rebel against its ally, on several grounds. First, institutional rules tended to secure union leaders against challenges from below as long as they remained loyal to the party. The party (through its control of the government) could remove union leaders, but members could not. As a result, internal competition for leadership was virtually nonexistent. Second, the SUTGDF enjoyed both a closed shop and a monopoly of representation. Every Mexico City worker had to belong to the union. Third, the union had in its contract a separation exclusion clause. The city was obligated to fire workers who were not union members. Thus, union leaders could get challengers fired by simply stripping them of their union membership.

Fourth, the union received financial subsidies from the state to pay for its offices and to release its leaders for full-time union work. In addition, union leaders enjoyed special privileges that enabled them to buy off dissidents. For example, uniforms, gloves, and other protective clothing paid for by the city were not distributed to workers by the city government but by union leaders. Union leaders used these goods to maintain control, either indirectly by selling them on the black market to generate slush funds, or directly by withholding equipment from members who did not demonstrate loyalty.

Finally, the culture of PRI unionism strongly discouraged autonomous mobilization. Official mobilizations – such as the annual May Day rally – were organized like military operations, down to where each section of each union should stand and what slogans they should chant. Attendance was mandatory. To sweeten the pot, the union offered free t-shirts, hats, and lunches to those who showed up. For union leaders, the May Day rally, "afford[ed] the workers' movement an institutionalized means of showing its solidarity with the government. Thus, union leaders reveal to prominent technocratic policymakers the number of faithful and – through placards, chants, and mini-demonstrations during the event – express opinions on actual or prospective programs" (Grayson, 1989: 60). But these occasions were highly scripted. In interviews, union leaders of the SUTGDF recognized that "this was never a combative union." It lacked a "spirit of struggle," or even internal dissident movements of significance (interviews 7D, 4D, with SUTGDF section officials).

Several of these factors changed when the PRD took power in December 1997, creating new incentives to protest. Most obviously, the new mayor was one of the PRI's bitterest enemies: Cuauhtémoc Cárdenas of the PRD. It is difficult to explain the almost visceral hatred of Cárdenas felt by many PRI leaders except in terms of a sense of betrayal: that the son of a PRI founder, who had benefited so long from the PRI system of promotion and advancement, should have attacked it frontally by launching an independent presidential campaign in 1988. To make matters worse, he almost won. In forcing the PRI to unusual extremes to retain power, he publicly exposed the corruption and fraud at the heart of the system. Cárdenas's successful campaign for mayor in 1997 revived nearly moribund hopes for avenging his 1988 defeat. It was evident from his first day in office that the new mayor would not be staying long. He had the 2000 presidential campaign clearly in view. Thus, the PRI had every incentive to use all the weapons at its disposal, including the SUTGDF, to harass, discredit, and undermine his administration.

Initially, Cárdenas's government attempted to avoid confrontation with the union, hoping that "if we leave them alone, they were going to leave him alone." Instead, "the union's response was attack, attack, attack" (interview 2B, with PRD government official). In the first two years of his administration, the SUTGDF protested nearly as many times as in the previous five years put together. And they protested much more aggressively. Nearly 40 percent of SUTGDF actions during the PRI governments involved a march or demonstration, 33 percent a strike, and 19 percent a street blockage or building takeover. Against the PRD (1998–2003), in contrast, less than 30 percent of SUTGDF protests involved a march or demonstration. Strikes rose to 40 percent of all actions, while street and building takeovers rose to 30 percent. However, median estimated attendance declined slightly from 250 people to 200. Thus, the level and aggressiveness of SUTGDF activity increased dramatically after the transition to a non-PRI government, but the union's ability to mobilize members without the help of material incentives, supplied in the past partly with municipal money, actually declined.

Many of the protests against the PRD government had clear political overtones. Over three-quarters of labor protests during the 1992–1997 PRI administrations focused on material issues like wages and working conditions. During the first two years of PRD administration (the Cárdenas years), this percentage declined to just over half (56 percent), mostly because of an increase in the number of protests demanding the resignation of bosses. Although some of these actions undoubtedly reflected pent-up discontent with certain incompetent, corrupt, or abusive bosses, this category also included demands against many of the newly named PRD heads of departments and heads of delegations.[8] Calls for the resignation of a public official accounted for 29 percent of SUTGDF protests against Cárdenas.

The desire to attack Cárdenas clearly increased SUTGDF protests, but the transition to a non-PRI government had a number of other, more subtle effects. First, the PRD's victory raised the level of competition within the union by challenging the old system of leadership nomination. Cárdenas refused to choose a candidate for Secretary General of the SUTGDF, forcing the union into an unaccustomed situation: it entered the April Congress to elect its new leadership without a designated candidate. Nobody knew what to do. Fighting over the rules and the candidates broke out, but the union failed to reach any decisions. Eventually, the national Secretary of Government (*Gobernación*) was forced to step in to name a new leader.[9] Subsequent Congresses of the SUTGDF became even more conflictual, with multiple candidates disputing control of the union. The breakdown in the tradition of appointment from above triggered an upsurge of activism at the sectional level. In several cases, the approach of internal

---

[8] Mexico City is divided into sixteen "Delegations," each of which has its own *Jefe Delegacional*, or delegation head. During the PRD administration of 1997–2000, these delegation heads were nominated by Cárdenas and ratified by the Mexico City Assembly. In most cases, the PRD-controlled assembly was able to push through its nominations, but in a few cases, particularly where PRD discipline broke down, Cárdenas had to withdraw his initial nominee and propose an alternate. Still, they were PRD *delegados*. In the 2000 mayoral election, heads of delegations were directly elected and included delegates from the PAN as well as the PRD.

[9] The Secretary of *Gobernación*, one of the most important figures in Mexican national government, traditionally takes responsibility for internal political order. Even after the transition to a PAN presidency, the Secretary of *Gobernación* has continued to collect information on social movements and political dissidents and intervened to negotiate conflicts.

sectional elections with multiple candidates led to competitive efforts to mobilize the workers in protests ostensibly directed at the municipal government.[10] Candidates used these protests to demonstrate their popular support, to raise their name recognition among eligible workers, and to prove their commitment to defending workers' rights.[11]

Nevertheless, the SUTGDF's responsiveness to these new incentives was limited by generalized distrust of union leaders among the membership as well as the SUTGDF's own negative attitude toward protest. In fact, one PRD official noted that it was harder to deal with organizations of his own party than those of the PRI. PRD organizations, he said, were used to mobilization. In contrast, the PRI union was "trained and brought up" to respect government (interview 6B, with PRD government official, October 2000). All of the SUTGDF leaders I interviewed agreed that protests had increased under the PRD. Many even indicated dissatisfaction with the PRD government's response to their demands. Yet they also accepted that old attitudes were holding them back; "we have to change our mentality," in order to make progress said one section leader (interview 8D, with SUTGDF section leader, November 2000). While recognizing that the new autonomy of the union from the Mexico City government created opportunities, union leaders simultaneously expressed nostalgia for the predictability of the past and lamented the loss of internal order and discipline. "Now there is no party line from above," said one; the sections "have been orphaned" (interview 7D, with SUTGDF section leader, October 2000).

One of the most significant problems involved in changing the union's internal culture was the lack of credibility of union leaders among members.[12] In at least one case, union leaders threatened a

---

[10] For example, elections in Section One (garbage workers) and Section Twenty-three (inspectors) produced conflicts between rival candidates for control of the section that spilled over into the streets.

[11] Alternatively, one of the union leaders in Section One blamed the PRD for increased protests during election season, arguing that the PRD government chose to try to take away union privileges during elections because it knew the union would be divided at that time. Either way, the fact that elections had become more competitive – increasing internal divisions – accelerated the dynamics leading to protest (interview 10D, with SUTGDF leader).

[12] Interview 5D, with SUTGDF section leader. The same issue – lack of credibility of union leaders – also came up in interviews 10D and 4D.

strike and then called it off due to fear that workers would not participate. Some protests involved only union leaders. By 2000, the main union conflicts involved such issues as who would distribute uniforms and equipment, who had the right to name delegation-level officials for the supervision of garbage collection, whether the city would pay for commemorative union baseball hats for the May Day rally, and how to distribute municipal government money for the annual union *fiesta* of each section. Such issues had little impact on workers but a big impact on the ability of union leaders to use material rewards to motivate participation. The PRD's attacks on leadership privileges created a climate of crisis for union leaders even though the economy was performing well. Nevertheless, they did not attract much sympathy from workers. The union had difficulty sustaining mobilization over time, with protest rates declining under the second PRD administration.

However, the PRD made little headway in competing with the PRI for the support of the union. Even PRD-sympathizing union leaders complained that union members have "no weight," within the party and that the PRD "has had no real influence [in unions]" (interview 2B, with former union organizer in the PRD government, October 2000). Indeed, at the time of my interviews in 1999 and 2000, most of the PRD-leaning leaders were afraid to identify themselves publicly as PRD.[13]

A second factor that changed after the PRD took power was the climate of receptiveness to union demands. While criticizing union leaders, the PRD expressed deep sympathy for ordinary workers trapped inside the SUTGDF and made some efforts to improve salaries and working conditions. In 1998 and 1999, salaries for Mexico City workers increased more than inflation and more than the salaries of federal workers (Executive Director of Labor Studies, 1999: 1). Union organizers argued that mobilization worked better against the PRD because the PRD felt more pressure to respond (interview 3D, with PRD-sympathizing organizer of an [illegal] police union). Moreover,

---

[13] In fact, all of the union officials – even loyal *priistas* – were extremely reluctant to talk on the record. Thus, I was forced to make these interviews anonymous. I located PRD-sympathizers through contacts from my previous research on the PRD (e.g., Bruhn, 1997), who provided personal introductions.

said one PRD official, "we know and they know that we can't use force [against workers] and it ties our hands." Another PRD-sympathizing union leader (of SUTGDF) thought that the PRD would have to be very careful in trying to undermine the PRI "mafias" who controlled the union, in order to avoid appearing antilabor (interview 6B, with PRD government official, November 2000; interview 4D, with SUTGDF leader). Despite these incentives to increase demands, the SUTGDF had a lot more trouble sustaining mobilization than its Brazilian counterpart.

Conclusions from the Case of the SUTGDF

My conclusions from this analysis are similar to my findings from the Brazilian case. Once again, organizational culture matters. In the SUTGDF, neither the leaders nor the members of the union shared a positive orientation toward protest. Moreover, because of the lack of leadership competition, leaders had little incentive to be responsive to member demands. When they chose causes for protest, they often failed to select issues that mattered to members. Predictably, members did not trust their leaders to represent their interests. As the union lost material resources once derived from its control of the municipal government, it had increasing difficulty maintaining mobilization even when leaders wanted to increase protest and believed the PRD government would be responsive to labor demands.

After the PRD's victory, the system of leadership appointment from above began to deteriorate. Increased leadership competition quickly resulted in competitive protests. Frequently, factions within a union section would engage in protest just prior to an internal election, as a means of gauging each other's strength. While the effects were limited, it is nonetheless noteworthy that even small increases in leadership competition can be tied so directly to decisions to engage in protest.

Shifts in political opportunity structure also affected strategies. When the PRD won, the natural attractiveness of protesting against a Leftist target was compounded by the appeal of bringing down a political rival. In the case of the SUTGDF, it seems likely that national PRI leaders ordered at least some of these protests in order to embarrass Cárdenas. In addition, the PRD administration seized the opportunity to undermine PRI union leaders by taking away historic privileges. These actions sparked protests, although relatively unpopular ones. Protest rates by the municipal employee union increased much more when the Left took power in Mexico City than in São Paulo. Municipal employee protests nearly tripled in Mexico City but increased by only 56 percent in São Paulo. In Brasilia, municipal employee protests are three times higher under the PT government than under the conservative government. However, in this case, the economic context that discouraged protest in São Paulo in 2001–2002 also discouraged protest in 2001–2002 in Brasilia. The limited number of cases may be concealing to some extent how economic opportunities affect the prospects for protest.

The significance of protest during honeymoon years seems more idiosyncratic in the Mexican case and less related either to demonstrating autonomy or to agenda setting. In the first two years of the Cárdenas administration, protest was primarily aimed at discrediting him as a potential presidential candidate. In the fall of 2000, when most of my union interviews were conducted, the PRD had just won reelection to the city government, and the PRI had lost the presidency. Union leaders were extremely alarmed at the prospect of losing federal subsidies as well as municipal power and were confused about how to respond. There was a sudden and dramatic (33 percent) decline in protest in the next year, the first year of the López Obrador administration. The contradictory effects demonstrate no clear or consistent pattern. Ultimately, I can only conclude that the SUTGDF was not a union inclined to strategize about when to protest, mostly reacting to external events or actions. Its behavior does not provide much support for my agenda-setting explanation of honeymoon year protests.

SUTGDF Versus SINDSEP

Despite the similar conclusions, the behavior of the SUTGDF raises an important challenge to the argument made in Chapter 4 about the importance of organizational culture, leadership competition, likelihood of protest success, and organizational autonomy. From these factors, the SINDSEP should protest at much higher rates than the corporatist SUTGDF. In fact, the "passive" SUTGDF mobilized an average of 7.2 times a year when the PRI was in power, more than the "combative" SINDSEP mobilized against the PT (4.2 times a year).

The most obvious explanation is that party alliance matters after all in helping to set the ambient level of protest. All types of organizations, from unions to urban popular movements, protest more in Mexico than in Brazil, and almost all popular organizations in Mexico are less closely tied to parties than their counterparts are tied to the PT. Thus, Brazilian organizations may feel less need (or willingness) to protest even though the specific event of their ally winning power produces no significant change in their protest behavior. A higher level of ambient noise could in turn force organizations into more protest than might be necessary where protest is more unusual. A second possibility is that the lower level of protest by the SINDSEP reflects a wider range of possible targets for public employees in São Paulo. The municipal government of São Paulo manages fewer services than Mexico City. Electricity and water are provided by state-level agencies. Subway workers and most police also report to the state government. In addition, the SINDSEP is newer, has fewer institutional resources, and lacks a closed-shop privilege.

Nevertheless, in order to understand what is going on here, we also need to take apart the records of SUTGDF protests. Protest patterns at this level appear far more related to internal competition than the overall picture of corporatist control would lead us to expect. During the PRI years, 21 percent of all SUTGDF protests involved conflict over an internal election for union leaders at the sectional level, usually complaints of fraud. Internal dissidents led these protests. Most such protests were smaller than other SUTGDF events during this period, with an average of only forty-eight participants. Moreover, a few sections accounted for the vast majority of all protests, specifically Section Twelve (medical workers) and Section Seventeen (treasury workers). Together these two groups were responsible for nearly 60 percent of *all* SUTGDF protests during the PRI administrations. These same sections held all of the protests against fraudulent internal elections. Again, one must suspect that the presence of small dissident factions within these two sections explains a lot of the surprising protest against the PRI government.

In all likelihood, the officialist currents of the SUTGDF were even better at containing protest against the PRI than my initial analysis suggested. Instead, dissident movements with no internal institutional recourse found themselves driven to protest in the streets.

Competition within Mexican unions more frequently spilled outside of institutional rules precisely because competition was so strongly prohibited inside them. The existence of institutional and democratic outlets for challengers in the SINDSEP may help union leaders process many internal conflicts without public protest.

The cases of the SUTGDF and the SINDSEP therefore strongly confirm the hypothesis that competition within unions for leadership is associated with competitive protest dynamics. The goal of these protests is not always to achieve some material goal; it may be to impress potential supporters or intimidate rivals. At some point, leadership competition may become dysfunctional for an organization. Pointless protest – one of the Murillo scenarios – may be the result. Nevertheless, it is not necessarily irrational from the point of view of individual leaders.

UNION PROTEST: BEYOND THE SUTGDF AND THE SINDSEP

Because these case studies are each limited to a single union, they cannot help us very much toward an understanding of two other findings in the statistical analysis: the greater tendency of unions to protest and the effect of partisan alliance. This section looks more broadly at unions in the Mexican and Brazilian context, comparing the behavior of independent unions and Leftist unions, Leftist and non-Leftist unions, in order to understand what happens when we combine the effects of party alliance with the effects of union status. It also constructs separate models for unions and non-unions in order to uncover clues to the general finding of union aggressiveness.

Independent Unions

The statistical results presented in Chapter 3 found a lower probability of mobilization by independent organizations. However, the analysis did not separate independent unions from other types of independent organizations. Were independent organizations less likely to protest or simply less likely to be unions? In Mexico, independent unions protested on average roughly twice as often as PRI unions.

However, three particular unions drive the calculation, accounting for nearly half of all independent union protests.[14] If these unions are excluded, the rate of protest by independent unions would drop to 1.13 protests per union per year, versus 0.95 protests per PRI union per year. In Brazil, PT-affiliated unions protest twice as often as independent unions in São Paulo and 4.5 times as often as independent unions in Brasilia.

Looking at mobilization by unions across time in Mexico finds evidence that increasing mobilization *preceded* decisions to become independent. The Mexican telephone workers' union is an example.[15] The leader of the union, Francisco Hernández Juárez, first rose to power in 1976 by means of an internal dissident movement that succeeded in overthrowing the *charro* (corrupt) leadership of Salustio Salgado.[16] Hernández Juárez won in part because of the existence within the union of an even more radical Leftist current, the Democratic Line. After the statutes changed to allow secret ballots in internal elections, Hernández Juárez successfully positioned himself as the middle ground between traditional *charrismo* and the radical left. He took over the union. Increasing strikes and protests were associated with this internal power struggle, many of them led by the Democratic Line faction in an effort to discredit Hernández Juárez. But after the Democratic Line was definitively repressed in 1982, elections once again shrank to virtual one-party rule by Hernández Juárez, with "formal elections only serv[ing] to legitimate what had been decided upon drawing up the candidate list" (de la Garza Toledo, 2001a: 27). By 1986, Hernández Juárez had moderated his

---

[14] The high average of the bus drivers' union (SUTAUR) reflects an atypical wave of protest sparked by the federal government's sudden privatization of the public bus system in Mexico City and its official dissolution of the union. It should legitimately be excluded as not typical of independent unions. In contrast, the activity of two teachers' unions (STUNAM and CNTE), representing teachers at the federal university UNAM and public school teachers represent fairly common behavior by teachers' unions. In both Mexico and Brazil, teachers were highly mobilized.

[15] I draw heavily on the work of Enrique de la Garza Toledo (2001b) throughout this section.

[16] The term "*charro*" in this context refers to corrupt leaders of corporatist labor unions. It derives from the association with a famously corrupt union leader in the 1920s who dressed like a *charro* (cowboy).

behavior so dramatically that Fidel Velázquez, leader-for-life of the CTM and the quintessential *charro*, backed his candidacy for president of the PRI-controlled Labor Congress (CT).

After 1990, with his leadership consolidated, Hernández Juárez gradually moved toward his eventual decision to leave the PRI and form an independent union central. However, this choice coincided with a marked decrease in protest. Instead, he engaged in a highly successful model of negotiations with the Mexican telephone company, TELMEX. In exchange for protection of jobs, the union ceded many aspects of control over working conditions and wages and actively engaged workers in efforts to improve productivity. Using this strategy, Hernández Juárez survived the financial crisis of TELMEX as well as its subsequent privatization. The fact that the union had the ability to protest may have given Hernández Juárez some leverage in these negotiations. But he deliberately did not use it.

Similarly, in the case of the National Social Security Workers' Union, a wave of protests preceded the decision to become independent. As in the case of the telephone workers, these protests targeted corruption and lack of democracy within the union as well as declining wages and job security. Between 1986 and 1989, the state's contribution to the Mexican Institute of Social Security declined by 50 percent according to one calculation. Moreover, average workloads increased, salaries eroded, and, "the result was very clear: deterioration of the conditions of work in general" (Ravelo and Sánchez, 2001: 76). In 1988, dissident union leaders began to stage small-scale demonstrations and hunger strikes protesting the acquiescence of the National Executive Committee of the union to these policies. Matters reached a head in the 1989 National Congress, when 298 delegates rejected the new collective contract proposed by the leadership. The president of the union was forced to resign. But "after the great protest of these months, we see a process of restoration of power of the [National Social Security Workers' Union] in workplaces." Despite some democratizing changes in the statutes, it remained a "union democracy vigorously monitored" by the National Executive Committee (Ravelo and Sánchez, 2001: 80, 89). Protests peaked prior to the union's decision to break with the PRI and declined dramatically after it declared independence, falling from thirty-one protests in 1993–1997 to just six protests in the ensuing five years.

Quantitative Analysis

To further test the effect of independence on unions, I split each city's dataset into two parts, one containing only unions (including transportation workers) and one containing only non-unions. I then reran the models from Chapter 3 for each subset, using the negative binomial procedure as before. Tables 5.1, 5.2, and 5.3 present models for "all targets," in order to include the maximum range of union types. Unstandardized coefficients are reported, and for significant variables, the percentage increase or decrease in the expected protest count given a unit increase in the independent variable is reported. Each table presents the comparison between the union sample and the non-union sample. In these comparisons, several interesting contrasts emerge.

First, independent unions protested significantly more than party-allied unions only in Mexico City, where they are mostly compared with PRI unions: forty-one PRI unions, forty-three independent unions, and ten "other party" unions held at least one protest. In São Paulo and Brasilia, where independent unions are compared with the PT-allied unions, the effect of independence is insignificant, though positive in both cases.[17] In contrast, independence is significant and negative in the dataset excluding unions.

This contrast between "union" and "non-union" models points to the possibility that low rates of protest do not imply a choice not to protest, but instead higher rates of extinction: independent urban popular movements (for example) might quit protesting because they cease to exist. In this scenario, party alliance might increase organizational survival rates more dramatically among non-unions than among unions, resulting in a lower extinction rate among those that forge ties to parties. Unions do not need external alliances to survive; at least in Brazil and Mexico, they get subsidies from member dues and/or the state, monopoly protection, and official status in contract negotiations. Alternatively, the decision to seek party alliance may

---

[17] In São Paulo, I counted forty-nine PT unions and eighteen independent unions. In Brasilia, I counted thirty-six PT unions and fifteen independent unions. In neither case did I find unions affiliated with other parties that held a protest. Running the models with only "PT" or "Independent" does not change the significance of any other variable, but it does increase the coefficient of the party alliance variable remaining.

TABLE 5.1. *Number of Protests, Mexico City: All Targets*

	Unions	Non-unions
Organizational Resources		
Neighborhood association	(not applicable)	.14
Student	(not applicable)	−.08
Vendor	(not applicable)	−.22
CGH (1999 student strikers)	(not applicable)	2.70*** (1,389.5%)
Age	−.01	−.13*** (−12.2%)
Identity		
Left party ally	.19	.17
Independent	.73***(106.9%)	−.61*** (−45.6%)
Protests in previous year	.19*** (20.5%)	.20*** (21.7%)
POS		
Allied to party in power	.36	.07
Honeymoon year	−.16	−.10
Election year	.09	.04
Interaction: Honeymoon, allied to party in power	−.41	−.59* (−44.5%)
Interaction: Election, allied to party in power	.22	−.24
Economic Grievance		
Inflation (natural log)	.13	−.18** (−16.1%)
Pseudo R^2	.10***	.11***

***significant at .01   **significant at .05   *significant at .1

indicate higher levels of politicization that could also lead organizations to be more active politically, to protest more, than independent organizations. More detailed analysis of the non-union set will be necessary to tease out these implications. Chapters 6 and 7 will pursue the matter further.

Second, age takes a greater toll on non-unions than on unions. In none of the three cities did union age have a negative effect on protest; in fact, it has a *positive* and significant effect on union protests in São Paulo. However, among non-unions, age had a negative and strongly significant impact in all three cases. Again, the significance of age may indicate that low protest among older movements results from extinction rather than deliberate choices not to protest. Unions clearly have more protection from premature demise in the legal context of Brazil and Mexico.

TABLE 5.2. *Number of Protests, São Paulo: All Targets*

	Unions	Non-unions
Organizational Resources		
Neighborhood association	(not applicable)	−.61*** (−45.4%)
Student	(not applicable)	Dropped
Vendor	(not applicable)	Dropped
MOCO (bus drivers' union)	.39	(not applicable)
Age	.04** (4.1%)	−.15*** (−13.6%)
Identity		
Left party ally	.46	.89*** (143.1%)
Independent	.34	−.67*** (−48.9%)
Protests in previous year	.21*** (23.3%)	.31*** (36.5%)
POS		
Allied to party in power	−.22	−.06
Honeymoon year	−.03	.31** (37%)
Election year	.13	.38**(46.5%)
Interaction: Honeymoon, allied to party in power	−.40	.06
Interaction: Election, allied to party in power	−.57	−.17
Economic Grievance		
Inflation (natural log)	.12*** (12.6%)	−.01
Pseudo R^2	.09***	.12***

***significant at .01 **significant at .05 *significant at .1

Third, unions generally respond to high inflation by protesting *more*, while non-unions generally respond to high inflation by protesting *less*, though these effects are not statistically significant in every case.

Finally, using all targets dilutes the effect of the honeymoon year variable. In the models presented here, non-unions seem more likely than unions to respond to cues from the strategic context. But when models are constructed using only protests against the local government, the effect of honeymoon years increases and becomes more significant. In Sao Paulo, the effect of honeymoon year becomes positive and significant for unions and produces a 95.9 percent increase in the expected protest count. For non-union protests, the effect of the honeymoon variable on expected protest count increases to a 125.3 percent boost versus 14.2 percent in the all target models. In Mexico City, honeymoon year reaches statistical significance in the non-union model and produces an increase of 47.4 percent in the expected

TABLE 5.3. *Number of Protests, Brasilia: All Targets*[a]

	Unions	Non-unions
Organizational Resources		
Neighborhood association	(not applicable)	−.79*** (−54.8%)
Student	(not applicable)	−.32
Vendor	(not applicable)	Dropped
Age	.003	−.19*** (−17.6%)
Identity		
Left party ally	2.32* (919.1%)	1.44*** (324%)
Independent	.72	−.94*** (−61%)
POS		
Allied to party in power	−.01	−.10
Honeymoon year	.22	.44** (55.5%)
Interaction: Honeymoon, allied to party in power	−.71	−.49
Economic Grievance		
Inflation (natural log)	.58* (78.2%)	.13
Pseudo R^2	.05***	.18***

***significant at .01 **significant at .05 *significant at .1

[a] The Brasilia dataset contains only two pairs of consecutive years. "Protests in previous year" was thus only available for two years. Inclusion of this variable would have cut half the cases from the sample. Similarly, none of the years in the Brasilia dataset was an election year, so this variable is also omitted.

protest count. Other differences between local and all-target models were minor. This result is interesting because it suggests that in protesting more during the first year of an administration, protesting groups really are trying to get the attention of the local government in particular. The impact of honeymoon years is not an accidental artifact of some other characteristic of those years that affects all protesting groups, including those making demands on other targets.

CONCLUSIONS

Chapters 4 and 5 use cases of municipal employee unions to evaluate the claim that, "other things being equal, union leaders are more willing to restrain their militancy when their allied parties are in the government and increase it when their allies are in the opposition" (Murillo, 2001: 15). In the examples examined here, all Leftist governments became the target of increased protest, regardless of the political affiliation of the unions. Whoever was seen as the softer target – including one's own party ally – could expect more mobilization as a result of the increased likelihood of successful protest. Cultural framing of protest as a demonstration of independence further increased incentives to protest. Finally, internal competition for union leadership tended to stimulate mobilization. However, the size of the stimulating effect depended on whether the political culture of the organization viewed protest favorably.

In the case of Mexico and the SUTGDF, strict institutional limits on internal competition, a political culture hostile to protest, and the likelihood of a negative reaction by PRI governments to unauthorized protest inhibited most protest against PRI governments. After these constraints were removed by PRD victory, protest began to increase. In addition to political motives to discredit the PRD, unions perceived the PRD as more vulnerable to protest than the PRI, which led them to undertake even politically risky protests for issues not considered very important by union members. However, none of these factors prevented the proliferation of low-intensity protest by internal dissidents at the height of PRI dominance. In fact, one might argue that the very absence of internal mechanisms for competition tended to channel these conflicts into the streets.

In Brazil, the political culture of both unions and parties created a context where protest was popular. Ultimately, though, PT unions protested against PT governments because it made strategic sense, not because they were helplessly addicted to protest. For union leaders, protest made it possible for them to sustain credibility (not *pelegos*). The visibility of protest made it an attractive signaling device for internal as well as external audiences, indicating the numbers and commitment of one's own followers as well as one's ability to secure concessions from the target. And protest seemed likely to succeed against the sympathetic PT – particularly compared to the PT's rivals, which were especially conservative and repressive. Finally, the PT's diverse collection of popular allies made it important to get demands on the agenda early, as others would make parallel claims.

If we summarize these findings as we did for the quantitative analysis in Chapter 3, the results are similar (see Table 5.4). Given only two cases, it is difficult to determine the relative weight of these variables. The directions, however, are fairly clear. A culture of protest

TABLE 5.4. *Summary of Results: Unions and Protest*

Variables	Operationalization	Results
Organizational Resources		
Type of resources	Unions versus non-unions Interviews Labor law	**Unions consistently protest more**
Institutionalization	Age, union statutes	Only decreases protest for *non*-unions
Leadership competition	Interviews, union statutes	**Increases protest**
Identity		
Past history of protest	**Protest lagged** **Records of protest**	**Increases protest**
Positive view of protest	**Left party ally** **Interviews** **Internal documents**	**Increases protest**
Independent of parties	**Independent**	**Increases protest by unions, but decreases protest by non-unions**
POS		
Allied to party in power	SINDSEP vs. SUTGDF	Protest always higher against the Left, regardless of union alliance
Electoral cycle effects	Honeymoon year	**Increases protest, only if local government target**
	Interviews and internal documents	
	Election year	Insignificant
	Interaction, in-group with honeymoon	Insignificant
	Interaction, in-group with election	Insignificant
Economic Grievance	Inflation (logged)	**Generally increases protest by unions, decreases protest by non-unions**
	Concern about unemployment	**Decrease in strikes but not protest**

tends to encourage protest. Internal competition tends to encourage protest, even (or especially) when it has no institutional means of expression. But ultimately, the decision to resort to protest must provide some likelihood of attaining benefits. Sometimes it is better to do something ineffective than to do nothing at all, just to be seen. However, repeated demonstrations with no payoffs will eventually discourage members and discredit leaders. Leaders may shift to less costly forms of protest (e.g., demonstrations rather than strikes) if they think the likelihood of success is low. Thus, despite the apparent irrationality implied by the failure of political opportunity variables to reach statistical significance, the calculations of these unions were fundamentally rational. They just reflected considerations derived from *internal* structures and incentives as well as external goals.

6

Clients or Citizens? Neighborhood Associations
in Mexico City

The differences between unions and non-unions highlighted at the end of Chapter 5 are further explored in the next two chapters through case studies of the most common type of non-union organization: urban popular movements. This chapter begins by elaborating upon the resource differences between urban popular movements and unions and speculating about how these differences might affect protest behavior. The second section recapitulates the independent variables under analysis and provides a preliminary comparison of urban popular movement protests in Mexico City, São Paulo, and Brasilia. The final section analyses urban popular movement behavior in Mexico City, using case studies of five movements. Chapter 7 continues the analysis through parallel case studies of urban popular movements in Brazil and concludes with additional quantitative analysis and some comparative conclusions.

Overall, the findings are quite similar to those of previous chapters. A pro-protest organizational culture, history of protest, and internal leadership competition all continue to promote protest. However, the urban popular movement cases highlight the ways in which resource scarcity causes urban popular movements to calculate the value of protest and the timing of windows of opportunity in different ways than unions and other non-union organizations.

URBAN POPULAR MOVEMENTS IN LATIN AMERICA

Neighborhood organizing reflects the increasingly urban nature of Latin American societies, the effects of rapid migration to cities that

overwhelmed housing and service provision, and the deep social differences that spatially and physically mark urban centers. As a result,
Escobar and Álvarez note that "no observer of contemporary social
movements in Latin America can overlook the salience of urban popular movements" (1992: 12). Urban popular movements are among
the most common popular organizations in Latin America; in Mexico
City, according to one survey, 20 percent of all organizations were
urban popular movements – the largest single category (Álvarez
Enríquez, 1997: 278).

Definitions of "urban popular movement" generally include its
location (in neighborhoods), its social base (poor and lower middle
class), and its focus on consumption demands (especially housing and
basic services). In contrast to unions and other class-based organizations that are rooted in relations of production, "urban popular
movements ... emerge from the sphere of reproduction and respond
to a different set of conflicts and contradictions, mostly focusing on
urban living conditions" (Schönwälder, 2002: 17. See also Foweraker,
1990: 5).

Four characteristics distinguish the urban popular movement sector
from the public employee unions discussed in the last two chapters.
First, unions enjoy a monopoly over representation in a given geographical territory, but neighborhood associations have no such protection. Rather, they must compete with other associations for members,
frequently within the same or adjoining territories. Some movements
even turn to violence to block the infiltration of other movements
into "their" territory. The lack of barriers to the formation of new
associations also tends to increase external competition: organizations
split rather than tolerate high levels of internal dissent. The effects
of leadership competition on protest may differ where it is mostly
external rather than mostly internal.

Second, unions enjoy a fairly stable income guaranteed by the state
in both Mexico and Brazil. Neighborhood associations, in contrast,
have very unpredictable sources of financing, potentially including contributions by members, support from nongovernmental organizations,
or grants from the state for specific projects. Lack of resources makes
it hard for urban popular movements to sustain collective action on
the basis of material rewards to participants; as a result, neighborhood associations may become more dependent on protest as a means

of organizational maintenance. The material demands of urban popular movements (services and resources from the state) also make them vulnerable to clientelistic exchanges of resources for votes, as many authors have noted (e.g., Cornelius, 1975; Gay, 1994; Eckstein, 1977). In Brasilia, for example, the bulk of the neighborhood associations have clientelistic ties to the conservative Right rather than the PT, based upon the exchange of land for political support.[1]

Third, the territorial basis of neighborhood associations makes them an attractive source of support for political parties. Such organizations – unlike most unions – control a concentrated bloc of votes in specific electoral districts. Their votes are worth bidding for. Strategically inclined neighborhood associations can take advantage of bidding wars to support different parties from one election to the next. Their alliance patterns may therefore change over time more frequently than those of unions.

Finally, in contrast to municipal employees – whose only real option involves targeting the municipal government – housing movements typically engage in multitarget strategies. In part, multitarget strategies reflect the empirical division of administrative responsibilities. Local government, for example, is usually the most appropriate target for land titles, land expropriation, or building permits. Local governments also typically have primary responsibility for basic infrastructure such as street paving and water service. National and state levels of government have more resources to finance major housing projects.

However, targeting strategies may also reflect movement perceptions of the susceptibility of different targets. For example, even if the national government has little to do with providing water service, a movement that sees it as a soft target might aim its protest at the

---

[1] The local government of Brasilia enjoys one unusual advantage: it owns most of the unoccupied land in Brasilia and the surrounding regions due to the federal expropriation of land for the new capital during its construction phase. Sixty percent of the total area in the Federal District belongs to the state. Thus, Joaquim Roriz could hand out massive amounts of land to poor residents of the city's periphery during his first term as Brasilia's governor (1988–1994), on condition that they form a housing association supporting his political aspirations. Nearly 90,000 families benefited directly – according to one estimate, accounting for almost a third of total homes in the Federal District. Positive evaluations of his actions helped boost his campaign for reelection in 2000. See de Campos Gouvêa (1998: 255), Dillon Soares (2000: 11–13).

national government in the hope of getting it to put pressure on a local agency. Thus, a change in the local party in power could trigger shifts in targeting as well as rates of protest: either to spare one's political ally by targeting a different level of government or to exploit the connection by mobilizing against the most sympathetic target.

VARIABLES AND MEASUREMENT

The principal variables under analysis are by now quite familiar to the reader. One measurement problem, however, deserves further discussion: the variable "party alliance." In comparison with unions, urban popular movements proved excruciatingly difficult to track down and identify in terms of party alliance. Many movements were too small to have regular offices where leaders could be located, were ephemeral reactions to some proposal by the government (e.g., the "Over my Dead Body" movement which objected to the construction of a highway overpass), or no longer existed. Even though I could make an educated guess about the independence of most of these movements, I could not rule out the possibility that party activists directed the movement unbeknownst to me. I chose, therefore, a conservative approach, only assigning alliance characteristics when I was unambiguously able to confirm them through various sources. The result is a rather alarming percentage of movements with "unknown" alliance. In Mexico City, for example, of 172 total movements, I failed to classify 145 (84 percent).[2] Luckily, these "unknown" movements account for less than 30 percent of all protests. Their average number of protests is 0.2 per group per year versus 1.3 for independent urban popular movements, 2.8 for PRI-allied movements, and 3.4 for PRD-allied movements. The situation is similar in São Paulo, where fifty-five of seventy-three urban popular movements (75 percent) are unidentified as to party affiliation. Once again, these movements have dramatically lower rates of protest. The average number of protests is 3.7 for independent groups (0.2 per year), 7.5 for PT groups (0.9 per year), and 1.4 for the unknown groups (0.09 per year).

---

[2] In Brasilia, nineteen out of twenty-five groups (76 percent) are unidentified as to party affiliation. Here, however, they account for 65 percent of all protests. I thus focus on Mexico City and São Paulo in what follows.

Mobilization and Decline

Although the Left was the preferred target of all municipal employee unions, it was not targeted to the same extent by urban popular movements. In fact, protest by *all* non-PRI neighborhood associations in Mexico City declined by 50 percent or more when the PRD won power. The lone PRI movement increased its rate of protest, though most of the increase is concentrated in the first PRD administration. The drop in protest levels suggests that PRD-affiliated neighborhood associations do spare their allies – though not more than independent associations.

Despite their apparent willingness to defer to the PRD, Mexican movements of all political tendencies still protested far more frequently against the local government – even against the PRD – than urban popular movements in Brazil, as Figure 6.1 shows dramatically. In São Paulo, PT-affiliated neighborhood associations accounted for virtually all cases of neighborhood associations.[3] Like the Mexican associations, they protested less against the PT than against comparable conservative administrations. Most unusually, however, protest rates tended to increase over time, from an average of 2.5 protests a year during the first PT administration (1989–1992) to 2.75 under Maluf (1993–1996), to 13.5 under Pitta (1997–2000). Protest then declined when the PT was elected again in 2000. But this rate – 10 protests per year – was substantially higher than it had been under the previous Erundina and Maluf administrations. PT movements always protested more frequently than the independent groups.[4]

Unlike unions, urban popular movements engaged in target-shifting in order to spare their party ally direct pressure. Brasilia offers the clearest evidence. None of the PT-allied mobilizations targeted the

---

[3] In Brasilia, protests by all types of urban popular movements – PT movements, movements affiliated to other parties, and movements without a known affiliation – increase when the PT as opposed to the PMDB is in power. The most likely reason for this unusual pattern is that in Brasilia – in contrast to Mexico City and São Paulo – conservative clientelistic networks captured most urban popular movements. Thus, movements in Brasilia *are* sparing their allies when they protest more against the PT than against the PMDB.

[4] I found only one group that I could clearly identify as affiliated with another party. It protested four times in 1989 – the first year of the Erundina administration – and never thereafter. I have thus omitted it from the table.

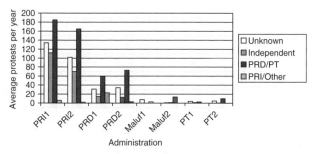

FIGURE 6.1. Urban Popular Movement Protest.

local government when the PT was in power, but all of them targeted the local government when Roriz (PMDB) was in power. However, these figures are based on a handful of demonstrations. More robust results emerge from São Paulo. PT-allied urban popular movements targeted the local government 29 percent of the time when the PT was in power versus 52 percent of the time when it was not. Independents, meanwhile, targeted the local government at the same rate regardless of whether the PT was in power. Less striking but still suggestive are Mexico City patterns. PRD-allied urban popular movements targeted the local government 40.7 percent of the time when the PRI was in power compared to 36.9 percent of the time when the PRD took over. Independent urban popular movements and the lone PRI movement increased targeting of local government after the PRD won: the independents increased their targeting by just a little, from 37 percent of the time to 39 percent of the time, and the PRI increased it from 62.5 percent of the time to 100 percent of the time. Even when urban popular movements maintained the same level of protest, they switched targets, though the substantive powers of different levels of government did not change. Municipal employee unions – who cannot effectively switch targets – do not have this option.

Nevertheless, these patterns challenge the arguments developed in Chapter 4 in two ways. First, municipal union protest against PT governments is explained as a result of their need to demonstrate independence from the PT and the greater chance of protest success in targeting a sympathetic administration. PT-affiliated urban popular movements should have had similar incentives. By not targeting their friends directly, they could engage in protest without confronting the party. But they could not demonstrate their independence from the PT by targeting governments controlled by other parties, and they could not increase the likelihood of protest success unless they protested against the most sympathetic target – their own party ally. Yet PT urban popular movements did not increase or even maintain levels of protest against the local government when the PT won. Why did they give their local government a break when unions did not?

Second, the urban popular movements that identified with the Left had a strongly mobilizational political culture, also singled out as contributing to mobilization even against allies. In the case of Mexico when the PRI was in power, three of the most active groups were urban popular movements allied to the PRD. Moreover, PRD party leaders could not punish "disloyal" movements. Yet these three groups went from 275 protests during the six PRI years (1992–1997) to a pathetic 36 protests during the six PRD years (1998–2003). Overall, PRD-affiliated urban popular movements went from a collective 350 protests during the PRI years to 133 during the PRD years, even though the number of movements affiliated to the PRD increased substantially after it won power. What explains the collapse of protest activity by PRD urban popular movements?

In the next section, I consider these questions in the light of a total of five case studies in Mexico City, though I focus for the sake of clarity on examples that represent extremes of behavior. The set of cases is first placed within the historical and political context that shaped neighborhood organizing in Mexico.

BARRIO ORGANIZATION AND POLITICAL CHANGE IN MEXICO

Historical Development

Historically, the PRI used clientelism to control neighborhoods through local settlement leaders; this pattern remained common through the 1990s (see Ward, 1989; Cornelius, 1975; Coulomb and Sánchez Mejorada, 1992; Eckstein, 1977). The development of independent urban popular movements is marked by three critical turning points in 1968, 1985, and 1988. The first turning point, the 1968 student movement, started with a march in support of the Cuban Revolution by high school and college students in July 1968. Police entered the campus of several high schools and the National Autonomous University to break up the demonstrations. Faculty and students considered the police actions a violation of the university's legal autonomy. They organized a series of protests, adding to their original complaints about police repression a growing list of demands for democratization, better living conditions for the urban poor, and postgraduation career opportunities. The government – usually tolerant of student marches – grew concerned about the increasing size, aggressiveness, and external support for student protests. In addition, large protests would embarrass the PRI when world attention focused on Mexico City as the host of the 1968 Olympic Games. On October 2, 1968, ten days before the Games, the government ordered army snipers to fire on demonstrating students in the Plaza of Tlatelolco in Mexico City, killing hundreds. The massacre shocked the nation. Tlatelolco brought home the reality of authoritarianism to the families of the usually privileged middle classes and inspired a generation of antisystem protest leaders.

Upon their release from prison in the early 1970s, some ex-student organizers became leaders in the guerrilla movements of the 1970s, convinced that peaceful protest could not bring down the PRI. Others scattered across the country to organize a more effective popular opposition. As Vivienne Bennett documents (1992), these former students, many of them belonging to a maoist current known as the Mass Line, were primarily responsible for the growth of independent urban popular organization in the 1970s. The Mass Line considered electoral participation "absolutely incorrect ... reformist and ... a class compromise." Instead, they followed a strategy of creating "liberated zones, completely controlled by revolutionary forces" (Serna, 1997: 14). Organizers moved into the shantytowns and set up neighborhood associations with their own courts, security forces, and schools. The idea was to promote self-help rather than petitioning the state or seeking positions in it. Thus, urban struggles were mostly "located in the periphery and their capacity of interlocution with the state was limited to aspects of housing and service provision" (Serna, 1997: 15).

The second turning point came in September 1985 when a major earthquake hit Mexico City. The 8.1 magnitude earthquake leveled nearly 400 buildings, many of them large apartment buildings in the city center. It also triggered an explosion of popular organizing. The seeming inability of the government to organize searches for survivors, inspect damaged buildings, or deliver critical emergency assistance forced many Mexico City residents to organize themselves. Over half of Mexico City's urban popular movements in 1995 were created in this post-earthquake period, 21 percent of them in 1985 alone (Serna, 1997: 36). Whereas the social base of previous movements drew largely on informal workers and the poor, the victims of the earthquake included professionals, renters, and employees. They did not engage in the typical pattern of squatting on unoccupied land and then building their own housing. These new activists needed massive financial assistance to rebuild large apartment complexes. They immediately targeted the state and sought to negotiate.

Just as these organizations got off the ground, a third turning point occurred: the emergence of the first credible Leftist party, capable of winning elections. Prior to 1988, "a position of incredulity dominated in Mexico regarding whether the country could change its political situation through the ballot box. Particularly within various popular organizations ... significant tendencies advocated abstention from elections." The 1988 presidential candidacy of Cuauhtémoc Cárdenas, evoking as it did fond memories of his presidential father, attracted enormous popular support. Indeed, "With regard to the [urban popular movements] and the political organizations that direct them, there were more than a few that finally found themselves forced or pressured by their 'bases' to join the *neocardenista* campaign" (Regalado, 1991: 50–51).

After the elections, only a minority of these movements followed up by allying with the PRD. By 1995, 65 percent of urban popular movements in Mexico City had participated in elections, but only 37 percent had an exclusive relationship to the PRD (Serna, 1997: 21, 42). Some remained independent. Others succumbed to the temptation offered by the National Solidarity Program, a social spending initiative created by President Salinas (1988–1994) to fund small-scale projects administered by the movements themselves. The program carried with it the informal political requirement of backing away from the PRD.

In 1997, the approach of the first election in which Mexico City residents could choose their own mayor again stimulated popular movement interest in elections, and in the PRD. PRD candidate Cuauhtémoc Cárdenas quickly became the front-runner. Moreover, Mexico City's recent institutional reforms had strengthened the powers of the local Legislative Assembly, the Asamblea Legislativa del Distrito Federal (ALDF). Thus, electing a local legislator on the PRD ticket seemed not only within reach but more rewarding than before. Suddenly, movement leaders discovered that their latent sympathies for the PRD demanded a closer connection. In exchange for PRD candidacies, they offered the support of their movements. When Cárdenas won a convincing victory in the mayoral race, he swept the legislative elections as well. Of the PRD's forty *asambleistas* – a legislative majority – thirty-five came directly from urban popular movements. Mayor Cárdenas also named several urban popular movement leaders as administrators of housing-related municipal offices.

The Case Studies

For closer analysis, I selected five urban popular movements from the list of possible cases. All shared one important characteristic: they protested frequently for at least some period in their history. In part, I based this choice on pragmatic considerations. It was hard to find contact information for even the most well-known organizations, let alone the smaller and less active ones. More importantly, organizations that never protested or that protested only once demonstrate no meaningful variation in the dependent variable, making analysis of the causes of changing tactics rather moot. In essence, then, I am controlling for the existence of a mobilizational political culture. These organizations also tended to be larger, older (with most dating to 1985–1987), and more institutionalized.

I also selected cases based on variation in the independent variable, party alliance. Two organizations continuously supported the PRD from its foundation, one forged an alliance in 1997 after being independent for ten years, one remained independent, and one was affiliated with the PRI. Loyalty to the PRD therefore runs across the range: highly integrated, recently integrated, neutral, and hostile. Their social bases also were slightly different, with two organizations based in the periphery of the city in self-constructed shantytowns and three based in the city center among renters and earthquake victims. In this analysis, I will focus primarily on three of these organizations: the loyal Asamblea de Barrios (a renter association), the opportunistic Frente Popular Francisco Villa, and the antagonistic PRI ally, Antorcha Popular (squatter associations).

Asamblea De Barrios

The Asamblea de Barrios (AB) is one of the first and most important PRD-allied urban popular movements. The AB was founded in April 1987 to extend the struggle for better housing to those whose housing deficit preceded the earthquake itself, the "life-long victims," as they put it. The original founders – veterans of the earthquake victims' movement – decided to conduct a census of people seeking housing, whether or not they were earthquake victims. And "in a few days, the 'group of soliciters' became enormous" (Cuéllar Vázquez, 1993: 72). Less than six months later, Cárdenas announced his candidacy for president. AB was one of the first popular movements to officially endorse him. When Cárdenas called for the formation of the PRD after the election, AB enthusiastically supported the new party. In recognition of their loyalty, AB leaders were repeatedly rewarded with PRD candidacies. In 1991, AB won one seat in the Mexico City local legislature; in 1994, it won two seats, and in 1997, six seats plus several important administrative posts in offices related to housing (Arzaluz Solano, 2002: 30).

Asamblea de Barrios was the single most active urban popular movement in terms of protest, with 205 recorded protests between 1992 and 2003. Most of these (90 percent) were peaceful marches and demonstrations, highlighted by colorful tactics like staged wrestling matches between their superhero mascot *Superbarrio* and masked figures representing such enemies as "neoliberalism" or "Catalino Creel, the voracious landlord," who always went down to defeat.[5] In 1995, AB had chapters in eleven of the sixteen Delegations (administrative subdivisions) of Mexico City (Serna, 1997: 30). However, by 2002, Asamblea de Barrios had splintered into nine groups, dividing

---

[5] Wrestling matches between masked wrestlers are a prominent part of popular culture in Mexico. The loser is literally "unmasked." The winner remains anonymous behind his spandex suit. See Schwarz (1994).

up these territories as the preserves of individual AB leaders (Arzaluz Solano, 2002: 31).[6]

Frente Popular Francisco Villa

The second PRD ally came relatively late to party activity – during the 1997 mayoral election – after nearly ten years of independent organization. The Frente Popular Francisco Villa (FPFV, or Popular Front of Francisco Villa) grew out of an accidental convergence between radical students in the department of political science at the National Autonomous University and squatters expelled by force from their precarious shacks near the university campus in 1988. The students, part of the 1987 student movement, were occupying the buildings of the political science department at the time.[7] They offered the nearly 3,000 displaced families temporary shelter in political science buildings and nearby fields. The FPFV was formally created one year later, in 1989. The FPFV expanded rapidly due to a combination of aggressive protest tactics that generated visibility and the deliberate colonization of "ripe" areas for new organization. Student organizers would move into targeted slums and begin to mobilize their new neighbors – "ant work," as one leader described it (interview C2, Mexico City, September 2000). By 1995, the FPFV operated in nine delegations.

From its origins, the FPFV had a more radical vision of social change than many of its competitors. Indeed, for many FPFV leaders, housing itself is "a tactical question, not a strategic one" (interview C1, Mexico City, September 2000). Housing demands are a way to get people involved. "People are very practical, they don't want to

---

[6] One of these splinter groups, the Asamblea de Barrios-Patria Nueva, was a second case study. A third also formed in direct response to the earthquake but chose to remain independent: the Union of Rooftop Dwellers and Renters (Unión de Cuartos de Azotea e Inquilinos, or UCAI).

[7] This mobilization, led by the CEU (Consejo Estudiantil Universitario/University Student Council) against fee increases and for university reform, was the first important mobilization by students since 1968. Many of the student leaders of CEU forged connections to the urban popular movements in 1985, when they organized rescue brigades to dig for survivors and even held off the Mexican army at one point to continue their search in the ruins of a municipal hospital. In the forty-eight additional hours they bought, seven babies and one adult were rescued. These actions made the students into heroes among the urban popular movement sector.

fight for state reform … [but] they mobilize for housing" (interview
C4, Mexico City, October 2000). The FPFV planned to use this base
to work for what every leader I interviewed cited as the FPFV's ultimate
goal: the construction of a socialist system based on self-management
(*autogestión*). In the 1988 election, the FPFV did not support Cárdenas.
In fact, it called for abstention.

The FPFV has been characterized by broader networks of alliances
with other social organizations than most urban popular movements.
The university provided the nexus for most of these connections. Many
of the events in which the FPFV participated after 1997 invoked solidarity with the 1999–2000 student strike that paralyzed UNAM
for nearly a year. However, the policy of solidarity began earlier. In
1995, FPFV support for striking bus workers marked it for growing
government attention and repression. At one point, a top FPFV leader
was arrested (and later cleared) for the murder of a judge involved in
the bus workers' conflict.[8] After 1996, the FPFV came under increasing scrutiny from military intelligence due to rumored ties with the
guerrilla group known as the Popular Revolutionary Army.

This growing scrutiny contributed to the FPFV's decision to ally
with the PRD in 1997.[9] In part, leaders sought political cover, as well
as benefits from the PRD's expected victory in the upcoming mayoral
elections. However, the decision to ally with a party and participate
in elections provoked a major split. Approximately 40 percent of
FPFV members left to form the Frente Popular Francisco Villa Independiente, which remained independent.[10]

Antorcha Popular

Antorcha Popular is the urban wing of Antorcha Campesina, a peasant
organization founded in Puebla in 1974. The founder, Aquiles Córdova

---

[8] The judge, Abraham Polo Uscanga, was found shot in his office in 1995. He was
believed to be sympathetic to the bus union, which makes the hypothesized
involvement of the FPFV in his murder somewhat illogical. The murder has never
been officially solved.

[9] By 1997, nine of the FPFV's leaders had been assassinated or killed in clashes with
police. "This caused us to widen our policy of alliances" (interview C1, Mexico
City, September 2000).

[10] The estimate comes from an interview (C4) with a leader of the FPFV who stayed in
the original organization and supported the alliance with the PRD.

Morán, belonged to the post-1968 generation of radicals and was specifically associated with the Marxist guerrilla organization known as the Liga Espartaco (Spartaquist League).[11] In the 1980s, members of Antorcha Campesina who had migrated to Mexico City created a sister organization to expand the movement into urban areas. This became known as Antorcha Popular. However, Antorcha Popular remains a subordinate branch of the larger organization still run by Aquiles Córdova Morán.

Antorcha formally affiliated with the PRI in 1988. The organization had by then become – in the words of one of its own leaders – "notorious" for its aggressive and often violent forms of struggle. As *antorchistas* put it, "organizing people in [rural] communities is something that implies confrontation with local caciques" (interview C12, Mexico City, November 2000). Most external evaluations put it in less flattering terms, arguing that by the mid-1980s Antorcha had become an armed paramilitary organization at the service of elements within the PRI. Its affiliation to the PRI bought political protection.[12] While Antorcha frequently confronts other factions of the PRI as well as opposition governments, it "tries not to break with the state." It deliberately does not seek to run its own schools or create a parallel local authority. Rather, it attempts to "secure a better distribution of wealth through services," from the state (interview C13, Mexico City, November 2000).

Little is known about Antorcha's geographical distribution or numbers, though leaders claim 500,000 members nationally (interviews C12 and C13, Mexico City, November 2000). It is one of the few large organizations that either was omitted from or refused to participate in Serna's survey of Mexico City popular movements. However, its most visible presence is in Mexico City's periphery, where it has often invaded land parcels and demanded assistance in housing and services.

As Figure 6.2 demonstrates, party loyalty seems to affect protest rates. The PRD-loyal AB protested seventy-six times against the PRI

---

[11] Antorcha's annual sports and culture festival is still known as the *Espartaqueada*. See www.antorchacampesina.org.mx.

[12] Interview C12, Mexico City, November 2000: "the PRI could give us better coverage than the PRD, and also ... we had several years of strong attacks by the very same groups that were supporting Cárdenas."

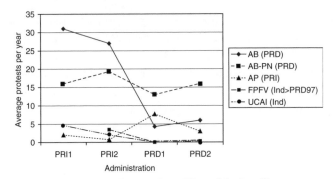

FIGURE 6.2. Protest Over Time: Mexico City.
Annual protests are calculated in terms of years of activity. For example, if a group's first protest is not until 1993, its total protests under the 1992–1994 PRI administration would be divided by two rather than by three (the years of the administration).

local administration versus eighteen times against the PRD. Protests against other targets also collapse after the PRD wins. Conversely, the PRI-loyal Antorcha exhibits very low rates of protest when the PRI is in power, followed by a spike in protest rates after the PRD wins. The only organization that maintained a similar level of mobilization after PRD victory, the FPFV, retargeted its protests. During the PRI years, while independent, the FPFV targeted the local government 59 percent of the time versus only 32 percent of the time after it became a PRD ally and the PRD won power. Instead, "solidarity marches" became increasingly relevant: 53 percent of protests from 1998 to 2003 were co-sponsored with another type of organization (not an urban popular movement) compared to 46 percent prior to 1998. The targets of these other organizations sometimes included the local government, but they also involved protest against university authorities (the student strike), federal authorities, or employers. The share of FPFV events making purely housing-related demands – housing, services, and land titles – declined from 37.8 percent of pre-1998 demands to 21.8 percent of post-1998 demands.

How do the variables under analysis correlate to these trends? In particular, how and why does the FPFV defy the trend toward demobilization over time? Several variables can be ruled out because they either did not change or were the same for all cases. A culture of protest was held roughly constant by the selection process. All of these organizations had a history of protest. The organizations were of roughly similar age. Finally, the severity of the grievance (the housing crisis) did not decrease. Indeed, one study by the National Population Council found a 75 percent *increase* in the housing deficit in the Metropolitan Zone of Mexico City, with roughly half of local residents living in marginal housing conditions (González, 2001: 49). The PRD claimed that in 2001–2002, the municipal housing agency issued 62,000 loans for housing and worked with 300 popular organizations – more than the 40,000 housing units built in the two years after the earthquake.

However, government data suggest that this effort began rather suddenly in 2001, when the budget for housing and urban development doubled. Prior to 2001, spending was fairly flat, increasing a total of 6 percent between 1998 (a PRI-formulated budget) and 2000. And after 2001, spending flattened out again, increasing less than 1 percent from 2001 to 2003. During the boom year, housing and urban development spending represented roughly 3 percent of the municipal budget. The government spent three times as much on general public works projects, including the construction of a double-decker highway intended to relieve traffic congestion for middle-class commuters.[13] Asamblea de Barrios leaders admit that their shift in tactics did not reflect a significantly different housing situation. Rather the deficit is "just as enormous as before" (interviews C9 and C11, Mexico City, October 2000).

Party alliance, in contrast, looks on the surface to be strongly associated with declines in mobilization. There is a roughly linear relationship between the decline in average protest and the degree of loyalty to the PRD. The AB's decline is the most sudden and dramatic and dates precisely to the inauguration of Cárdenas. The rate of protest by the PRI-affiliated AP increases. And the FPFV – whose leaders frequently noted that "we participate in the PRD but we do not trust it" – maintained a fairly high rate of protest, though shifting targets somewhat to non-PRD levels of government.[14] Like their union

---

[13] Much of this information is available on-line, at www.finanzas.df.gob.mx. Earlier data were photocopied from municipal accounts.

[14] Others highlighted the idea that their alliance is only with "certain currents" in the PRD (interview C4, Mexico City, October 2000). At the FPFV's 2000 Congress, speakers made a point of repeating that the PRD alliance was "tactical, not strategic," that, "the PRD is not our party," and that even holding positions in the party hierarchy "does not convert us into its unconditional supporters." One of the

counterparts, these urban popular movement leaders understood the connection between party alliance and protest success. As a leader of one independent urban popular movement lamented, "it's harder for those of us who are independent than those that are in parties ... it is easier to get them to listen to you if you have a legislator" (interview C8, Mexico City, October 2000).

To some extent, the AB's demobilization resulted from the personal choices of its mostly middle-class leaders. Unlike the PT union leaders, they swiftly redefined their relationship to the state after the PRD victory as one of "co-responsibility," of "ceasing to position ourselves as a movement merely of opposition ... now it's about being co-participants." And, they noted that "it's not so easy to march against yourself" (interviews C9 and C11, Mexico City, October 2000).

Literally, of course, the same person cannot simultaneously be outside a government office leading a march and inside the office listening to the protest. AB leaders were much more likely to have assumed positions in the local legislature and the local administration than union leaders in Brazil. This decapitation of movement leadership occurs to some extent in many cases where party allies take power. As Ramírez Sáiz notes (2002: 8),

the most plausible interpretation [of urban popular movement demobilization] is its political participation ... during the electoral campaigns the leader directs most of his efforts to that activity. In practical terms, he is absent from the organization. And, if he is elected, the achievement of popular representation means the loss of a leader for the movement ... the organizations are frequently decimated and disarticulated, as much if the candidate is elected as if he doesn't win any post.

However, decapitation covered virtually all of the AB's top leaders. Those protests in which the AB participated after the PRD's election rarely targeted the PRD. After 2000, most of the locally targeted

few portions of the proposed statutory reforms struck down by the delegates to the Congress would have made it the responsibility of the Electoral Commission of the FPFV to "guarantee attendance at all events and activities of the [PRD]" (FPFV, 2000: 8). The question raised by many activists was whether it would be "possible to use the PRD and not let [ourselves] be used by it" (interview C5, Mexico City, October 2000).

demonstrations took place in a specific delegation, Benito Juarez, where a member of the conservative National Action Party (Partido Acción Nacional, or PAN) had been popularly elected to head the delegation. There, AB demonstrated in support of PRD government goals and against the rival PAN's "distortion" of them. AB had become a tool for advancing the PRD's agenda.

AB also justified its declining protest rates as the result of "hope that this [PRD] government will resolve problems" (interview C11, Mexico City, October 2000). More specifically, movement leaders argued that their access to legislative and administrative positions was an acceptable substitute for mobilization. For AB leaders, the PRD's electoral victory meant that, "now, you have a voice because you are in the PRD" (interview C9, Mexico City, October 2000). Thus, "it is logical that when the PRD enters, people will mobilize less against the government" (interview C11, Mexico City, October 2000). Moreover, leaders claimed, AB members would not protest even if asked, because members believed that responsibility for achieving results ought to lie with their (AB) legislative representatives (interview C3, Mexico City, September 2000).

The AB example points to the importance of internal organizational structures and leadership competition on the propensity to protest. Asamblea de Barrios lacked even minimum formal mechanisms to elect leaders. According to Cuéllar Vázquez (1993: 72), "the leadership of AB was put together without having been proposed or elected and without having met any formal conditions. Their representativeness was constructed on the basis of moral authority and a preoccupation with not becoming bureaucratic and maintaining daily direct contact with the represented." Their claim to authority was "never legitimated in any other way." Rather than institutionalizing a formal organization, AB held an open assembly every Thursday, where members learned what the organization's leaders were up to and leaders had a chance to listen to complaints and suggestions. This situation, seen as defending direct participation, in practice gave leaders wide latitude. The AB's free-wheeling style made it especially vulnerable to decapitation when its leaders joined the new PRD municipal government.

What kept the FPFV from falling into the same decapitation trap? For one thing, the FPFV began with a higher level of distrust of the PRD. This led the 2000 Congress of the FPFV to require all its candidates for office or appointed government positions to sign a resignation letter in advance and leave it with the leadership, to be used if the individual defied organizational directions.

Second, the FPFV has a more developed institutional structure, though not a democratic one. Officially, it subscribes to the principle of democratic centralism, in which "members are subordinate to the organization, the minority is subordinate to the majority, the lower levels are subordinate to the higher levels, [and] the entire organization is subordinate to its leadership." Moreover, not just anyone can run for leadership posts. Members of the National Political Commission, for example, "should be the most advanced elements of the organization ... have great moral and political authority among the masses and the cadres of the organization ... [be] experienced in the practical labor of mass work, [and] possess a high degree of theoretical preparation."[15] At the 2000 Congress of the FPFV, the members of the National Political Commission were reelected by acclamation, despite the efforts of some members to propose new names for election to the Commission.[16]

Nevertheless, the centralized and collegial structure of its leadership functioned better as a bulwark against decapitation than the personalistic style of AB. The FPFV limited the number of leaders in each region authorized to seek a candidacy or accept a public position in order to preserve the continuity of full-time movement leaders and to keep those elected/appointed dependent on the central leadership. For example, one founder of the FPFV was allowed to take an

---

[15] The national political commission is the primary national leadership during the two-year period between congresses. However, a much smaller seven-member Political Commission actually runs the organization, makes most strategic decisions, and has formal responsibility for overseeing the work of the other commissions. All quotes and information from the FPFV statutes approved during their fourth national Congress, October 27–29, 2000, in Mexico City (FPFV, 2000: 1–2).

[16] Rather than confront the existing CPN directly, a motion was made to expand the membership of the CPN by several new members, who were publicly named. Those running the meeting tabled the motion for "further discussion" and never voted on it. Instead, the delegates simply voted – out loud, with no secret ballot – on an alternative motion to reconfirm the existing members. I was told by one of the FPFV delegates that it really wasn't the right time to expand the CPN; those who aspired and lost "will have to wait" their turn, and develop more as leaders before they could join the CPN. However, two of the rejected candidates were among the original founders of the FPFV (interview C10, Mexico City, October 2000).

administrative position in the PRD government (issuing building permits) but was told to request placement in a different region of the city than the one he himself organized so that he could not use his government authority to create a clientelistic personal base. In a way, the FPFV's authoritarian internal structure helped preserve the organization's "need" to protest: leaders without an elected or appointed position enhanced their influence by mobilizing the movement's bases to counteract the influence of rivals in the local government.

Add to this situation a context of intense external competition for members. Altogether, 172 urban popular movements held at least one recorded protest in Mexico City between 1992 and 2003 – not counting the tiny and often ephemeral groups whose names (if any) did not make the papers. Rivalry between movement leaders frequently created splits within organizations, sometimes leading to violent conflicts over the division of territory and members. With ineffective internal democracy, the availability of alternative organizations is the biggest source of member influence over leaders: they can vote with their feet. What is a neighborhood leader to do?

In Mexico City, four principal mechanisms were used. First, movement leaders attempted to keep members loyal by delivering material rewards. Mexico's municipal employee union was much less successful than popular movements in winning political positions, especially in the legislative assembly. SUTGDF officials ranked lower on PRI candidate lists than PRI-affiliated urban popular movements. In the PRD, urban popular movements constituted virtually the entire territorial structure of the party in many districts. Since the PRD won legislative majorities in both 1997 and 2000, the result was an ample number of seats for popular movement leaders. Moreover, even a limited number of positions helped urban popular movements considerably. Many urban popular movement demands can be met by the actions of an individual in a position to grease the right administrative wheel at the right time and to secure building permits, land titles, or a loan from the municipal housing agency. Salary demands are far more visible, expensive, and hard to secure through the action of any single elected or appointed official.

Second, urban popular movement leaders used protest as advertisement, to attract new members and to keep existing members committed to the organization. Asamblea de Barrios specialized in this use of protest. The colorful figure of *Superbarrio*, public wrestling matches, dramatic symbolic "closures" of public buildings, and cultural events all conspired to put Asamblea de Barrios regularly on the front pages of newspapers, creating the image of an active organization. Internally, leaders could use mobilization "to prove they were the ones behind the resolution of the demand." In one case, according to a government official, the popular movement staged a protest *after* he had already privately agreed to their demands (interview 7B, Mexico City, October 2000). It is, of course, much less risky to protest for something you know has already been granted! Finally, protest was used to publicize a group's perception that they have not gotten the rewards they feel they deserve and lays a foundation for increased claims on party and government resources. In this case, the target of publicity is the party – a message that the group's support is worth keeping.

Third, protest was used to reward more active militants with selective payments. The mechanism among successful organizations involved an elaborate point system. Leaders kept track of the number of meetings attended by individuals, the number of times members contributed dues, participation in security patrols at movement set-tlements, and – most importantly – the number and type of protests attended. Protests invariably counted for more points than attendance at regular meetings. The number of points determined any family's priority on the list of those who qualified for housing projects the movement secured. After this, participation determined to whom residents in a housing project could sell the unit at a later date. FPFV settlements did not permit the sale of units to nonmembers, falling back on the point system to determine which member could purchase a unit that fell vacant. The AB, in contrast, permitted the sale of units to nonmembers. The point system not only kept participation in the movement high but also reinforced loyalty to the movement: points did not transfer if the member switched movements. A point system works less well when a movement shifts toward securing public goods – water service or electricity. It simply is not possible to limit participation in public goods to those with more points.

However, such a system stimulates further protest, even when goals could be achieved in another way, because members need to continue to win points. Among the Mexican cases, the FPFV relied most on a point system. Target-switching kept the point system compatible with the FPFV's other goals of winning political cover from the PRD and maintaining access to municipal government resources. Protest in a "solidarity" demonstration counted toward a member's total points but did not irritate the PRD.

Finally, movement leaders offered selective benefits in addition to those secured from the state. Long-standing FPFV settlements – where housing and services have already been secured – required resident participation in garbage collection and security patrols. They had their own schools and markets. They presented cultural programs and dances, including parties for *quinceañeras* – celebrations for girls turning fifteen – that are common among the middle class but often financially out of reach for the poor. They organized informal sector workers who lived in FPFV settlements – especially street vendors and taxi drivers – in unions to defend access to taxi licenses or street territories. By broadening the spectrum of demands they made, the FPFV increased opportunities for protest. Most importantly, however, they fortified member identity and thus the capacity to call upon members for mobilization when necessary. None of the other organizations I looked at relied upon member solidarity and identity as much as the FPFV.

CONCLUSIONS

The model that emerges from this analysis is complex. For urban popular movements, the *capacity* to protest varies as much as the *will* to protest. High rates of protest are a function of both capacity and will. If the will is absent, the capacity lies unused and eventually atrophies. If the capacity to protest is low, the will to protest suffers because the likelihood of protest success diminishes. Different factors influence capacity versus will. PRD victory affected primarily the will to protest, declining for PRD allies with improved access to municipal resources. But other factors also influenced the will to protest. In particular, internal competition emerges as significant. The FPFV had a more radical political culture than the AB. But equally important, it did not rely on a single leader. Only part of the leadership participated in government at any one time. The rest had to rely on their ability to sponsor protest to keep their names in the public eye. The will to protest thus reflects an organization's dependence on protest as part of a membership maintenance strategy.

The capacity to protest reflects two main factors: size and access to resources. Size matters not only because more people at a protest make a bigger impression but also because only the largest organizations have the ability to develop the kind of internal differentiation and record-keeping that stimulated protest in the FPFV. Serna's survey (1997: 46) found that 30 percent of all organizations had three or fewer internal commissions, a measure of institutional complexity. Just 6 percent had ten or more. When internal competition results in a split, the will to protest may remain the same or even increase as both new groups attempt to prove their superior ability to deliver the goods. But the capacity to sustain protest or to hold impressive protests may diminish for both groups. The FPFV's continued protest levels even after a major split reflect its participation in an increasing number of protests sponsored by other groups – maintaining the appearance of activity and disguising the size of the FPFV's individual contribution. For most groups, however, the splintering of an original organization produces disillusionment, reduced size and resources, and a decline in protest.

Most of the groups in my database were unable and/or unwilling to sustain protest. Of the 172 named groups, 104 (60.5 percent) protested only once in twelve years. Many other groups never protested at all and never got into my database. Neighborhood organization in Mexico is a rare and precarious thing. Just 5 percent of the population of Mexico City reported participation in a neighborhood association in 2003 (Mendez and León, 2003: 5B). And whereas most Mexican unions date their foundation to the 1930s – the SUTGDF, for example, was founded in 1936 – the oldest urban popular movements analyzed here date to the mid-1980s. None survived intact into the second PRD administration. Indeed, within ten years of foundation, all had suffered at least one major split and many had splintered into three or four competing organizations. For the urban poor, the dominant method of securing public aid continues to run through clientelistic exchanges rather than organization and mobilization. The experience of PRD administrations simply demonstrates that even previously mobilized groups can find clientelism appealing as well. By 2003, the Mexico City PRD had become a party dependent on clientelistic relationships with urban popular movements in many districts.

Protest and alliance strategies must be viewed in this light. Alliance with a party can stabilize the flow of resources to a neighborhood association. Parties in Mexico receive government subsidies with which they develop an infrastructure – local offices, telephones, vehicles, loudspeakers, and so on – that they share with affiliated organizations. Independent organizations struggle to survive. These resource constraints explain in part why they protest less often than party-affiliated groups. However, party alliance also causes many splits within urban popular movements. As the unity of a movement erodes, its capacity for effective protest erodes as well.

7

Favelas and *Cortiços*

Neighborhood Organizing in São Paulo

As Chapter 6 demonstrated, neighborhood associations in São Paulo were less inclined to limit protest when their party ally won power than their counterparts in Mexico City, although small changes were observed. Yet the Brazilian movements were more organically linked to the PT than most of the Mexican movements were to the PRD. This chapter explores how the PT-affiliated movements largely escaped the decapitation effects that afflicted the AB despite similarly high levels of loyalty to their party. The organizational solutions are strikingly similar to those of the FPFV. The chapter concludes with a quantitative analysis of urban popular movement behavior more broadly in the two cities and a summary of findings from Chapters 6 and 7.

HISTORICAL DEVELOPMENT

As in Mexico City, membership in any neighborhood association is relatively rare in São Paulo. A 1999 study found that just 2.5 percent of metropolitan residents in Brazil participated in a neighborhood association as of 1996, compared to 15.7 percent who belonged to a union (Costa Ferreira, 1999: 98). There is also a long history of clientelistic relations between politicians and the urban poor, superseded only in the late 1970s and early 1980s by the emergence of a more independent and active urban popular movement sector. The central issues that motivate organization are similar: access to land and services for self-constructed shantytowns on the city's periphery (the *favelas*) and improvement of unsafe living conditions in the tenement houses located in the city center (the *cortiços*). However, several characteristics distinguish urban organizations in São Paulo from their counterparts in Mexico City.

First, the clientelistic networks constructed in São Paulo were tied to individual politicians rather than a hegemonic political party like the PRI. The Neighborhood Friends' Societies (Sociedades de Amigos de Bairro or SABs) formed in the 1950s under the direction of ambitious politicians seeking to form an electoral base. In São Paulo, the most famous example was Jânio Quadros. When he ran for mayor, the "transformation of many [electoral] committees in favor of Jânio into SABs in the poor periphery of the city was in large measure a deliberate operation ... to consolidate his electoral base." Quadros used an initially electoral structure to negotiate the exchange of votes for favors (Singer, 1980: 87). The newly constituted neighborhood organizations that took delivery of benefits after the election served Quadros well in his political rise from mayor to governor and eventually president of Brazil.

The fact that clientelistic exchanges created personal rather than party loyalties meant that they could survive the military's proscription of political parties after the 1964 coup. Many individual politicians remained active, especially among the conservative set that had spent the most time building clientelistic machines. Quadros survived politically to become mayor of São Paulo once again from 1986 to 1988 – an impressive demonstration of the longevity of his personal networks. However, these networks were vulnerable to their leader's loss of state access or death. No party loyalty served as a bulwark in lean times, making their bases open to raids by competing organizations.

A second characteristic differentiating São Paulo and Mexico City is the political orientation of competing organizations. In Mexico, the first wave of independent movements was led by activists who saw organizing the urban poor as a step toward socialist revolution. In São Paulo, progressive Catholic priests played the role of movement entrepreneurs. The Ecclesial Base Communities (Comunidades Eclesiais de Base, or CEBs) originated as grassroots groups of Catholic believers, instituted for the purpose of responding to Vatican II's call to make the church more relevant and responsive to the needs of believers. The social gospel of what became known as liberation theology redefined the church's relationship to the status quo. Long a bulwark supporting conservative political regimes, the church (or at least some elements within it) began to defend popular causes such as human rights and social equality. Levine and Mainwaring (1989: 209–210) define CEBs in terms of

a striving for community (small, homogeneous); a stress on the ecclesial (links to the church); and a sense in which the group constitutes a *base* (either the faithful at the base of the church's hierarchy or the poor at the base of the social pyramid). Most CEBs are small groups ... [that] gather regularly ... to read and comment on the Bible.

Despite these apparently innocuous activities, many CEBs became forums for the poor to reflect on the causes of poverty, to attribute blame, and to call for action to change their circumstances rather than waiting for death and the prospect of heaven to bring relief. Thus, CEBs "encouraged new religious practices that embody more critical conceptions of authority" (Levine and Mainwaring, 1989: 205).

Liberation theology had a particularly strong impact in Brazil due to three factors: First, a progressive National Brazilian Bishops' Council (also known as the Conferencia Nacional dos Bispos de Brasil, or CNBB) was created relatively early in Brazil, in the 1950s, that quickly embraced the "preferential option for the poor" of post–Vatican II (1960s) liberation theology. Second, Brazilian educator Paulo Freire had pioneered a student-led form of literacy training, widely used in CEB Bible studies, which focused on consciousness-raising, curriculum with relevance to the lives of the students, and equality between student and teacher. Third, Brazil's largest city – São Paulo – happened to have an especially progressive and politically active archbishop, Paulo Evaristo Arns. Only about 80 of Brazil's 350 bishops actively promoted CEBs, but because they included the top Catholic cleric in São Paulo – at that time "the most populous archdiocese in the world" – São Paulo became a center for the proliferation of CEBs in Brazil (Levine and Mainwaring, 1989: 215).

During the 1970s, the CEBs were also a relatively safe place for leftists to hide out. According to Frei Betto (Brother Betto), "the CEBs did not attract the attention of the military. ... So, many leftist militants hibernated in the CEBs and with that, they became the great greenhouse for new militants and at the same time, the seed of popular movements."[1] Frei Betto himself worked in the CEBs and helped found the combative Landless Workers' Movement in the 1980s.

Particularly in its initial phase, the CEB movement focused on self-empowerment within a civil sphere far from the state. Since a military junta governed Brazil at the time, a focus on elections and parties seemed both irrelevant and risky. The Brazilian military regularly held elections with two official political parties, established by military decree to replace the political parties of Brazil's Second Republic that were outlawed by the military. In theory, one party supported the military government and one acted as the loyal opposition. In reality, neither party allowed itself the luxury of real opposition; Brazilian wits called them the parties of "yes" and "yes, sir." Politicians who did not face personal bans (*cassação*) could join one of these two parties. However, these limitations left the CEBs with few sympathetic public officials to petition. Before 1964, the Communist Party dominated independent organizing in São Paulo's poor urban neighborhoods, but communists were banned from political participation after 1964.

The focus on self-help rather than petitioning the state for benefits mirrors to some extent the reaction of the *maoist* student leaders to Mexico's authoritarian regime. Some liberation theology priests embraced socialism and its goals of radical social transformation. Yet for many, the goals were more limited: democracy, political empowerment, and compassionate attention to the needs of the poor. After Brazil's democratic transition, the CEB movement began to withdraw from political activism and turn its attention back to religious instruction and social programs. Recent studies (e.g., Hewitt, 1998: 171) note an overall decline in the number of active CEBs, as well as "drastically diminished involvement in politics ... overall the sample [of CEBs in São Paulo] appears to be transforming itself into a much more conservative, 'devotional' force ... with increasingly strong ties to the Catholic Charismatic movement." Most of the Leftist militants

---

[1] From an interview with Frei Betto, published in Rossiaud and Scherer-Warren (2000: 47).

who once provided leadership to the CEBs found it safe to organize openly in democratic Brazil, leaving more religiously oriented leaders in charge of the CEBs. Most urban popular movements in São Paulo are no longer led by priests or nuns, though local churches still provide meeting places and infrastructure for many groups.[2]

The third characteristic distinguishing São Paulo and Mexico City cases is the more limited range of alliance patterns in São Paulo. Virtually all of the urban popular movements I found and identified by party alliance had been tied to the PT since their foundation. These people knew each other, shared similar perspectives, and contributed to common mobilization efforts. The 1977 Anti-Scarcity Movement and the 1979 Movement against the High Cost of Living brought together multiclass coalitions of organizations, led by the CEBs but attracting independent unions as well as human rights organizations. The Amnesty Movement of 1978–1979 again joined CEBs with unions and popular movements. Later, urban popular movements intervened on behalf of union leaders jailed after the independent strikes led by Lula and the Metalworkers' Union.

It was only natural, then, that when Lula called for the formation of a Workers' Party, he should attract the sympathy and attention of many urban popular movements from the CEB sector. The PT's formation is unique not just because of the leadership provided by unions, but also because of the inclusion of popular movements, women's movements, rural workers, and the urban poor. This early immersion in the PT left leaders of urban popular movements in São Paulo with strong feelings of ownership of the PT, akin only to the sentiments of AB leaders toward the PRD. Most Mexican movements sought out the PRD more or less reluctantly. Their suspicion of parties mirrored that of newly independent unions. They managed to overcome it, in part because of the rewards, but also in part because they came to believe that they could control the PRD. This was the explicit strategy of the FPFV: to use their territorial organization to "penetrate" and control party committees in their zones of influence (interview C4, Mexico City, October 2000). In contrast, most urban popular

---

[2] Two of the three "base" meetings that I attended took place in church buildings, and the third at the site of a building invasion occupied by the movement.

movements in São Paulo strongly identified with the PT. I was able to find only three independent neighborhood associations and one association affiliated with another party.[3]

Paradoxically, strong identification with the PT persists despite their limited influence over the PT. Unlike urban popular movements in the PRD, they must share power with union leaders as well as the well-organized veterans of pre-PT Leftist parties. In the PT, the main rivals of urban popular movement leaders are not party hacks but other popular organization leaders. In 1993, 15 percent of PT state-level legislators were linked to neighborhood associations, but 30 percent were linked to unions (Shidlo, 1998: 85). This situation may induce greater solidarity among urban popular movement organizations: in order to maintain a strong PT commitment to their priorities (as against other concerns), they have to act together.

In general, the urban popular movement sector in São Paulo displays a remarkable degree of concentration and coordination compared to Mexico City. In Mexico City, 172 different neighborhood associations protested at least once in twelve years. In São Paulo, only 73 organizations protested at least once in fifteen years. Two of the most active organizations in terms of protest are actually networks of other urban popular movements. The only major coordinating network that formed in Mexico – the National Coordinator of Urban Popular Movements (CONAMUP) – had more than one hundred affiliated organizations at its height but its size hid intense internal political differences. To maintain maximum numbers of affiliates with different political orientations, CONAMUP abdicated control over their individual strategic choices. CONAMUP began to fall apart when the PRD emerged in 1989 and dissolved completely by 1994.[4]

---

[3] One of these independent organizations protested a total of four times (once in 1998, twice in 1999, and once in 2003), and I was unable to secure interviews with its leaders. The others may not even exist any more – none has protested since 1999 at the latest. I participated in a series of conferences in São Paulo from June to September 2004 to promote discussion of urban issues, attended by virtually all urban popular movements of significance, but I never met representatives of these movements.

[4] Founded in 1981, the CONAMUP was dominated by *maoist* organizers. However, debates over electoral participation and political orientation made the survival of the CONAMUP contingent on a nonpolitical stance. The emergence of the PRD as a viable electoral option made the debate over electoral participation more than just a moot point and widened these cleavages, leading inexorably to a split in 1988. Two

The PT movements devised a system to manage competition that protects all of them and amplifies their power to protest when they jointly decide on action. However, as I will discuss below, this very coordination may act to inhibit protest overall.

Two of the five cases I analyzed in São Paulo were coordinating networks. The other three focused on São Paulo's tenement houses (renters rather than shantytown dwellers). Because the internal organization of all of these movements was quite similar, I will focus for the sake of clarity on two organizations: the União de Movimentos de Moradia (Union of Housing Movements, or UMM) and the Forum dos Cortiços.[5]

The UMM

The UMM formed in 1987 as a network of housing movements in São Paulo and the surrounding metropolitan region. The impetus for its formation came from leaders involved in CEBs, the Housing Pastorate (a Catholic mission focused on housing), and the *favela* movement, which had recently staged a series of land invasions involving 200,000 people. Luiza Erundina – an adviser to the Unified Movement of Favelas – played an important role in bringing the UMM together, just prior to launching her successful campaign for mayor of São Paulo.

One of the main reasons for creating the UMM was to take advantage of the opportunity offered by the projected constitutional convention, scheduled for 1988. In part as a result of pressures by the UMM, the new constitution gave greater autonomy and a larger share of federal funds to Brazilian cities. By 1993, Brazilian cities could expect to receive 21 percent of total tax revenue (Assies, 1993: 43). The

new *coordinadoras* – the pro-PRD Convención Nacional del Movimiento Urbano Popular and the anti-party Asamblea Nacional del Movimiento Urbano Popular – emerged from its ashes. Both had disappeared by 1994. See Serna (1997).

[5] The other organizations were the Central de Movimentos Populares (Popular Movements' Central, or CMP), a coordinating network, the Movimento de Moradia do Centro (Housing Movement of the Center, or MMC), and the Unificação das Lutas de Cortiço (Unification of Cortiço Struggles, or ULC). The reason for their similar statutes is the fact that historically speaking, all of the groups were related. The CMP grew out of the UMM, and the UMM is today also a member of the CMP. The MMC, ULC, and Forum de Cortiços belong to the CMP as well.

1988 Constitution also created "Management Councils" (*Conselhos Gestores*) and made them "legally indispensable for the transfer of federal funds to states and cities" (Tatagiba, 2002: 308). In order to receive money from specified federal programs, cities had to set up a Management Council to oversee the use of funds. More importantly, these Management Councils had to be constructed on the basis of equal representation of the state and civil society. Councils could be linked to specific government programs (e.g., school lunch programs, housing programs, and health programs), to citizenship rights (e.g., childrens' rights, women's rights), or to issues (e.g., culture, sports, or transportation). By 1996, an estimated 65 percent of all Brazilian cities had at least one Management Council (Tatagiba, 2002: 306). While doubts remain about the effective power of the councils, they did give a place at the table to movements that had never before had a formal role in policy making. The UMM also sponsored in 1991 a law that set aside 1 percent of the state-level value-added tax in a National Fund for Popular Housing. This fund is the largest single source of funding for low-income housing projects in Brazil. In São Paulo, an additional (1995) law required the state government to reserve 10 percent of these funds for self-constructed housing projects administered by the movements themselves.

UMM statutes establish democracy as the basic organizing principle. Its largest body is the Plenary of Affiliated Entities, made up of two representatives per affiliated urban popular movement "plus one additional representative for each 250 (two hundred fifty) participants that it contains." The UMM demands discipline: organizations that are behind in their dues to the UMM do not have the right to a vote at the plenary.[6] The plenary meets once a year and elects the nine members of the General Board via a system of lists (*chapas*) identical to the system used in the SINDSEP, and proportional representation with a 10 percent threshold. As in the SINDSEP, these *chapas* were usually prenegotiated. According to interviews (L2 and L5, July and

---

[6] I must note, however, that in my visits to the UMM offices at least half of the organizations were listed as behind on their dues. Perhaps they catch up just before the plenary – or, perhaps the UMM simply does not enforce this provision. Interviews did not clarify which situation occurred, though leaders did say they planned to enforce it. Citations are from the Estatuto da União dos Movimentos de Moradia da Grande São Paulo e Interior, printed from the UMM computer, August 2003.

August 2003), the UMM has never had more than one *chapa* – the consensus list – on voting day. However, during negotiations, representatives of affiliated groups received shares of power roughly proportional to their size. The real elections took place within affiliated groups as they decided which individuals would serve on the UMM board. Despite the potential for abuse created by negotiations, high turnover does occur. Eight of the nine board members in 2003 were serving their first term. The General Board runs UMM affairs and decides strategy. No board member can receive "any type of remuneration" for service on the board.

Forum dos Cortiços

The Forum dos Cortiços operates in São Paulo's tenement houses, mostly located in the center of the city. In contrast to other Brazilian cities, such as Rio de Janeiro, the phenomenon of shantytowns on the city's periphery did not play a big role in resolving housing shortages for new migrants to São Paulo. A short boom in *favela* settlements occurred in the 1970s as the extension of bus lines made commuting to jobs in the city center feasible. However, the shared rental housing known as the *cortiço* – the oldest form of urban housing for the poor in São Paulo – experienced renewed growth in the 1980s and 1990s as the service sector grew, locating jobs in the center rather than on the industrial periphery, and as collective transport became ever more expensive, unpleasant, unreliable, and time-consuming. According to one estimate, 28 percent of the population of São Paulo lived in *cortiços* by 1990.[7]

Literally meaning "beehive," the *cortiço* resembles its metaphorical name: tiny rooms, divided and subdivided with improvised walls, and crowded to the gills with low-income families, workers, and students. Cooking, bathing, and sanitary facilities must usually be shared with other tenants and are often jerry-rigged and unsafe. Buildings rarely

---

[7] These estimates come from the progressive nongovernmental organization POLIS (Simões Junior, 1991: 20) and the Câmara Municipal de São Paulo (2003: 21). The count of *cortiço* dwellers is made harder by the difficulty of classifying any one building as a *cortiço* versus counting all residents in a *favela* zone.

become *cortiços* until after they have been abandoned by more financially stable clients and often were not intended as residences at all. Yet half of the *cortiço* renters surveyed in 1997 paid more than 28 percent of their meager incomes for the pleasure of living in them, and a quarter paid more than 43 percent of their income (Bonduki, 2000: 75). They pay, essentially, for the central location of *cortiços* – near jobs, schools, and shopping – which saves them time and the expense of commuting. Over half of surveyed *cortiço* residents walk to work. The free bus tokens that many jobs provide can then be sold on the black market, offering an additional source of income. *Cortiço* residents frequently move from one *cortiço* to another and most of them – 95 percent in one 1990 survey – work regularly, giving them less time to participate in organizations (Simões Junior, 1991: 27). These factors make organizing in the *cortiços* especially challenging. Base groups frequently meet in movement offices or churches rather than neighborhoods because *cortiço* dwellers change residences so often.

The Forum dos Cortiços is the youngest group of the five I looked at, and the result of a split from one of the other four (the Unificação das Lutas de Cortiço/Unification of Cortiço Struggles, or ULC). In 1998, its founder Veronica Kroll broke with the ULC (of which she was a key leader) over what she called "differences of opinion." The Forum was one of several groups that left the ULC around this time. Groups that left – including the Forum – argued that the ULC had become too moderate, too close to the government, and that it had directly supported the campaign activities of party candidates. Kroll also cited the ULC's lack of support for building invasions as a source of disagreement.

Like the UMM, the Forum dos Cortiços elects a general coordinating body every two years, voting by lists with proportional representation of each list. Compared with the UMM, Forum was dominated by a small group of leaders, headed of course by Veronica Kroll. This pattern was typical of many of the smaller organizations, as leaders leveraged control of their local organizations into citywide and state-level activism. Nevertheless, leadership bodies were typically much larger than the half dozen or so that dominated Mexico's AB, and formal institutional mechanisms provided for regular leadership elections. The Forum had a General Coordinating Committee with sixty members and a smaller (fifteen- to twenty-person) executive leadership, elected by the General Coordinating Committee. Both groups met every week. At these meetings, leaders would report back on developments in individual housing projects (base communities), discuss strategies, and prepare to relay organizational policy to the base groups during their next meeting.

Patterns of Mobilization in São Paulo

Like their Mexican counterparts, these urban popular movements spared their party ally, though the decline in mobilization was not nearly as dramatic. Arranging the São Paulo administrations in chronological order, we see increasing protest over time from the first PT administration through the second conservative administration and decreasing slightly when the PT took over again (see Figure 7.1). This pattern is consistent with an interpretation that the urban popular movements – in contrast to unions – deliberately spared the PT.

Moreover, there is evidence of retargeting. Two of the organizations never targeted a PT local government, but directed 40 to 50 percent of their protests at the local government when the Maluf faction was in power. Two other organizations targeted both PT and non-PT local governments, but they targeted the non-PT governments at a higher rate. The gap is substantial: UMM targeted the local

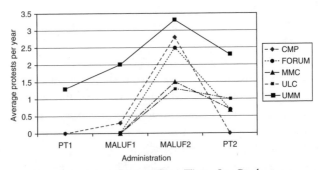

FIGURE 7.1. Protest Over Time: São Paulo.
Annual protests are calculated in terms of years of activity. For example, if a group's first protest is not until 1991, its total protests under the 1989–1992 PT administration would be divided by two rather than by four (the years of the administration).

government three times as often when the PT was out of power. Nor does this pattern reflect the unique wave of protest against corruption in Pitta's government. On the contrary, São Paulo's urban popular movements are narrowly focused on housing. With the exception of the one national-level coordinating network (CMP), these movements made demands for housing in 100 percent of their protests under both PT and non-PT governments. Even the CMP made the removal of Pitta an additional demand in less than 10 percent of its protests.

The PT-linked movements in São Paulo movements closely resemble the FPFV in terms of their institutional rules, level of internal differentiation, and management of internal competition, though most of the PT groups were more democratic and open to leadership rotation. The norm, for example, was to represent factions proportionally to their strength and to negotiate beforehand; in contrast, the FPFV reelected its entire existing leadership by acclamation. This system for electing leaders tended to reward those who could mobilize supporters. In one group, members elected their top leaders every two years at a public meeting. Voting was by lists with proportional representation of each list. There was thus a premium on turnout: she who could convince more people to come and vote for the list she headed was likely to end up on the council.

As in the FPFV, leadership was collegial, especially at the top levels. Unlike the FPFV, PT movements made an effort to include new movement leaders in existing coordinating networks. The fact that eight of the nine UMM executive board members in 2003 had never served before resulted from a deliberate decision by previous board members not to run again. They argued that it was necessary to give midlevel organizers a chance to grow as leaders (interview L5, São Paulo, August 2003). This strategy of cultivating a broad leadership – not all of whom would participate in government – also provided a bulwark against decapitation, just as in the FPFV. It was typical (though not required) for PT movement leaders who took government positions to resign from day-to-day leadership in the movements so that other leaders could take their place and devote their full attention to movement affairs.

Also as in the FPFV, all of the PT movements employed a point system awarding credit to members for participation in organization activities, including protest. I watched at meetings of local base organizations as members stood in line to pay their dues, sign the attendance sheet, and get their point books updated. In part to sustain the point system between mobilizations, the base-level groups kept to a rigorous schedule of meetings every two weeks, usually on Sundays when most businesses are closed in São Paulo. The primary purpose of the meetings was to inform members of progress on their housing projects and to alert them to upcoming events at which they could earn points. Leaders also led discussions of overall strategy and talked openly about internal conflicts. Attendance was usually thirty to fifty people, making real discussion possible.

In one meeting, most of the discussion turned on whether the point books accurately rank-ordered two members who both wanted a disputed place in the movement's new housing project. To resolve the issue, leaders at the meeting handed out copies of the rules for accumulating points: local meetings were worth four points; participation in courses or cultural activities was worth three points; paying dues was worth one point; but attending a demonstration was worth five points, and participating in an occupation (of buildings or land) was worth seven. The handout further elaborated that arriving thirty minutes late to a meeting meant you did not get points; arriving without identification meant you did not get points; only adults (age 18 or older) could represent a family at a meeting; and you could not increase your points by attending the meetings of two separate base groups belonging to the movement. One could get an excuse for absence only in the case of marriage, illness, and death (if proof was provided). And, the rules recommended, "try not to come drunk." Most importantly, "only those with the most points will have a right to vacancies" in housing projects.[8]

Benedito Roberto Barbosa, a UMM founder, admits that "in the beginning, [the people] participate because of the points, but later they understand that it is necessary to fight for their own homes and for those of other people ... because now they have participated in a process of consciousness-raising."[9] Nevertheless, the point systems remain in place. Elaborate systems of record-keeping were the rule

---

[8] All information comes directly from the actual handout that I collected at the meeting.
[9] From an interview with Benedito Roberto Barbosa, published in Rossiaud and Scherer-Warren (2000: 84).

rather than the exception among São Paulo urban popular movements, though they were absent in the unions (which have other sources of funding and control over members). And they consistently rewarded mobilization more than other kinds of participation.

These characteristics kept PT movements from reducing mobilization as dramatically when the PT won power as the AB did when the PRD won. Nevertheless, mobilization did decline more than in the case of the FPFV, up to 50 percent. Why? In part, loyalty to the PT functioned much as loyalty to the PRD functioned in the AB. Movement evaluations of the prospects for protest success also differed. As in Mexico, Brazilian movements believed that Left electoral victory would improve their access and their odds of getting demands met. However, Brazilians saw the effect of Left *losses* much more negatively. PRD movements saw the PRI as vulnerable to mobilization and pressure. PT movements did not see the conservative Maluf governments in similar terms. They spared the PT because they did not need to protest as much. They spared Maluf because they did not think protest would work.

The contrast is evident in the comparison between Erundina's administration and that of Maluf. The Erundina administration turned over housing funds to popular movements by authorizing *mutirão* projects – literally, mutual help. *Mutirão* allowed movements to design and build self-managed housing projects with municipal financing. Participants would pay for technical assistance (e.g., architectural design) but build the houses with their own labor. In this way, they could reduce costs and get what they wanted. Because Erundina lacked a legislative majority, "what advanced under Erundina was what the Executive could do alone" (interview L2, São Paulo, July 2003). Still, *mutirão* projects enabled her to satisfy urban popular movement constituents in accordance with the participatory values of the movements.

When Maluf took over in 1993, he immediately froze all of the funds intended for these housing projects, alleging lack of technical competence. The fact that most of the beneficiaries were PT organizations made his decision easy. He reoriented public works spending to a series of high-profile road projects intended to ease traffic congestion for the middle class. He did not completely ignore low-income housing. But his housing initiative involved hiring contractors to build large apartment buildings, like project Cingapura, after the high-rise apartment buildings he admired in Singapore. Not coincidentally, Maluf made his fortune in the construction industry and got a lot of his campaign donations from this sector. For the next eight years, the *mutirão* projects remained in a state of suspended animation.

Initially, the PT movements reacted to this cutoff of funds with outrage and protest. But when Maluf did not budge, they began to see the handwriting on the wall. The UMM, for example, protested six times against Maluf in the first year of his government, but only twice in the next three years. In a 1994 interview, UMM director Paulo Conforto evaluated the situation thus: "at the beginning of [Maluf's] government people held big demonstrations ... but obviously, people are not fools. Everyone can tell when they are beating their head against a wall. And they begin to look for another moment to be able to continue the struggle" (Da Silva, 1994b: 87). Similarly, UMM leader Benedito Roberto Barbosa argued that "Maluf began with the principle that the *mutirantes* are dominated by PT groups and therefore are his enemies. ... [W]e understand that with Maluf we will have a hard time getting any kind of resources" (Da Silva, 1994b: 73). The UMM, he went on to argue, should instead seek resources outside the São Paulo municipal government, from domestic and foreign NGOs and from the governor's office (occupied by a member of the Social Democratic Party). The PT-affiliated municipal employees union made similar calculations about the receptiveness of Erundina and Maluf. However, unlike the municipal employees, neighborhood associations could solve at least some of their problems by retargeting.

Likewise, the aggressiveness of their tactics reflected calculations about success and the likelihood of repression. One of the most aggressive tactics used by urban popular movements is building occupation, the takeover of vacant buildings. Residents may occupy these buildings for years at a time, hoping to put pressure on the owners to transfer title or on the government to relocate them to more adequate housing. Shortly after the disappointing reelection of the Maluf faction in 1996, the number of building invasions began to rise. Despite the odds against success, some leaders believed that further postponement of the demand agenda could endanger the morale of the movement and the credibility of movement leaders as effective organizers. They argued that "struggle makes you grow" (interview L4, São Paulo, July 2003).

Nevertheless, once the PT won power, many leaders I interviewed argued that invasions "just don't make sense now."[10] Rather, movements should take advantage of their institutional access as long as the PT remained in office. Only one leader continued to claim that occupations remained an important tactic to force the government to negotiate. Significantly, for this leader, there was no difference between a PT and a non-PT government: "the movement has to stand on its own two legs" (interview L3, São Paulo, July 2003). Moreover, he said, occupations could make the housing problem more "visible to society" (Câmara Municipal de São Paulo, 2001: 37). Even so, none of the buildings his organization occupied belonged to the local government.[11]

Empirically, there was a big difference in the material rewards obtained by the Brazilian movements under PT governments versus the rewards obtained by movements from the Mexico City government. Suplicy's first innovation – a simple executive order to resume funding approved during the Erundina administration – allowed many of the paralyzed *mutirão* projects to finish construction. According to municipal data, the Suplicy administration funded 7,500 *mutirão* projects begun between 1989 and 1991 and suspended during the entire Maluf period; by 2003, 2112 projects had completed work (Secretariat of Housing and Urban Development, 2003a: 1, 14).

Suplicy also expanded the role of Management Councils in which popular movements could participate. In Mexico City, movement access to government positions went mostly through the election of legislators, and the mayor's power of appointment when the PRD won. The few efforts to create participatory councils came at the initiative of individual politicians and failed to become institutionalized (Sánchez Mejorada and Álvarez Enriquez, 2003; Olvera, 2003b). In São Paulo, six of the PT's sixteen local legislators came from urban popular movements during the Erundina administration, the height of their influence. But the PT never managed to win a legislative majority. This may explain the importance attributed to the Management Councils.

---

[10] Interview L8, São Paulo, August 2003. Also, interview L2, São Paulo, July 2003.

[11] This targeting strategy also reflected an analysis that by occupying buildings owned by banks and financial agencies (of the federal and state government), they could secure the loans needed to refurbish and repair the buildings at the same time as they achieved the transfer of property title.

Of the sixteen popular movement representatives holding positions on São Paulo's Housing Council, six listed their affiliation as the UMM.[12] Three others belong to movements that in turn are affiliated to the UMM. Elections for these positions were citywide and open to all. Thus, organizations that could get their members out to vote benefited. Leaders did note that "you have to be careful not to turn into a militant of the meeting," a reference to the time sucked up by constant meetings without tangible results. Nevertheless, "at least they listen to you" (interview L8, São Paulo, August 2003).

These calculations of risks and probability of success help explain not only why protest does not change as dramatically from PT to non-PT governments as in Mexico, but also why the overall level of protest has been so low in São Paulo. When the PT won, affiliated movements did not protest because they felt, given their increased access to public administration, that they had "much more hope of having their demands attended with new housing programs" (Ruscheinsky, 1997: 18). This was particularly true during the administration of Erundina, a former adviser of the housing movement. When the PT lost, urban popular movements did not protest because they felt it would do no good. This was particularly true of the Maluf government. Thus, "The Housing Movement suffered a strong blow to its prospects with the governments of the right ... [but] an identity crisis at the beginning of the *petista* government" (Ruscheinsky, 1997: 18).

Another factor that helps explain São Paulo's relatively low rates of protest is the existence of complex networks to manage competition among urban popular movements. In a very real sense, these cases are not truly independent but a series of nested organizations: the MMC and the Forum de Cortiços belonged to the ULC until 1998; the ULC belonged to the UMM, and the UMM belonged to the CMP. They adopted similar organizational structures because they shared the same set of organizers. Individual movements could make their own decisions about protest but usually deferred to the coordinating networks to which they belonged. They did have internal conflicts – one former movement leader noted that "they fight so much among each other that they don't need an enemy" (interview M3, São Paulo, July 2003).

---

[12] Secretariat of Housing and Urban Development (2003b: 14). Also interview L5, São Paulo, August 2003.

Yet the respect for and desire for coordinated action is noteworthy. The PT *coordinadoras* use majority decision-rules as a last resort, but the effort to agree on tactics among radical and moderate groups tends to moderate the tactics of the *coordinadoras* as a whole.

Some of this sense that the urban popular movements have to act together in order to succeed comes from the experience of repression under the military government, and some comes from the vastly more conservative opposition in São Paulo. Furthermore, the way in which these groups manage their environment by coordinating may cut down on the number of successful new urban popular movements. What we can say for sure is that the PT groups enjoy a far more hegemonic position in São Paulo than elsewhere. Only 70 movements protested at least once in São Paulo versus 172 in Mexico City. Of these 70 movements, 44 (62 percent) protested only once, virtually the same percentage that protested only once in Mexico City. There are just a lot more Mexican movements that protest. So, the overall level of protest is higher, and any group that wishes to get the attention of local government has to get past a lot more noise in order to be heard. After the mobilizational "collapse" of the Asamblea de Barrios, it still protested on average three times a year against the local PRD administration. The most active São Paulo group protested only five times in its most active year against all targets.

PROTEST BY URBAN POPULAR MOVEMENTS: A STATISTICAL ANALYSIS

Creating a model of the protest strategies of urban popular movements proved considerably more difficult than creating one for unions, mostly because the number of cases is much smaller. In Brasilia, there are too few urban popular movement protests (only 13) for meaningful statistical analysis – and in São Paulo, the 125 protests available do not justify much confidence in the statistical stability of the findings.

Nevertheless, the findings are mostly consistent with the model for all non-union protests that was presented in Chapter 6 (see Table 7.1). Protest rate in the previous year has a significant positive effect. Age is significant and negative. Left-affiliated organizations protest significantly more than independent or other-party organizations. Honeymoon years have a positive and significant effect on protest in São Paulo,

TABLE 7.1. *Number of Protests, Urban Popular Movements: Local Government Target*

	Mexico City	São Paulo
Organizational Resources		
Age	−.11**(−10.1%)	−.13*(−12.1%)
Identity		
Left party ally	.65*(92.3%)	1.34*(280.9%)
Independent	−.12	.15
Protest in previous year	.29***(33.3%)	.16
POS		
Party ally in power	−1.22**(−70.4%)	−.73
Honeymoon year	.35	1.2***(233.3%)
Election year	−.36	−.62
Interaction: honeymoon year and ally in power	.02	−.45
Interaction: election year and ally in power	1.76***(481.4%)	18.6
Economic Grievance		
Inflation (natural log)	−.40*(−33.1%)	.01
Pseudo R^2	.14***	.17***

*** significant at .01   ** significant at .05   * significant at .1

and a positive (though not significant) effect on urban popular movements in Mexico City. Even though in general they spare their allies, housing movements make an exception for the first year of a new administration, anxious to establish their place at the head of the line for receiving resources.

Perhaps the most striking *new* result is the strong effect of the interaction term for election year with alliance to the party in power in Mexico City. Urban popular movements in Mexico City protest nearly 500 percent more often in election years, *but only if they are allied with the party in power*. This effect becomes more understandable in the context of the case study findings that urban popular movements in Mexico City have far greater advantages in securing party candidacies within the PRD than their PT-affiliated counterparts in São Paulo, because they do not have to compete with unions for nominations. My own observations suggest strongly that protests in these years have a lot to do with staking a claim to positions on the

PRD candidate list. Mexican urban popular movements then rely on these positions to secure benefits in the next administration. However, they only need to stage protests when the PRD is actually in power because this is when their rates of protest have fallen off significantly.[13] PT movements, in contrast, get fewer candidacies and therefore rely more on protest during the honeymoon year to get the attention of the new government.

When we break down the non-union set even further, running separate models for each type of non-union organization, we find that the statistically significant effect of honeymoon year in Mexico City is substantially dependent on the inclusion of street vendors in the sample. Street vendors increase their protest rates by nearly 600 percent in honeymoon years. In Mexico City, the local government has the authority to issue permits to sell on the streets in given territories, or to enforce general anti-street-vending laws. When a new administration comes in, vendor associations simply must establish their claim to territories or face significant economic hardship. Interestingly, they do this primarily when the new administration is *not* of their political party: the interaction effect between honeymoon year and alliance to the party in power is significant and negative. Different types of organizations respond quite differently to changes in the POS, depending on the particular incentives that they face.

CONCLUSIONS

As the PT debated the formation of the Popular Movements' Central (CMP), speakers noted the problem posed by the "ephemeral nature of the popular movements" (PT, 1993: 15). Most urban popular movements arise around specific demands connected to specific people – my house, my water service, restitution for my earthquake damage – which galvanize ordinarily passive people to do extraordinarily active things. Frequently, however, the resolution of initial demands combined with the costs of participation and the daily struggle for survival leads to diminishing participation. Housing movements can make themselves

---

[13] It should be noted that only two or three urban popular movements in my database were allied to the PRI in this period. Therefore, any organization "allied to the party in power" (not independent) was almost certainly allied to the PRD.

obsolete in the same way that "the Movement for Amnesty only existed as long as there were political prisoners," while "the union exists independently of whether the workers are on strike or not" (PT, 1993: 16). Urban popular movements face different constraints than unions regardless of whether they share the same party sympathies or cultural preferences for protest. They have less stable access to resources, less legal protection, greater risk of splits, and a high level of exposure to collective action problems.

Urban popular movements resolve these problems in a number of different ways. Alliance with a political party can help smooth out access to resources. The urban popular movements studied here stand out for the long life and high level of activity they demonstrate vis-à-vis the majority of movements (over 60 percent in all three cities) who demonstrated only once. They survived by expanding their agendas and/or expanding their territories. Party alliance can help movements do both, perhaps explaining why independent urban popular movements have become increasingly rare in both Mexico and Brazil while independent unions have become more common. Gay (1994: 77) notes correctly that affiliation with a political party can be "as much a liability as an asset, since both politicians and political parties could be voted out of office." PT-affiliated movements certainly found that out when Maluf won power and cut them off from housing funds. However, parties continue to deliver organizational support even when out of power. Particularly in cases where a single legislator may be able to deliver some goods even if the mayor belongs to another party, the level of access may wax and wane, but it rarely disappears altogether.

Yet alliance to parties carries with it the risk of cooptation by clientelistic politicians. Urban popular movement leaders experience strong pressure to secure what people believe to be achievable goals: a house, a paved street, electricity service. The relatively low cost of the benefits they seek makes even limited access to a legislator or a public official more valuable to urban popular movements than to unions who must make demands on behalf of a much larger group of people. To the extent that movement members perceive their leaders as corrupt and coopted, the movement loses prestige, legitimacy, and ultimately popular support.

Other movements made protest part of a membership maintenance strategy that also included party alliance. Periodic protests helped leaders avoid the appearance of cooptation. For at least some organizations, protest also became a means of ensuring member loyalty and participation in the movement. By converting protests into points, the FPFV and many PT movements made protest part of a selective reward system for militants and leaders. Thus, even when protest appeared less likely to result in benefits – or conversely, when benefits could be achieved without protest – giving up protest could create problems for movement leaders. By retargeting their protests – a strategy not available to municipal employees – these movements tried to have the best of both worlds: party alliance *and* regular protest.

Despite their efforts, urban popular movements were less able to sustain protest over time than unions, due to the lack of resources and the lower barriers to exit that frequently turned internal rivalries into a proliferation of new organizations. All of the cases examined here experienced at least one split or formed as the result of a split from an older organization. The vulnerability of urban popular movements to splits may contribute to the volatility they display in terms of protest and to their apparently high rate of extinction.

Nevertheless, the factors that explain protest by municipal employee unions also help us understand the behavior of urban popular movements. Leadership competition tends to increase protest, particularly when internal norms of leadership selection reward those who can mobilize more people. A political culture favoring protest makes leaders vulnerable to criticism if they do not lead regular protests. In the case of urban popular movements, this culture of protest is likely to have formed during the creation of the movement, selectively attracting members who are comfortable with protest and who believe it is useful in putting pressure on the government to resolve demands.

However, leaders and members of urban popular movements continue to evaluate the potential success of protest. In fact, compared to the public employee unions in Chapters 4 and 5, urban popular movement leaders seem to have more flexibility in the timing and targeting of protest than union leaders. The strategic opportunities presented by alternation in power produce complex changes in the behavior of urban popular movements. On the one hand, their windows of opportunity may be narrower and more infrequent. Where unions get to renegotiate their contracts every year, urban popular movements seem to concentrate on the moment right around a transition from

TABLE 7.2. *Summary of Results: Urban Popular Movements and Protest*

Variables	Operationalization	Results
Organizational Resources		
Type of resources	Role of protest in generating member loyalty	**Increases protest**
	Interviews	
Institutionalization	Age	**Decreases protest**
	Internal differentiation	**Increases protest**
Leadership competition	Interviews	**Increases protest**
	Internal statutes if any	
	Rules of leadership selection	
	Role of protest in determining leadership selection	
Identity		
Past history of protest	Protest lagged	**Increases protest**
	Records of protest over time by case studies	
Positive view	Left party ally	**Increases protest**
	Interviews	
of protest	Internal documents	
Independent of parties	Independent	**Decreases protest**
POS		
Allied to party in power	Qualitative evaluation, based on self-declaration	**Led to retargeting of protest**
Electoral cycle effects	Honeymoon year	**Increases protest in Brazil**
	Interviews regarding rationale for timing	
	Election year	Insignificant
	Interaction, in-group with honeymoon	Insignificant
	Interaction, in-group with election	**Increases protest in Mexico**
Economic Grievance		
	Inflation (logged)	**Decreases protest in Mexico**

one administration to another, either the election year (to secure candidacies) or the honeymoon year (to secure favors).

On the other hand, urban popular movements experience the same dilemma – loyalty to the ally versus greater chance of protest success against the ally – that municipal employee unions do, but their opportunities to choose protest without necessarily sacrificing loyalty, by means of retargeting, are much greater. Even when directed at a different target, protest may send the same message to a party ally: look at us, look at how much trouble we *could* cause if we wanted to, shouldn't we get a candidacy/housing loan/building permit? Table 7.2 sums up these findings in terms of the variables used in the previous chapters. Chapter 8 concludes with a comparison of findings from the quantitative results, unions, and urban popular movements.

8

The Dynamics of Protest

This book explores the question of why organizations change their protest strategies over time. It draws hypotheses from three standard models of contentious political action – POS, resource mobilization theory, and identity – and subjects them to a series of qualitative and quantitative tests to see whether they can explain organizational tactics. Because the evidence comes from only two specific contexts, the answers I reach must be considered preliminary and subject to further testing. Nevertheless, the results are strongly encouraging that work on this question will pay off: protest strategies vary across organizations and across time in regular and predictable ways. Table 8.1 summarizes the results of the analysis.

RESOURCE MOBILIZATION AND IDENTITY

The single most powerful explanatory factor is a previous history of protest. Organizations that protest a lot in one year are more likely to protest a lot the next year, and the year after that, and the year after that. Tilly (and Tarrow) are right: protest repertoires are fairly sticky characteristics of movement organizations. The question is, why? Are organizations just slow learners, mindlessly repeating the same tactics over and over regardless of changes in the external context? The evidence presented here suggests that far from endangering group goals, protest can be a rational and intelligent mechanism for improving the odds of group survival, provided that a few conditions are met. First,

TABLE 8.1. *Summary of Results*

Basic Variables	Quantitative Models	Unions	Urban Popular Movements
Organizational Resources			
Type of resources: union	**Increases protest**	More stable resources increase protest capacity	Resource scarcity $\rightarrow$ depend on protest OR extinction
Institutionalization/ age	**Decreases protest**	Insignificant	**Decreases protest**
Institutionalization/ differentiation	Not tested	Similar for all cases	**Increases protest**
Leadership competition	Not tested	**Increases protest**	**Increases protest**
Identity			
Past history of protest	**Increases protest**	**Increases protest**	**Increases protest**
Positive view of protest	**Increases protest**	**Increases protest**	**Increases protest**
Independent of parties	Insignificant	**Increases protest in Mex.**	**Decreases protest**
POS			
Allied to party in power	Insignificant	Protest higher against the Left	**Retargeting of protest**
Honeymoon year	**Increases protest**	Insignificant	**Increases protest in Brazil**
Election year	Insignificant	Insignificant	Insignificant
Interaction, in-group with honeymoon	Insignificant	Insignificant	Insignificant
Interaction, in-group with election	Insignificant	Insignificant	**Increases protest in Mexico**
Economic Grievance			
Inflation (logged)	Insignificant	**Increases protest by unions**	**Decreases protest**
Unemployment	Not tested	**Change type of protest action**	Not mentioned

there must be some competition for member support, either as a result of internal democratic elections or a competitive external environment where more successful leaders can "raid" one's own ranks. Competition within organizations is particularly useful, since it makes the organization less vulnerable to decapitation if the dominant leaders take a position in government or leave the organization. Thus, paradoxically, some constraints on the formation of new organizations may help sustain protest in a context of internal competition: they help an organization maximize the benefits of competition, avoid decapitation, and keep competition from resulting in splits and potentially undermining the organization's capability to sustain protest.

Second, members must see protest in a positive light. Organizational cultures that view protest positively and state actors negatively are priming their members to reward leaders that sponsor protest. The existence of a promobilization culture is never an accident. It frequently dates back to the foundation of the organization, which selectively attracts activists and leaders that share its views of mobilization. Movement identity then coheres around the stories of past protests, the shared experience of marches and demonstrations, and the songs, posters and symbols of previous mobilization campaigns.

Third, it is useful (though not necessary) if protest has become engrained in the internal structures of the organization as a means of leadership selection and/or member advancement. Urban popular movements that incorporated a point system as a mechanism for selective rewards (e.g., a spot in a housing project) and awarded more points for participation in protests created a permanent need for leaders to hold protests in order to reward their supporters. Though retargeting could (and did) occur, to spare political allies, leaders of such movements were dependent on protest for their positions. Once these organizations turn to the provision of public goods – where the enjoyment of the goods cannot be limited to those who contributed by their presence at protests – the usefulness of this system may decline, perhaps helping account for the relatively short life span and high extinction rate of urban popular movements.

Organizational dependence on protest is also a function of the nature and extent of the resources each type of group possessed. Urban popular movements lived a shoestring existence, frequently allying with parties to gain access to resources and relying on the use of protest to distribute selective rewards and retain members. At least in these cases, unions enjoyed a far more privileged existence, with the state providing guaranteed protection from competition and enforcing the collection of union dues. They had the capacity to sponsor protest, though not necessarily the will. Even the PRI-affiliated municipal employees union in Mexico City could muster the resources for a wave of protest against the PRD, at least until the PRD government began to cut off the slush funds and sources of corruption that union leaders used to bribe members to participate.

Moreover, in neither Mexico nor Brazil were unions incorporated into the kind of overarching corporatist peak bargaining systems common in Europe. They faced, therefore, far fewer penalties for *not* cooperating with parties. Mexico and Brazil may represent ideal situations for the kind of union propensity to protest that all of my quantitative tests demonstrated: neither exposed to the kind of pluralistic competition that makes protest and strikes risky in the United States nor sufficiently rewarded for using negotiation to give up protest as a weapon as in European social democracies. Further testing of these findings might help clarify why unions in my cases were so much more likely to protest than other types of organization.

Identity also fared very well in both the quantitative and qualitative analyses. This is the real explanation for the significance of Left party ally. To the extent that the economic Left in most countries is anti-status-quo, Left parties in general may attract more confrontational and argumentative people. In the special cases of Mexico and Brazil, this tendency is magnified. Both the PT and the PRD are examples of antisystem parties, founded in the course of a struggle against an authoritarian regime and with the explicit purpose of confronting that regime. Both attracted relatively few members in the beginning and, at least after the 1988 election in Mexico, relatively few votes. As Kenneth Greene (2007) argues, such parties – minority opposition parties with little or no chance of actually winning elections – are of interest only to people with extreme views who are driven by ideology more than the desire for power. Such people are less willing to compromise, more committed to radical change, and more likely to get satisfaction from their courage in standing up for principle against long odds. In other words, they are natural-born protesters. Left-leaning parties founded from a position of power, such as the PRI in its origins, did not develop an identity tied to protest. Independence in such a political context does not necessarily imply greater radicalism. Instead, it may indicate a desire to stay above the fray of party politics and maintain the freedom to negotiate with the state under all circumstances. It is partly for this reason that independence generally had a negative effect on protest rates in these cases.

POLITICAL OPPORTUNITY STRUCTURES: THE EFFECT OF PARTY ALLIANCE

The approach that seems to give us the least purchase on protest strategies is the one that I, initially, thought would be the most powerful: political opportunity structures. It seemed obvious (to me) that people should prefer not to protest against their allies, and the dramatic drop in protest by PRD-allied urban popular movements that emerged in the early stages of the data gathering also pointed in that direction. Yet in the multivariate models, the effect of alliance with the party in power, though negative, is not statistically significant. Indeed, in some situations, organizations protested more against their friends than against their enemies.

Ultimately, it became clear that organizational leaders do respond to shifts in the political opportunities. But "alliance to the party in power," it turned out, created as many opportunities for protest as for negotiation. In the first place, the probability of success from protest was higher when protesting against the ally, producing an increase in expected benefits. In contrast, protesting against the opponent, particularly in Brazil, dramatically lowered the probability of success. As soon as leaders realized they were beating their heads against a wall, protest began to seem less attractive.

In the second place, leaders compared the benefits of protesting or not protesting *within* the context of a single administration. As long as a protest increased the odds of getting versus not getting the benefit from an ally in government, even slightly, then protest could seem attractive. And given the competition for benefits among affiliated organizations, protest could give an organization first claim on resources.

Tying protest to calculations of expected benefits also helps clarify the fascinating finding of honeymoon year effects. In the aggregate models, protest increased significantly in the first year of a new administration. Interviews provided some reasons why, principally involving agenda setting. Urban popular movement leaders in São Paulo also talked about the bitter experience of losing their *mutirão* project funding when Maluf won. When Suplicy was elected, they wanted to get their bids in early so that even if she lost in four years, they would have time to complete their projects. Union leaders talked about the desire to recover from years of losses and economic hardship by targeting incoming PT administrations as soon as possible. Being able to demonstrate independence from the government was an added benefit.

As the models were broken down by organizational type, however, it became clear that different kinds of organizations see "windows of opportunity" in slightly different ways. It was not equally attractive for all organizations to protest during the first year of a new administration. For Mexican urban popular movements, the strategy that made the most sense in terms of controlling the agenda involved staking claim to as many *candidacies* as possible. Given the PRD's lack of union allies, they were generally quite successful. Thus, they focused their protesting in election years, but only when their ally (the PRD) was in power and might have forgotten about their ability to mobilize votes. Interestingly, the only other organization type that behaved this way was party – also focused on candidacies in election years. For Mexican street vendors, in contrast, the importance of hanging on to their territories when a new administration came in, especially if it was politically hostile, meant that the first year of the new administration was the window of opportunity, or perhaps more appropriately a window of threat. And for unions, honeymoon years were not necessarily the most propitious moment to set the agenda for relations with a new government, in part because annual contract negotiations provide a routine schedule of opportunities to lay union demands on the table.

Still, it would be worthwhile for students of unconventional politics to explore how marginalized organizations attempt to affect the political agenda. The conventional wisdom has pointed more to unusual moments of opportunity to affect the agenda, assuming that the rest of the time movements of the marginalized are basically just reacting to a government agenda. This may not be entirely true. At any rate, even marginalized movements may feel that they cannot afford simply to cede the field.

A second reason why the alliance variable did not perform as well as some of the others is that the expected benefits of protest do not result exclusively from responses by the target of the protest. The external delivery of resources generates obvious benefits, but the mere holding of a protest can generate benefits even if the official target does not respond. I have discussed some of these benefits, in terms of the role that protest plays in organizational solidarity. However, protest also seems to function as a signaling mechanism, both to members and to nonmembers *outside the actual target*. In part, this is Tilly's argument (1995: 369) that protest is designed to demonstrate that a group is Worthy, United, Numerous, and Committed (later abbreviated WUNC) in order to convince the target that it is better to give in to the group's demands, and in order to attract additional support from the public and other organizations. Clearly, protest functions in all of these ways. But *leaders* also see it as helpful to demonstrate their personal worthiness, competence, courage, and independence. They use protest to gauge their power vis-à-vis rivals for leadership. They use it to prove that even though they have accepted a position in the government, they are not the lapdogs of the mayor. If the protest produces results, so much the better, but protest may help them even if it doesn't.

PROTEST SPECIALISTS

Despite the apparent advantages of protest that I describe here, not all leaders or all organizations engage in protest. In fact, for most organizations, protest is a rare event, seldom repeated. Some organizations are clearly protest specialists. One might think of protesting as a specific ecological niche, along with clientelistic linkages, or incorporation in a political party, by which organizations attempt to survive. Protest appears to be a fairly uncommon niche, occupied by a few protest experts over time. This book focuses on the behavior of protest experts.

Given that these experts are responsible for most protest – and particularly the most disruptive protest – understanding even a little about how they tick is worthwhile. Since 1990, eleven Latin American presidents have been forced out of office before the end of their terms (Sader, 2005: 59). In at least two other instances (involving President Chávez of Venezuela) attempts to force out the executive failed. The leading role in forcing out an unpopular executive has been assumed by various types of popular movements, including unions, indigenous peasant organizations, and middle-class demonstrators. Militaries play at most a supportive role – refusing to repress demonstrations and/or letting the president know that he cannot count on the military's support. In two cases (Peru and Venezuela), the incidence of such "civil society coups" (Encarnación, 2002) followed the virtual collapse of the political party system. In two others (Bolivia and Ecuador), party systems have higher than average levels of electoral volatility and party system fractionalization.[1] These experiences certainly suggest that weak party systems create a representation gap that encourages confrontational politics. Reversing the arrow of causality, Simón Pachano argues that in the case of Ecuador, "labor and indigenous movements, by confronting the state directly and avoiding the intermediation of formal political institutions, have allowed representative institutions to atrophy. Thus, the success of protest politics ... has made Ecuador's polity a victim of 'chaotic representation.' "[2] Whichever way the causal arrow points, the source of failure is posited as the lack of connection between organized civil societies and parties.

Yet the examples of Ecuador and Bolivia themselves point toward a blurring of the lines between conventional and unconventional politics. The leader of mass protests in Bolivia, Evo Morales, held a seat in Congress from 1997 to January 2002, when he was expelled on charges of terrorism. A few months later he ran for president and narrowly lost to Gonzalo Sánchez de Lozada. His party, the Movement Toward Socialism (MAS), continued to hold 30 percent of senate seats and 21 percent of congressional seats throughout the successive waves of protest that brought down President Gonzalo Sánchez de Lozada in 2003 and President Mesa in 2005 (http://cdp.binghamton.edu/era/). In Ecuador, the Confederation of Indigenous Nationalities of Ecuador

---

[1] Average volatility in Latin America in the 1990s was 26.5 percent, compared to 30.6 percent volatility in Bolivia and 40.3 percent volatility in Ecuador. Average fractionalization in Latin America was .61 (Rae's Index) compared to .76 in Bolivia and .82 in Ecuador.

[2] Lucero (2001: 71); portion in quotes cites Pachano (1995).

(Confederación de Nacionalidades Indígenas del Ecuador, or CONAIE) that spearheaded the protests that forced out President Jamil Mahuad in 2001 subsequently formed an electoral organization (the Pachakutik Pluricultural United Movement). In 2002, one of the military officers who supported CONAIE and participated in the 2001 coup ran for president as the candidate of Pachakutik, and won. And in 2005, this same president (Lucío Gutierrez), having lost the support of the indigenous movement, was himself ousted by the congress following yet another wave of massive protests in which CONAIE participated. Even as these movements created political parties to represent their interests and enthusiastically entered the realm of electoral and institutional politics, they continued to use protest as a means of holding elected leaders accountable – including leaders originally supported by their own political parties.

Perhaps, one might argue, these situations were exceptional, reflecting unusually severe crises (or unusually poor leadership). Thus, movements in Bolivia and Ecuador engaged in tactics that most movements in normal noncrisis politics would not employ. This book suggests, on the contrary, that such behavior is quite ordinary. Organizations allied with political parties – particularly Left-leaning political parties – are if anything more likely to protest than independent organizations. And they routinely challenge even their friends in power.

THE ROADS NOT TAKEN

Protest of the ordinary sort – the kind that snarls traffic, shuts down schools, and waves banners – is a phenomenon produced by organizations. Understanding the connections between protest and more conventional forms of political action is an important first step toward explaining protest. Yet clearly much more remains to be done. The structural factors illuminated in this analysis leave the majority of protest unexplained. A proper model, ultimately, would have to incorporate decision making by governments and parties as well. To be sure, many protests are organized around proactive demands for a specific policy priority – land reform or public housing for example. But many others respond defensively to policy reforms initiated by the government. Protest in these circumstances is less a function of organizational characteristics than of what the government in its wisdom (or lack thereof) has decided to do. Modeling this process would require bringing in the role of legislatures, the bureaucracy, economic elites, and potentially international interests as well as parties and organizations. We are much closer to understanding why states choose to repress potential protesters than understanding how they choose policies that are likely to provoke protests. Political science in particular has been too cavalier about studying policy formation from a theoretical rather than a practical point of view (most of the good work here has been done by sociologists), and it clearly is a huge and daunting task. This book has necessarily tackled a much narrower question. Nevertheless, I believe its findings suggest the potential benefits of an approach that tackles the role of specific organized actors who shape the context for protest, on more than a case-by-case basis. Future research, hopefully, will take up this challenge.

A LAST WORD: STRUCTURE, AGENCY, AND THE KITCHEN SINK

In a 2004 article, Jack Goldstone calls for replacing the term "POS" with the broader term "external relational field, " arguing that "structures" is too static and state-centered a concept. Instead, we should think about not only states and police forces, but also about the other movements, countermovements, economic institutions, religious elites, media, critical events, symbolic and value orientations, civil society, and political party systems in which a specific movement is embedded. Though he accepts that this sounds like "replacing the cool, parsimonious term of POS with a kitchen sink full of all possible factors affecting movements," in fact the usage of POS has often referred to just such a full range of factors in analyzing social movement dynamics. Whether one accepts his term or not, the research agenda that he sees emerging "has two parts: one for studies of individual movements, the other for comparative studies of movement clusters or different movements across time and space" (Goldstone, 2004: 358–360).

This book clearly follows the second path. I have from the start focused on the search for patterns of behavior associated with one key element in the external relational field of popular organizations: the alliance with political parties, particularly as it intersects with control of the state in the context of municipal government. However, I have compared the effect of this factor to the effect of factors more endogenous to the movements. The results have been illuminating. The effects of changes in the political context cannot be understood without reference to the characteristics of organizations themselves. Vendor associations react differently than urban popular movements, which react differently than unions. Organizations constantly calculate their costs, benefits, risks, and probabilities of success with respect to external actors, but they also constantly consider the demands of organizational survival – which differ, systematically, by organizational type and even political context.

The search for a complete model of protest behavior is daunting and probably impossible. Although institutional differentiation may make urban popular movements on average more likely to survive and to continue protest, there will always be the occasional Gegê, leader of the Brazilian Movement for Housing in the Center (MMC) in São Paulo. A short, intense man with dreadlocks and a trademark colorful knit beret, Gegê dominates the MMC via highly personalistic leadership. He also refuses to be "decapitated" and insists on an aggressive schedule of building invasions.

Nevertheless, the search for regularities is useful. It may help focus our attention on particular elements of structure, or particular relationships with external actors, or on particular aspects of organizations. It provides a validity check on the rich analysis of individual movements and helps us understand the extent to which a specific movement is typical of others. As we learn how to lower the costs of gathering the kind of data necessary for this type of analysis, it will surely become an important part of the research agenda on contentious politics.

Appendix

This appendix deals with problems of bias created by coding from newspaper accounts: the issues of bias created by newspaper preferences, bias caused by the coder, and bias created by missing information.

BIAS CREATED BY NEWSPAPER PREFERENCES

The newspapers themselves clearly differed in the kinds of events they reported, the way in which events were portrayed, and the attention they devoted to covering protest in general. The Leftist *La Jornada* in Mexico City was the hands-down champion of protest reporting, covering on average 71.3 percent of events. *Reforma* covered 51.4 percent of events on average. *La Jornada* had a large network of connections within many progressive movements, who informed their friends when a protest was occurring and expected favorable coverage. The sympathies of *La Jornada* were so well - known that many smaller groups actually picketed the offices of the newspaper, not to protest the paper's policies but to make sure reporters knew about their grievances. However, rates of coverage also varied widely by year, with no clear trend across time from which estimates of coverage could be extrapolated. In its worst year, *Reforma* covered 38.9 percent of events in the recorded record; in its best, 58.9 percent. *La Jornada* ranged between 58 percent and 77 percent of recorded events.

La Jornada accounts of protest were also more sympathetic to the protesters. One representative headline, for example, reported, "Teachers Protest at the SNTE." The headline of its conservative competitor, *Reforma*, for the same event was, "Kidnapping at the Ministry of Gobernación." *La Jornada*'s estimates of attendance were 32 percent higher than those of *Reforma*. Violence, when it occurred, was usually attributed to the police or provocateurs. The two papers chose different groups to highlight in very large events. Reporting on a march against violence in 1997, for instance, *Reforma* emphasized human rights organizations as the sponsors; *La Jornada* focused on the participation of political parties.

In São Paulo, I used the Estado de São Paulo, and Folha de São Paulo. Only about 30 percent of total recorded events were covered by both newspapers. Nor was this percentage stable over the entire fifteen-year period. The percent of recorded events covered by both papers in any given year ranged from 24 percent to 33 percent, with no perceptible trend. The estimated size of events as reported in Folha is 32 percent greater than in Estado – a further hint that size estimates are unreliable and vary substantially by the source. Folha consistently reports larger size estimates than Estado, in twelve out of fifteen years.

As expected, large events were more likely to be reported in both papers in each city. The average estimated size of duplicated events was 17,417 compared to 999 for unduplicated events in Estado and 1,302 for unduplicated events in Folha. The average size of events reported in both *Reforma* and *La Jornada* was 19,383, compared to 1,738 for unduplicated events in *Reforma* and 2,461 for unduplicated events in *La Jornada*. Strikes and other aggressive events also seem more likely to appear in both papers than peaceful events like demonstrations.

Less predictably, different newspapers may focus on certain kinds of protesters. For example, union sponsors account for 45 percent of Folha events versus 36 percent of Estado events. Estado, in contrast, focuses more on urban popular movements, transportation workers, and street vendors. These differences are fairly minor, with the exception of unions, but it is worth considering whether editorial perspectives or source-relationships affect the interest shown by the newspapers in specific kinds of events.

On the other hand, when both newspapers did cover an event, the results were consistent on the main elements of the report. The most consistent coding was sponsor type. Sponsor type matched in the Mexican newspapers 97 percent of the time, and in the Brazilian newspapers almost 99 percent of the time. In 5.2 percent (Brazil) to 8.6 percent (Mexico) of duplicated reports, in addition to a primary sponsor type mentioned in both accounts, a second or third sponsor type was listed in only one account. For example, a protest involving unions might or might not mention the supportive participation of a student group. Also quite reliable are descriptions of the protest targets. Target type matched in 96.3 percent of duplicated Brazilian reports and 97.7 percent of duplicated Mexican reports.

Less consistent was the coding of tactics. In Brazilian newspapers, my coding of tactical choices differed 24.3 percent of the time, of which 10.5 percent involved nonmatches with no overlap. In Mexican newspapers, tactics did not match 16 percent of the time, and additional tactics appeared in 11 percent of duplicated reports. The vast majority of these disparities involved confusion between "marches" and "demonstrations." At least part of the time, discrepancies reflected *when* reporters arrived at an event – before or after a march reached its destination. In my analyses, I simply combined march/demonstration into a single category of relatively nonaggressive events.

Adding a second newspaper significantly expanded the number of organization names I was able to collect. The names of the groups did not match (different names with no names in common) just 3.6 percent of the time in Brazil and 2.7 percent of the time in Mexico. However, it was fairly common for one article to mention more groups than the other. About 26–27 percent of the time, at least one organization name was reported only in one of the two accounts. The additional name reported is the only indication of identity in either report 40 percent of the time in Brazil and 35 percent of the time in Mexico; the other newspaper does not give an organization name at all. For my research question, using two newspapers proved truly providential: losing so many organization names could have significantly affected analysis of behavioral trends.

Thus, the main variables I used in this analysis – group name, group type, and target – had error rates of between 3 and 5 percent, with slightly higher rates of divergence for tactics. Adding a second newspaper, on the other hand, increased the number of organization names by more than 25 percent.

Size estimates presented much more serious problems. In Brazil, duplicated reports gave the *same* estimate of attendance only 23 percent of the time, with an average difference of over 3,000. I averaged the two size estimates in duplicated reports and compared the difference between them to the averaged value. In using this approach, I minimize the proportional effect of the differences. If consistently taken over the smaller of the two estimates, for example, the average difference I report would be magnitudes greater. Nevertheless, the difference between the two papers was 43 percent of the averaged estimated size of the demonstration. Although the modal difference was zero, typically where the same source was quoted for the estimate (police or organizers), nonmatching estimates were almost three times as likely as matches. If size estimates were given by both papers, they matched 26 percent of the time and did not match 74 percent of the time. Variance of over 100 percent between two estimates was common, in large and small events alike.

In Mexican newspapers, the erratic reporting of size is even more notable. When size estimates are given in both reports, the estimates match less than 20 percent of the time. Thus, though the modal difference is zero, as in Brazil, the reliability of size estimates in any given paper must be questioned. The largest difference between the newspapers in the Mexican case is nearly 200 percent and differences of well over 100 percent are frequent. Absolute differences were also on average more than three times larger in Mexico: 5,137 versus 1,584 in Brazil. Nearly 11 percent of the estimates in the Mexican papers differ by at least 10,000, and 18.9 percent differ by at least 5,000. The median percentage difference is 40 percent of the event size versus 28.6 percent in Brazil.

As the size of events increases, the potential for large absolute errors does too. I found literally dozens of cases where an estimate of 100 by one newspaper was matched to an estimate of over 1,000 by the other, or an estimate of 450 participants by one newspaper contrasted with an estimate of 3,500 by the other. These findings should give us pause about using size estimates in statistical analyses. Particularly when based only on one source, they are not reliable for single events.

CODER ERROR

At least part of the error rate reflects coder unreliability (mine). Since I was the only coder, it is impossible to generate intercoder reliability tests. To simulate this figure, I went to an electronic database of Latin American newspapers provided by Factiva. Due to the expense of a subscription to Factiva, I had to use the trial version, and time constraints kept my data analysis to comparing coding of 2003. Moreover, Factiva did not include either of the two Mexican newspapers I used. Since I wanted to compare the results from simple electronic searches to the results from hard-copy searches, I therefore limited my search to the São Paulo newspapers. Factiva is searchable by keyword, so rather than develop an elaborate protocol, I conducted keyword searches for only a few important words, which might appear in the headline or anywhere in the body of the story.

In all, searches of both newspapers plus Factiva resulted in a total of 178 events. The Factiva searches found a record of 65 percent of these events. Hard-copy searches did slightly better, finding 74 percent. Thus, 26 percent of these events were found only in Factiva, possibly due to what Earl et al. (2004) refer to as error resulting from coder fatigue, although at least some of the missed articles came from sections of the newspaper that I did not concentrate on in my hard-copy searches because they rarely contained reports on protests. Even so, 35 percent of events were found only in the hard-copy searches; human beings still do better than electronic searches, though more elaborate search programs might well reverse this pattern.

Since Factiva merely compiles original newspaper articles, I can also compare how I coded an article in Factiva from a particular newspaper versus my previous coding from the same article in the same newspaper. The results are similar to the comparison between newspapers. I was most likely to code tactics differently – adding an extra tactic in one coding of the same article roughly 10 percent of the time, and 5 percent of the time coding tactics differently. Again, most of these differences involved confusion between marches and demonstrations. These error rates are much lower than nonmatches in the comparison between newspapers, which failed to match 10.5 percent of the time. Thus, differences in how newspapers report events probably account for about half of the discrepancy in tactic types in my general database; coder error accounts for the rest.

Targets matched at roughly the same rate in my double-coding of single articles as across newspapers: 96 percent of the time. Sponsors matched more frequently, 99 percent of the time. Size, unsurprisingly, is now consistent, since I only had to write down the same newspaper estimate the second time I read the article. My practice was to code one newspaper through at least one year before beginning the next. Thus, my coding of the original reports was separated by weeks, months, and sometimes as much as a year. The Factiva coding took place more than two years after finishing the primary coding and data entry. Low error rates therefore are not a result of remembering and being familiar with a story from having seen it recently, but represent reasonably reliable coding.

MISSING DATA

The main problem I had with missing information concerned alliance characteristics. I could not find many of the groups that protested, particularly in the earliest years of the sample, much less identify their alliance characteristics. The question is whether these "unknown" groups have significantly different characteristics that would bias my estimates. I suspect that they do. Based on impressionistic evidence, it seems plausible that these organizations are more likely to be small, to not have attracted the attention or interest of parties, and therefore to be independent. If so, then my estimates of the effect of party alliance are low – party alliance has a more significant positive effect and independence a more significant negative one than I find. Empirically, the behavior of the unknown groups looks most like independents, but all groups are most likely to be concentrated in the category of ten or fewer total protests. The drop-off between one protest and five protests is dramatic in all three cases.

Size estimates were also frequently missing. In almost one-third of events in Mexico City and 29 percent in São Paulo, neither newspaper even attempted to estimate the number of people participating. This is less problematic than missing data on alliance, since I did not rely heavily on size estimates in my analysis.

EVENT CODING SHEET

Name of newspaper: _____ Article date: __/__/__ Page: ____
Title of Article: _____
I. Event classification
Type of event: _____ Two or more events from same article: _____
Date of <u>event</u>: __/__/__ Duration of event: _____
                 Dates (if more than one day): _____
Location of event: _____
                   City/Country
Specific site of event: _____
Destination of event (if nonfixed): _____
Number of people involved: _____
Type of demand: _____
           Specific demand: _____

_____

Primary target of behavior: _____
Description of event:
II. Organizational classification
Primary sponsoring organization/s: _____
           Specific organization/s:

_____

_____

If organization is unnamed, describe as fully as possible:
Primary leaders of event:

CODING KEY:

Type of Event:

1. demonstration (a fixed, nonregularly scheduled, public rally unconnected with electoral campaigns, lasting less than one day)
2. march (nonfixed, nonregularly scheduled event with starting point and destination)
3. picketing/plantón (a fixed presence lasting more than one day)
4. strike (a work stoppage or slowdown lasting any length of time)
5. building invasion

6   street blockage
7   hunger strike
8   other (please describe fully)

Type of Organization Sponsoring:

1   political party
2   union (any workers' organized representation, officially recognized or not, except street vendors, police, and transportation [see below])
3   peasant organization
4   local/neighborhood association
5   students
6   elected official/government
7   ethnic organization
8   human rights organization
9   street vendors
10 business (formal sector only)
11 military/police
12 religious organization
13 environmental group
14 other (please describe fully)
15 transportation workers

Target of Event:

1   federal government
2   local government
3   private employer
4   other private business interest
5   school authorities
6   international actor
7   political party (support)
8   political party (oppose)
9   social/popular movement
10 union/peasant organizatoin
11 other (please describe fully)
12 state-level government

Type of Demand Made:

1 electoral
2 ethnic
3 working conditions/wages
4 human rights
5 crime/public security
6 environment
7 macroeconomic policies
8 expansion of vendor access
9 contraction of vendor access
10 housing policies
11 educational policies
12 transportation/traffic/parking
13 other public services
14 removal of a public official
15 support of a public official
16 anticorruption
17 probusiness policies
18 land invasions/regularization; conflicts over land use
19 debt resolution
20 antigrowth – opposed to new construction
21 other (please describe fully)
22 democracy
23 agrarian demands

Site:

0 no location (e.g., strikes)
1 Zocalo/Av. Paulista/Planalto
2 federal government building
3 local government building
4 street
5 other
6 state government building

Selected Sources

General Works

Alcántara, Manuel, and Elena M. Barahona, eds. 2003. *Política, dinero, e institucionalización partidista en América Latina.* Mexico City: Universidad Iberoamericana.

Almond, Gabriel. 1960. "Introduction." In *The Politics of the Developing Areas.* Edited by Gabriel Almond and James Coleman. Princeton, NJ: Princeton University Press, pp. 3–64.

Aminzade, Ronald. 1995. "Between Movement and Party: The Transformation of Mid-Nineteenth Century French Republicanism." In *The Politics of Social Protest: Comparative Perspectives on States and Social Movements.* Edited by J. Craig Jenkins and Bert Klandermans. Minneapolis: University of Minnesota Press, pp. 39–62.

Aminzade, Ronald, et al. 2001. *Silence and Voice in the Study of Contentious Politics.* New York: Cambridge University Press.

Anderson, Christopher. 1998. "Parties, Party Systems, and Satisfaction with Democratic Performance in the New Europe." *Political Studies.* Vol. 46 (July): 572–588.

Andrews, Kenneth. 2001. "Social Movements and Policy Implementation: The Mississippi Civil Rights Movement and the War on Poverty, 1965 to 1971." *American Sociological Review.* Vol. 66, No. 1 (February): 71–95.

Andrews, Kenneth. 1997. "The Impacts of Social Movements on the Political Process: The Civil Rights Movement and Black Electoral Politics in Mississippi." *American Sociological Review.* Vol. 62, No. 5 (October): 800–819.

Banfield, Edward C. 1961. *Political Influence.* New York: Free Press.

Barr, Robert. 2005. "Bolivia: Another Uncompleted Revolution." *Latin American Politics and Society.* Vol. 47, No. 3 (Fall): 69–90.

Baumgartner, Frank R., and Bryan D. Jones. 1993. *Agendas and Instability in American Politics.* Chicago: University of Chicago Press.

Bond, Doug, et al. 1997. "Mapping Mass Political Conflict and Civil Society: Issues and Prospects for the Automated Development of Event Data." *Journal of Conflict Resolution.* Vol. 41, No. 4 (August): 553–579.

Borja, Jordi. 1992. "Past, Present, and Future of Local Democracy in Latin America." In *Rethinking the Latin American City.* Edited by Richard Morse and Jorge Hardowy. Baltimore: Johns Hopkins University Press: 131–143.

Bratton, Michael, and Nicolas van de Walle. 1997. *Democratic Experiments in Africa: Regime Transitions in Comparative Perspective.* New York: Cambridge University Press.

Budge, Ian, et al., eds. 2001. *Mapping Policy Preferences: Estimates for Parties, Electors, and Governments 1945–1998.* New York: Oxford University Press.

Bugajski, Janusz. 2002. *Political Parties of Eastern Europe: A Guide to Politics in the Post-Communist Era.* Armonk, NY: M. E. Sharpe.

Burgess, Katrina. 2004. *Parties and Unions in the New Global Economy.* Pittsburgh: University of Pittsburgh Press.

Burstein, Paul. 1985. *Discrimination, Jobs and Politics: The Struggle for Equal Employment Opportunity in the United States since the New Deal.* Chicago: University of Chicago Press.

Burstein, Paul, Rachel L. Einwohner, and Jocelyn A. Hollander. 1995. "The Success of Political Movements: A Bargaining Perspective." In *The Politics of Social Protest: Comparative Perspectives on States and Social Movements.* Edited by J. Craig Jenkins and Bert Klandermans. Minneapolis: University of Minnesota Press: 275–295.

Canache, Damarys. 2002. *Venezuela: Public Opinion and Protest in a Fragile Democracy.* Miami, FL: North-South Center Press.

Chalmers, Douglas, et al., eds. 1997. *The New Politics of Inequality in Latin America: Rethinking Participation and Representation.* New York: Oxford University Press.

Chevigny, Paul. 1995. *Edge of the Knife: Police Violence in the Americas.* New York: The New Press.

Clemens, Elisabeth. 1996. "Organizational Form as Frame: Collective Identity and Political Strategy in the American Labor Movement, 1880–1920." In *Comparative Perspectives on Social Movements: Political Opportunities, Mobilizing Structures, and Cultural Framings.* Edited by Doug McAdam, John D. McCarthy, and Mayer N. Zald. New York: Cambridge University Press, pp. 205–226.

Collier, Ruth Berins, and David Collier. 1991. *Shaping the Political Arena: Critical Junctures, the Labor Movement, and Regime Dynamics in Latin America.* Princeton, N.J.: Princeton University Press.

Coppedge, Michael. 1994. *Strong Parties and Lame Ducks: Presidential Partyarchy and Factionalism in Venezuela.* Stanford, CA: Stanford University Press.

Cornelius, Wayne. 1978. "Introduction." In *Metropolitan Latin America: The Challenge and the Response.* Edited by Wayne Cornelius and Robert

V. Kemper. Latin American Urban Research Vol. 6. Beverly Hills, CA: Sage Publications.

Corrales, Javier. 2002. *Presidents without Parties: The Politics of Economic Reform in Argentina and Venezuela in the 1990s.* University Park, PA: Penn State Press.

Costain, Anne N. 1992. *Inviting Women's Rebellion: A Political Process Interpretation of the Women's Movement.* Baltimore: Johns Hopkins University Press.

Costain, Anne N., and Andrew S. McFarland, eds. 1998. *Social Movements and American Institutions.* Boulder, CO: Rowman and Littlefield Publishers.

Cowen, Michael, and Liisa Laakso, eds. 2002. *Multiparty Elections in Africa.* New York: Palgrave.

Crozat, Matthew. 1998. "Are the Times A-Changin'? Assessing the Acceptance of Protest in Western Democracies." In *The Social Movement Society: Contentious Politics for a New Century.* Edited by David S. Meyer and Sidney Tarrow. New York: Rowman and Littlefield, pp. 59–81.

Dalton, Russell. 1995. "Strategies of Partisan Influence: West European Environmental Groups." In *The Politics of Social Protest: Comparative Perspectives on States and Social Movements.* Edited by J. Craig Jenkins and Bert Klandermans. Minneapolis: University of Minnesota Press, pp. 296–323.

Dalton, Russell. 2002. *Citizen Politics: Public Opinion and Political Parties in Advanced Industrial Democracies.* 3rd edition. New York: Chatham House Publishers.

Dalton, Russell, and Manfred Kuechler, eds. 1990. *Challenging the Political Order: New Social and Political Movements in Western Democracies.* New York: Oxford University Press.

Dalton, Russell, and Martin Wattenberg. 2000. "Partisan Change and the Democratic Process." In *Parties Without Partisans: Political Change in Advanced Industrial Democracies.* New York: Oxford University Press, pp. 261–285.

Dalton, Russell, Ian McAllister, and Martin Wattenberg. 2000. "The Consequences of Partisan Dealignment." In *Parties without Partisans: Political Change in Advanced Industrial Democracies.* Edited by Russell Dalton and Martin Wattenberg. New York: Oxford University Press, pp. 37–63.

Davis, Charles L., Edwin E. Aguilar, and John G. Speer. 1999. "Associations and Activism: Mobilization of Urban Informal Workers in Costa Rica and Nicaragua." *Journal of Interamerican Studies and World Affairs.* Vol. 41, No. 3: 35–66.

Day, Alan, Richard German, and John Campbell. 1996. *Political Parties of the World.* 4th edition. New York: Cartermill Publishing.

Della Porta, Donatella, and Dieter Rucht. 1995. "Left-Libertarian Movements in Context: A Comparison of Italy and West Germany, 1965–1990." In

The Politics of Social Protest: Comparative Perspectives on States and Social Movements. Edited by J. Craig Jenkins and Bert Klandermans. Minneapolis: University of Minnesota Press, pp. 229–272.

DeNardo, James. 1985. *Power in Numbers: The Political Strategy of Protest and Rebellion.* Princeton, NJ: Princeton University Press.

Dietz, Henry. 1998. *Urban Poverty, Political Participation, and the State: Lima 1970–1990.* Pittsburgh: University of Pittsburgh Press.

Dietz, Henry, and Gil Shidlo, eds. 1998. *Urban Elections in Democratic Latin America.* Wilmington, DE: Scholarly Resources Books.

Dillon Soares, Gláucio Ary. 1993. "A violência política na América Latina." *Revista Brasileira de Ciências Sociais.* Vol. 8, No. 21 (February): 22–39.

Downs, Anthony. 1957. *An Economic Theory of Democracy.* New York: Harper and Row.

Duverger, Maurice. 1954. *Political Parties: Their Organization and Activity in the Modern State.* Translated by Barbara North and Douglas North. New York: Wiley.

Earl, Jennifer, Andrew Martin, John D. McCarthy, and Sarah A. Soule. 2004. "The Use of Newspaper Data in the Study of Collective Action." *Annual Review of Sociology.* Vol. 30: 65–80.

Eckstein, Susan, ed. 1989. *Power and Popular Protest: Latin American Social Movements.* Berkeley: University of California Press.

Eisinger, Peter K. 1973. "The Conditions of Protest Behavior in American Cities." *American Political Science Review.* Vol. 67: 11–28.

Ekiert, Grzegorz, and Jan Kubik. 2001. *Rebellious Civil Society: Popular Protest and Democratic Consolidation in Poland, 1989–1993.* Ann Arbor: University of Michigan Press.

Encarnación, Omar. 2002. "Venezuela's Civil Society Coup" *World Policy Journal.* Vol. 19, No. 2 (Summer): 38–49.

Escobar, Arturo, and Sonia E. Álvarez. 1992. "Theory and Protest in Latin America Today." In *The Making of Social Movements in Latin America: Identity, Strategy, and Democracy.* Edited by Arturo Escobar and Sonia E. Álvarez. Boulder, CO: Westview Press, pp. 1–15.

Fearon, James D. 2003. "Ethnic and Cultural Diversity by Country." *Journal of Economic Growth.* Vol. 8, No. 2 (June): 195–222.

Fearon, James D., and David Laitin. 2003. "Ethnicity, Insurgency, and Civil War." *American Political Science Review.* Vol. 97: 75–90.

Fillieule, Olivier. 1999. " 'Plus ça change, moin ça change': Demonstrations in France during the Nineteen–Eighties." In *Acts of Dissent: New Developments in the Study of Protest.* Edited by Dieter Rucht, Ruud Koopmans, and Friedhelm Neidhardt, New York: Rowman and Littlefield, pp. 199–226.

Finkel, Steven, and Edward Muller. 1998. "Rational Choice and the Dynamics of Collective Political Action: Evaluating Alternative Models with Panel Data." *American Political Science Review.* Vol. 92, No. 1 (March): 37–49.

Finkel, Steven, and Karl-Dieter Opp. 1991. "Party Identification and Participation in Collective Political Action." *Journal of Politics*. Vol. 53, No. 2 (May): 339–371.

Fitzsimmons, Tracy, and Mark Anner. 1999. "Civil Society in a Postwar Period: Labor in the Salvadoran Democratic Transition." *Latin American Research Review*. Vol. 34, No. 3: 103–128.

Flacks, Richard. 1994. "The Party's Over – So What Is to Be Done?" In *New Social Movements: From Ideology to Identity*. Edited by Enrique Laraña, Hank Johnston, and Joseph Gusfield. Philadelphia: Temple University Press: 330–351.

Francisco, Ronald. 1996. "Coercion and Protest: An Empirical Test in Two Democratic States." *American Journal of Political Science*. Vol. 40, No. 4 (November): 1179–1204.

Gamson, William. 1975. *The Strategy of Social Protest*. Homewood, IL: Dorsey Press.

Gamson, William, and David Meyer. 1996. "Framing Political Opportunity." In *Comparative Perspectives on Social Movements: Political Opportunities, Mobilizing Structures, and Cultural Framings*. Edited by Doug McAdam, John D. McCarthy, and Mayer N. Zald. New York: Cambridge University Press, pp. 275–290.

Garrett, Geoffrey. 1998. *Partisan Politics in the Global Economy*. New York: Cambridge University Press.

Gilbert, Alan, ed. 1996. *The Mega-City in Latin America*. New York: United Nations University Press.

Goldstone, Jack. 2003. "Introduction: Bridging Institutionalized and Noninstitutionalized Politics." In *States, Parties, and Social Movements*. Edited by Jack Goldstone. New York: Cambridge University Press, pp. 1–24.

Goldstone, Jack. 2004. "More Social Movements or Fewer? Beyond Political Opportunity Structures to Relational Fields." *Theory and Society*. Vol. 33: 333–365.

Guigni, Marco, Doug McAdam, and Charles Tilly, eds. 1999. *How Social Movements Matter*. Minneapolis: University of Minnesota Press.

Gurr, Ted Robert. 1970. *Why Men Rebel*. Princeton, NJ: Princeton University Press.

Gurr, Ted Robert, with contributions from Barbara Harff, Monty G. Marshall, and James Scarritt. 1993. *Minorities at Risk: a Global View of Ethnopolitical Conflicts*. Washington, DC: Institute of Peace Press.

Gusfield, Joseph. 1963. *Symbolic Crusade: Status Politics and the American Temperance Movement*. Urbana: University of Illinois Press.

Hall, Melvin. 1995. *Poor People's Social Movement Organizations: The Goal is to Win*. Westport, CT: Praeger.

Hannan, Michael. 2005. "Ecologies of Organizations: Diversity and Identity." *The Journal of Economic Perspectives*. Vol. 19, No. 1 (Winter): 51–70.

Haynes, Jeff, ed. 2001. *Democracy and Political Change in the 'Third World'*. New York: Routledge.

Heywood, Paul. 1996. "The Emergence of New Party Systems and Transitions to Democracy: Spain in Comparative Perspective." In *Stabilizing Fragile Democracies: Comparing New Party Systems in Southern and Eastern Europe.* Edited by Geoffrey Pridham and Paul Lewis. New York: Routledge, pp. 145–166.

Hibbs, Douglas. 1973. *Mass Political Violence: A Cross-National Analysis.* New York: Wiley.

Hipsher, Patricia. 1998. "Democratic Transitions as Protest Cycles: Social Movement Dynamics in Democratizing Latin America," In *The Social Movement Society: Contentious Politics for a New Century.* Edited by David S. Meyer and Sidney Tarrow. New York: Rowman and Littlefield, pp. 153–172.

Hirschman, Albert O. 1970. *Exit, Voice, and Loyalty: Responses to Decline in Firms, Organizations, and States.* Cambridge, MA: Harvard University Press.

Hocke, Peter. 1999. "Determining the Selection Bias in Local and National Newspaper Reports on Protest Events." In *Acts of Dissent: New Developments in the Study of Protest.* Edited by Dieter Rucht, Ruud Koopmans, and Friedhelm Neidhardt. New York: Rowman and Littlefield, pp. 131–163.

Hojnacki, Marie. 1997. "Interest Groups' Decisions to Join Alliances or Work Alone." *American Journal of Political Science.* Vol. 41, No. 1 (January): 61–87.

Huber, John, and Ronald Inglehart. 1995. "Expert Interpretations of Party Space and Party Locations in 42 Societies." *Party Politics.* Vol. 1, No. 1: 73–111.

Huntington, Samuel. 1968. *Political Order in Changing Societies.* New Haven, CT: Yale University Press.

Huntington, Samuel. 1975. "The United States." In *The Crisis of Democracy.* New York: The Trilateral Commission/New York University Press, pp. 59–118.

Jenkins, J. Craig. 1995. "Social Movements, Political Representation, and the State: An Agenda and Comparative Framework." In *The Politics of Social Protest: Comparative Perspectives on States and Social Movements.* Edited by J. Craig Jenkins and Bert Klandermans. Minneapolis: University of Minnesota Press, pp. 14–35.

Jenkins, J. Craig, and Bert Klandermans, eds. 1995. *The Politics of Social Protest: Comparative Perspectives on States and Social Movements.* Minneapolis: University of Minnesota Press.

Kingdon, John W. 1995. *Agendas, Alternatives, and Public Policies.* 2nd edition. New York: HarperCollins.

Kitschelt, Herbert. 1989. *The Logics of Party Formation: Ecological Politics in Belgium and Germany.* Ithaca, NY: Cornell University Press.

Klandermans, Bert, Marlene Roefs, and Johan Olivier. 1998. "A Movement Takes Office." In *The Social Movement Society: Contentious Politics for a New Century.* Edited by David S. Meyer and Sidney Tarrow. New York: Rowman and Littlefield, pp. 173–216.

Kohli, Atul. 1990. *Democracy and Discontent: India's Growing Crisis of Governability*. New York: Cambridge University Press.

Kohli, Atul. 1994. "Centralization and Powerlessness: India's Democracy in a Comparative Perspective." In *State Power and Social Forces: Domination and Transformation in the Third World*. Edited by Joel Migdal, Atul Kohli, and Vivienne Shue. New York: Cambridge University Press, pp. 89–107.

Koopmans, Ruud. 1999. "The Use of Protest Event Data in Comparative Research: Cross-National Comparability, Sampling Methods, and Robustness." In *Acts of Dissent: New Developments in the Study of Protest*. Edited by Dieter Rucht, Ruud Koopmans, and Friedhelm Neidhardt, New York: Rowman and Littlefield, pp. 90–110.

Koopmans, Ruud, and Dieter Rucht. 2002. "Protest Event Analysis." In *Methods of Social Movement Research*. Edited by Ruud Koopmans and Suzanne Staggenborg. Minneapolis: University of Minnesota Press, pp. 231–259.

Kornhauser, William. 1959. *Politics of Mass Society*. Glencoe, IL: The Free Press.

Kriesi, Hanspeter. 1995. "The Political Opportunity Structure of New Social Movements: Its Impact on their Mobilization." In *The Politics of Social Protest: Comparative Perspectives on States and Social Movements*. Edited by J. Craig Jenkins and Bert Klandermans. Minneapolis: University of Minnesota Press, pp. 167–198.

Kriesi, Hanspeter. 1996. "The Organization of New Social Movements in a Political Context." In *Comparative Perspectives on Social Movements: Political Opportunities, Mobilizing Structures, and Cultural Framings*. Edited by Doug McAdam, John D. McCarthy, and Mayer N. Zald. New York: Cambridge University Press, pp. 152–184.

Kuenzi, Michelle, and Gina Lambright. 2001. "Party System Institutionalization in 30 African Countries." *Party Politics*. Vol. 7, No. 2: 437–468.

Laraña, Enrique, Hank Johnston, and Joseph Gusfield, eds. 1994. *New Social Movements: From Ideology to Identity*. Philadelphia: Temple University Press.

Lawson, Kay, ed. 1980. *Political Parties and Linkage: A Comparative Perspective*. New Haven, CT: Yale University Press.

Levitsky, Steven. 2003. *Transforming Labor-Based Parties in Latin America: Argentine Peronism in Comparative Perspective*. New York: Cambridge University Press.

Lewis-Beck, Michael, and Brad Lockerbie. 1989. "Economics, Votes, Protests: Western European Cases." *Comparative Political Studies*. Vol. 22, No. 2 (July): 155–178.

Lipset, S. M. 2001. "Cleavages, Parties, and Democracy." In *Party Systems and Voter Alignments Revisited*. Edited by Lauri Karvonen and Stein Kuhnle. New York: Routledge, pp. 3–9.

Lipset, S. M., and Stein Rokkan, eds. 1967. *Party Systems and Voter Alignments: Cross-National Perspectives*. New York: Free Press.

Long, J. Scott, and Jeremy Freese. 2003. *Regression Models for Categorical Dependent Variables Using Stata*. Revised edition. College Station, TX: STATA Corporation.

López Maya, Margarita, ed. 1999. *Lucha popular, democracia, neoliberalismo: Protesta popular en América Latina en los años de ajuste*. Caracas, Venezuela: Editorial Nueva Sociedad.

López Maya, Margarita. 2002. "Venezuela despues del Caracazo: Formas de la protesta en un contexto desinstitucionalizado." Kellogg Institute Working Paper No. 287. Notre Dame, IN: Kellogg Institute for International Studies.

Lucero, José Antonio. 2001. "Crisis and Contention in Ecuador." *Journal of Democracy*. Vol. 12, No. 2 (April): 59–73.

Maguire, Diarmuid. 1995. "Opposition Movements and Opposition Parties: Equal Partners or Dependent Relations in the Struggle for Power and Reform?" In *The Politics of Social Protest: Comparative Perspectives on States and Social Movements*. Edited by J. Craig Jenkins and Bert Klandermans. Minneapolis: University of Minnesota Press, pp. 199–228.

Mainwaring, Scott, and Tim Scully. 1995a. "Introduction: Party Systems in Latin America." In *Building Democratic Institutions: Party Systems in Latin America*. Edited by Scott Mainwaring and Tim Scully. Stanford, CA: Stanford University Press, pp. 1–34.

Mainwaring, Scott, and Tim Scully, eds. 1995b. *Building Democratic Institutions: Party Systems in Latin America*. Stanford, CA: Stanford University Press.

McAdam, Doug. 1996. "Conceptual Origins, Current Problems, Future Directions." In *Comparative Perspectives on Social Movements: Political Opportunities, Mobilizing Structures, and Cultural Framings*. Edited by Doug McAdam, John D. McCarthy, and Mayer N. Zald. New York: Cambridge University Press, pp. 23–40.

McAdam, Doug, and Yang Su. 2002. "The War at Home: Antiwar Protests and Congressional Voting, 1965 to 1973." *American Sociological Review*, Vol. 67, No. 5 (October): 696–721.

McAdam, Doug, John D. McCarthy, and Mayer N. Zald. 1996. "Introduction: Opportunities, mobilizing structures, and framing processes – Toward a synthetic, comparative perspective on social movements." In *Comparative Perspectives on Social Movements: Political Opportunities, Mobilizing Structures, and Cultural Framings*. Edited by Doug McAdam, John D. McCarthy, and Mayer Zald. New York: Cambridge University Press, pp. 1–22.

McAdam, Doug, John D. McCarthy, and Mayer Zald, eds. 1996a. *Comparative Perspectives on Social Movements: Political Opportunities, Mobilizing Structures, and Cultural Framings*. New York: Cambridge University Press.

McAdam, Doug, Sidney Tarrow, and Charles Tilly. 2001. *Dynamics of Contention*. New York: Cambridge University Press.

McCarthy, John D. 1996. "Constraints and Opportunities in Adopting, Adapting, and Inventing." In *Comparative Perspectives on Social*

Movements: Political Opportunities, Mobilizing Structures, and Cultural Framings. Edited by Doug McAdam, John D. McCarthy, and Mayer N. Zald. New York: Cambridge University Press, pp. 141–151.

McCarthy, John D., Clark McPhail, and Jackie Smith. 1996b. "Images of Protest: Dimensions of Selection Bias in Media Coverage of Washington Demonstrations, 1982 and 1991." *American Sociological Review*. Vol. 61, No. 3 (June): 478–499.

McCarthy, John D., Jackie Smith, and Mayer N. Zald. 1996. "Accessing Public, Media, Electoral and Governmental Agendas." In *Comparative Perspectives on Social Movements: Political Opportunities, Mobilizing Structures, and Cultural Framings*. Edited by Doug McAdam, John D. McCarthy, and Mayer N. Zald. New York: Cambridge University Press, pp. 291–311.

McCarthy, John D., et al. 1999. "Electronic and Print Media Representations of Washington, D.C. Demonstrations, 1982 and 1991: A Demography of Description Bias." In *Acts of Dissent: New Developments in the Study of Protest*. Edited by Dieter Rucht, Ruud Koopmans, and Friedhelm Neidhardt, New York: Rowman and Littlefield, pp. 113–130.

Meyer, David S., and Sidney Tarrow, eds. 1998a. *The Social Movement Society: Contentious Politics for a New Century*. New York: Rowman and Littlefield.

Meyer, David, and Sidney Tarrow. 1998b. "A Movement Society: Contentious Politics for a New Century." In *The Social Movement Society: Contentious Politics for a New Century*. Edited by David S. Meyer and Sidney Tarrow. New York: Rowman and Littlefield, pp. 1–28.

Michels, Robert. 1962. *Political Parties: A Sociological Study of the Oligarchical Tendencies of Modern Democracy*. Translated by Eden and Cedar Paul. New York: Collier Books.

Migdal, Joel, Atul Kohli, and Vivienne Shue, eds. 1994. *State Power and Social Forces: Domination and Transformation in the Third World*. New York: Cambridge University Press.

Montero, José Ramón, Richard Gunther, and Mariano Torcal. 1997. *Democracy in Spain: Legitimacy, Discontent, and Disaffection*. Estudio/ Working Paper 1997/100 (June). Madrid: Instituto Juan March.

Moore, Will. 1998. "Repression and Dissent: Substitution, Context and Timing." *American Journal of Political Science*. Vol. 42, No. 3 (July): 851–873.

Morris, Aldon, and Carol McClurg Mueller, eds. 1992. *Frontiers in Social Movement Theory*. New Haven, CT: Yale University Press.

Morse, Richard, and Jorge Hardoy, eds. 1992. *Rethinking the Latin American City*. Baltimore: Johns Hopkins University Press.

Mueller, Carol. 1997. "International Press Coverage of East German Protest Events, 1989." Vol. 62, No. 5 (October): 820–832.

Murillo, Maria Victoria. 2001. *Labor Unions, Partisan Coalitions, and Market Reforms in Latin America*. New York: Cambridge University Press.

Myers, Daniel, and Beth Schaefer Caniglia. 2004. "All the Rioting That's Fit to Print: Selection Effects in National Newspaper Coverage of Civil Disorders, 1968–1969." *American Sociological Review*. Vol. 69, No. 4 (August): 519–543.

Myers, David. 2002. "The Dynamics of Local Empowerment: An Overview." In *Capital City Politics in Latin America: Democratization and Empowerment*. Edited by David J. Myers and Henry A. Dietz. Boulder, CO: Lynne Rienner Press, pp. 1–27.

Myers, David, and Henry A. Dietz, eds. 2002. *Capital City Politics in Latin America: Democratization and Empowerment*. Edited by David Myers and Henry A. Dietz. Boulder, CO: Lynne Rienner Press.

Nickson, R. Andrew. 1995. *Local Government in Latin America*. Boulder, CO: Lynne Rienner Press.

Nohlen, Dieter, ed. 1993. *Enciclopedia Electoral Latinoamericana y del Caribe*. San Jose, Costa Rica: Instituto Interamericano de Derechos Humanos.

Nohlen, Dieter, Florian Grotz, and Christof Hartmann, eds. 2001. *Elections in Asia and the Pacific: A Data Handbook*. Vols. I and II. New York: Oxford University Press.

Nohlen, Dieter, Michael Krennerich, and Bernhard Thibaut, eds. 1999. *Elections in Africa: A Data Handbook*. New York: Oxford University Press.

Norris, Pippa. 2002. *Democratic Phoenix: Reinventing Political Activism*. New York: Cambridge University Press.

Norris, Pippa, Stefaan Walgrave, and Peter Van Aels. 2005. "Who Demonstrates? Antistate Rebels, Conventional Participants, or Everyone?" *Comparative Politics*. Vol. 37, No. 2 (January): 189–205.

Oberschall, Anthony. 1993. *Social Movements: Ideologies, Interests, and Identities*. New Brunswick, NJ: Transaction Publishers.

O'Donnell, Guillermo, and Philippe Schmitter. 1986. *Transitions from Authoritarian Rule: Tentative Conclusions about Uncertain Democracies*. Baltimore: Johns Hopkins University Press.

Oliver, Pamela, and Gregory Maney. 2000. "Political Processes and Local Newspaper Coverage of Protest Events: From Selection Bias to Triadic Interactions." *American Journal of Sociology*. Vol. 106, No. 2 (September): 463–505.

Oliver, Pamela, and Daniel J. Myers. 1999. "How Events Enter the Public Sphere: Conflict, Location, and Sponsorship in Local Newspaper Coverage of Public Events." *American Journal of Sociology*. Vol. 105, No. 1 (July): 38–87.

Olson, Mancur. 1965. *The Logic of Collective Action: Public Goods and the Theory of Groups*. Cambridge, MA: Harvard University Press.

Olzak, Susan, and Johan L. Olivier. 1999. "Comparative Event Analysis: Black Civil Rights Protest in South Africa and the United States." In *Acts of Dissent: New Developments in the Study of Protest*. Edited by Dieter Rucht, Ruud Koopmans, and Friedhelm Neidhardt, New York: Rowman and Littlefield, pp. 253–283.

Opp, Karl-Dieter. 1988. "Grievances and Participation in Social Movements." *American Sociological Review*, Vol. 53 (December): 853–864.

Opp, Karl-Dieter. 1989. *The Rationality of Political Protest: A Comparative Analysis of Rational Choice Theory*. Boulder, CO: Westview Press.

Opp, Karl-Dieter, et al. 1995. "Left-Right Ideology and Collective Political Action: A Comparative Analysis of Germany, Israel, and Peru." In *The Politics of Social Protest: Comparative Perspectives on States and Social Movements*. Edited by J. Craig Jenkins and Bert Klandermans. Minneapolis: University of Minnesota Press, pp. 63–95.

Ortiz, David, et al. 2005. "Where Do We Stand with Newspaper Data?" *Mobilization*. Vol. 10, No. 3 (October): 397–499.

Oxhorn, Philip D. 1995. *Organizing Civil Society: The Popular Sectors and the Struggle for Democracy in Chile*. University Park: Penn State Press.

Pachano, Simón. 1995. *La representación caótica*. Quito: FLACSO.

Panebianco, Angelo. 1988. *Political Parties: Organization and Power*. Translated by Marc Silver. New York: Cambridge University Press.

Piven, Frances Fox, and Richard A. Cloward. 1977. *Poor People's Movements: Why They Succeed, How They Fail*. New York: Vintage Books.

Portes, Alejandro, and John Walton. 1976. *Urban Latin America: The Political Condition from Above and Below*. Austin: University of Texas Press.

Powell, G. Bingham. 1982. *Contemporary Democracies: Participation, Stability and Violence*. Cambridge, MA: Harvard University Press.

Pridham, Geoffrey, and Paul Lewis, eds. 1996a. *Stabilizing Fragile Democracies: Comparing New Party Systems in Southern and Eastern Europe*. New York: Routledge.

Pridham, Geoffrey, and Paul Lewis. 1996b. "Stabilizing Fragile Democracies and Party System Development." In *Stabilizing Fragile Democracies: Comparing New Party Systems in Southern and Eastern Europe*. Edited by Geoffrey Pridham and Paul Lewis. New York: Routledge, pp. 1–22.

Randall, Vicky, and Lars Svåsand. 2001. "Party Institutionalization and the New Democracies," *Democracy and Political Change in the 'Third World.'* Edited by Jeff Haynes. New York: Routledge Press, pp. 75–96.

Reilly, Charles A., ed. 1995. *New Paths to Democratic Development in Latin America: The Rise of NGO-Municipal Collaboration*. Boulder, CO: Lynne Rienner Press.

Remmer, Karen. 1991. "The Political Impact of Economic Crisis in Latin America in the 1980s." *American Political Science Review*. Vol. 85, No. 3 (September): 777–800.

Rice, Roberta. 2003. "Channeling Discontent: The Impact of Political Institutions on Patterns of Social Protest in Contemporary Latin America." Research Paper No. 40. Albuquerque: University of New Mexico Latin American Institute.

Roberts, Kenneth. 1998. *Deepening Democracy: The Modern Left and Social Movements in Chile and Peru*. Stanford, CA: Stanford University Press.

Robertson, Graeme B. 2004. "Leading Labor: Unions, Politics and Protest in New Democracies." *Comparative Politics*. Vol. 36, No. 3 (April): 253–272.

Rucht, Dieter. 1996. "The impact of national contexts on social movement structures: A cross-movement and cross-national comparison." In *Comparative Perspectives on Social Movements: Political Opportunities, Mobilizing Structures, and Cultural Framings*. Edited by Doug McAdam, John D. McCarthy, and Mayer N. Zald. New York: Cambridge University Press, pp. 185–204.

Rucht, Dieter. 1998. "The Structure and Culture of Collective Protest in Germany since 1950." In *The Social Movement Society: Contentious Politics for a New Century*. Edited by David S. Meyer and Sidney Tarrow. New York: Rowman and Littlefield, pp. 29–57.

Rucht, Dieter, and Friedhelm Neidhardt. 1999. "Methodological Issues in Collecting Protest Event Data: Units of Analysis, Sources and Sampling, Coding Problems." In *Acts of Dissent: New Developments in the Study of Protest*. Edited by Dieter Rucht, Ruud Koopmans, and Friedhelm Neidhardt, New York: Rowman and Littlefield, pp. 65–89.

Rucht, Dieter, Ruud Koopmans, and Friedhelm Neidhardt, eds. 1999. *Acts of Dissent: New Developments in the Study of Protest*. New York: Rowman and Littlefield.

Saideman, Stephen, David Lanoue, Michael Campenni, and Samuel Stanton. 2002. "Democratization, Political Institutions, and Ethnic Conflict: A Pooled Time-series Analysis, 1985–1998." *Comparative Political Studies*. Vol. 35, No. 1 (February): 103–129.

Scarritt, James, and Susan McMillan. 1995. "Protest and Rebellion in Africa: Explaining Conflicts between Ethnic Minorities and the State in the 1980s." *Comparative Political Studies*. Vol. 28, No. 3 (October): 323–349.

Schmitter, Philippe C. 2001. "Parties Are Not What They Once Were." In *Political Parties and Democracy*. Edited by Larry Diamond and Richard Gunther. Baltimore: Johns Hopkins University Press, pp. 67–89.

Schneider, Cathy Lisa. 1995. *Shantytown Protest in Pinochet's Chile*. Philadelphia: Temple University Press.

Schönwälder, Gerd. 2002. *Linking Civil Society and the State: Urban Popular Movements, the Left, and Local Government in Peru, 1980–1992*. University Park: Penn State Press.

Smelser, Neil. 1963. *A Theory of Collective Behavior*. New York: Free Press.

Snow, David, and Robert Benford. 1992. "Master Frames and Cycles of Protest." In *Frontiers in Social Movement Theory*. Edited by Aldon Morris and Carol McClurg Mueller. New Haven, CT: Yale University Press, pp. 133–155.

Spalding, Hobart A. 1977. *Organized Labor in Latin America: Historical Case Studies of Workers in Dependent Societies*. New York: New York University Press.

Stockton, Hans. 2001. "Political Parties, Party Systems, and Democracy in East Asia: Lessons from Latin America." *Comparative Political Studies.* Vol. 34, No. 1: 94–119.

Stokes, Susan. 2001. *Mandates and Democracy: Neoliberalism by Surprise in Latin America.* New York: Cambridge University Press.

Stolowicz, Beatriz, ed. 1999. *Gobiernos de Izquierda en América Latina: El desafío del cambio.* Mexico City: Plaza y Valdez.

Sussman, Glen, and Brent Steel. 1991. "Support for Protest Methods and Political Strategies among Peace Movement Activists: Comparing the United States, Great Britain, and the Federal Republic of Germany." *The Western Political Quarterly.* Vol. 44, No. 5 (September): 519–540.

Tarrow, Sidney. 1983. "Struggling to Reform: Social Movement and Policy Change During Cycles of Protest." Occasional Paper #15. Western Societies Program, Cornell University.

Tarrow, Sidney. 1989a. *Struggle, Politics and Reform: Collective Action, Social Movements, and Cycles of Protest.* Occasional Paper #21. Western Societies Program, Cornell University.

Tarrow, Sidney. 1989b. *Democracy and Disorder: Protest and Politics in Italy 1965–1975.* New York: Oxford University Press.

Tarrow, Sidney. 1994. *Power in Movement: Social Movements, Collective Action and Politics.* Cambridge: Cambridge University Press.

Tarrow, Sidney. 1999. "Studying Contentious Politics: From Event-ful History to Cycles of Collective Action." In *Acts of Dissent: New Developments in the Study of Protest.* Edited by Dieter Rucht, Ruud Koopmans, and Friedhelm Neidhardt, New York: Rowman and Littlefield, pp. 33–64.

Ten Eyck, Toby A. 2001. "Does Information Matter? A Research Note on Information Technologies and Political Protest." *The Social Science Journal.* Vol. 38: 147–160.

Tilly, Charles. 1978. *From Mobilization to Revolution.* Reading, MA: Addison-Wesley.

Tilly, Charles. 1995. *Popular Contention in Great Britain: 1758–1834.* Cambridge, MA: Harvard University Press.

Tilly, Charles. 2003. "Afterword: Agendas for Students of Social Movements." In *States, Parties, and Social Movements.* Edited by Jack Goldstone. New York: Cambridge University Press, pp. 246–256.

Tilly, Charles, Louise Tilly, and Richard Tilly. 1975. *The Rebellious Century: 1830–1930.* Cambridge, MA: Harvard University Press.

Tóka, Gábor. 1998. "Party Appeals and Voter Loyalty in New Democracies." *Political Studies.* Vol. 46: 589–610.

Valenzuela J. Samuel. 1992. "Labour Movements and Political Systems: Some Variations." In *The Future of Labour Movements.* Edited by Marino Regini. London: Sage Press, pp. 53–101.

Van Dyke, Nella. 2003. "Protest Cycles and Party Politics: The Effects of Elite Allies and Antagonists on Student Protest in the United States, 1930–1990.

In *States, Parties, and Social Movements*. Edited by Jack Goldstone. New York: Cambridge University Press, pp. 226–245.

Vilas, Carlos. 1997. "Participation, Inequality, and the Whereabouts of Democracy." In *The New Politics of Inequality in Latin America: Rethinking Participation and Representation*. Edited by Douglas Chalmers et al. New York: Oxford University Press, pp. 3–42.

Walker, Jack. 1991. *Mobilizing Interest Groups in America*. Ann Arbor: University of Michigan Press.

Wallace, Michael, and J. Craig Jenkins. 1995. "The New Class, Post-industrialism, and Neocorporatism: Three Images of Social Protest in the Western Democracies." In *The Politics of Social Protest: Comparative Perspectives on States and Social Movements*. Edited by J. Craig Jenkins and Bert Klandermans. Minneapolis: University of Minnesota Press, pp. 96–137.

Wignaraja, Ponna, ed. 1993. *New Social Movements in the South: Empowering the People*. London: Zed Books.

Wilkie, James, ed., with Eduardo Aleman and José Guadalupe Ortega, co-editors. 2002. *Statistical Abstract of Latin America*. Vol. 38. Los Angeles: UCLA.

Williams, Glyn. 2001. "Understanding 'political stability': Party action and political discourse in West Bengal." *Third World Quarterly*. Vol. 22, No. 4: 603–622.

Zapata, Francisco. 2003. *¿Crisis en el sindicalismo en América Latina?* Kellogg Institute Working Paper No. 302. Notre Dame, IN: Kellogg Institute for International Studies

Selected Sources – Mexico

"Aceptan marchas reguladas." 2001. *Reforma*. 2 February 2001: 4B.

Aguilar García, Javier. 2001. *La población trabajadora y sindicalizada en México en el período de la globalización*. Mexico City: Fondo de Cultura Económica.

Alonso, Jorge. 1986a. "Movimientos sociales en el Valle de México: Una introducción." In *Los movimientos sociales en el Valle de México*. Vol. I. Edited by Jorge Alonso. Mexico City: CIESAS, pp. 17–52.

Alonso, Jorge, ed. 1986b. *Los movimientos sociales en el Valle de México*. Two volumes. Mexico City: CIESAS.

Álvarez Enríquez, Lucía, ed. 1997. *Participación y democracia en la Ciudad de México*. Mexico City: UNAM/La Jornada.

Álvarez Enríquez, Lucía. 1998. *Distrito Federal: Sociedad, Economía, Política, Cultura*. Mexico City: UNAM.

Aranda Sánchez, José. 2001. *Un movimiento obrero-popular independiente en México*. Toluca, Mexico: Universidad Autónoma del Estado de México.

Arzaluz Solano, Socorro. 2002. "Asamblea de Barrios y acción colectiva." *Ciudades*. No. 55: 26–32.

Barragán, Pedro Moctezuma. 1999. *Despertares: Comunidad y organización urbano popular en México 1970–1994.* Mexico City: Universidad Iberoamericana.

Becerra Chavez, Pablo Javier. 2001. "Gobierno y legislación electoral en el Distrito Federal." In *Reforma político-electoral y democracia en los gobiernos locales.* Edited by Rodolfo Vega Hernández, et al. Santiago de Querétaro: Fundación Universitaria de Derecho, Administración, y Política, pp. 1–26.

Bennett, Vivienne. 1992. "The Evolution of Urban Popular Movements in Mexico Between 1968 and 1988." In *The Making of Social Movements in Latin America: Identity, Strategy, and Democracy.* Edited by Arturo Escobar and Sonia E. Álvarez. Boulder, CO: Westview Press, pp. 240–259.

Bensusán, Graciela, and Arturo Alcalde. 2000. "Estructura sindical y agremiación." In *Trabajo y trabajadores en el México contemporáneo.* Edited by Graciela Bensusán and Teresa Rendón. Mexico City: Miguel Ángel Porrúa, pp. 163–192.

Bensusán, Graciela, and Teresa Rendón, eds. 2000. *Trabajo y trabajadores en el México contemporáneo.* Mexico City: Miguel Angel Porrúa.

Borjas Benavente, Adriana. 2004. *Partido de la Revolución Democrática: Estructura, organización interna y desempeño público, 1989–2003.* Vol. 2. Mexico City: Ediciones Gernika.

Bouchier, Josiane. 1990. "El movimiento urbano popular y la Coordinadora Nacional del Movimiento Urbano Popular." In *Movimientos sociales en México.* Edited by Sergio Zermeño and Aurelio Cuevas. Mexico City: UNAM, pp. 203–219.

Bruhn, Kathleen. 1997. *Taking on Goliath: The Emergence of a New Left Party and the Struggle for Democracy in Mexico.* University Park: Penn State Press.

Bultmann, Ingo, et al., eds. 1995. *¿Democracia sin movimiento social? Sindicatos, organizaciones vecinales y movimientos de mujeres en Chile y México.* Caracas: Editorial Nueva Sociedad.

Carr, Barry. 1991. "Labor and the Political Left in Mexico." In *Unions, Workers, and the State in Mexico.* Edited by Kevin J. Middlebrook. La Jolla, CA: Center for U.S.-Mexican Studies/UCSD, pp. 120–152.

Castillo Palma, Jaime, Elsa Patiño Tovar, and Sergio Zermeño, eds. 2001. *Pobreza y organizaciones de la sociedad civil.* Puebla, Mexico: Universidad Autónoma de Puebla.

Cornelius, Wayne. 1975. *Politics and the Migrant Poor in Mexico City.* Stanford, CA: Stanford University Press.

Cornelius, Wayne, Todd Eisenstadt, and Jane Hindley, eds. 1999. *Subnational Politics and Democratization in Mexico.* La Jolla, CA: Center for U.S.-Mexican Studies.

Cross, John. 1998. *Informal Politics: Street Vendors and the State in Mexico City.* Stanford, CA: Stanford University Press.

Coulomb, Rene, and Cristina Sánchez Mejorada, eds. 1992. *Pobreza urbana, autogestión y política*. Mexico City: Centro de la Vivienda y Estudios Urbanos.

Cuéllar Vázquez, Angélica. 1992. "Asamblea de Barrios." In *Crísis y sujetos sociales en México*. Vol. 1. Edited by Enrique de la Garza Toledo. Mexico City: Miguel Ángel Porrúa, pp. 225–252.

Cuéllar Vázquez, Angélica. 1993. *La noche es de ustedes, el amanecer es nuestro: Asamblea de Barrios y Superbarrio Gómez en la Ciudad de México*. Mexico City: UNAM.

Davis, Diane. 2002. "Mexico City: The Local-National Dynamics of Democratization." In *Capital City Politics in Latin America: Democratization and Empowerment*. Edited by David Myers and Henry Dietz. Boulder, CO: Lynne Rienner Press, pp. 227–263.

De Grammont, Hubert C. 2001. *El Barzón: Clase media, ciudadanía y democracia*. Mexico City: Plaza y Valdés.

De la Garza Toledo, Enrique. 1992. *Crísis y sujetos sociales en México*. Vol. 1. Mexico City: Miguel Ángel Porrúa.

De la Garza Toledo, Enrique. 2001a. "La democracia en tiempos del poscorporativismo: El caso del Sindicato de Telefonistas de la República Mexicana." In *Democracia y cambio sindical en México*. Edited by Enrique de la Garza Toledo. Mexico City: Plaza y Valdés, pp. 21–51.

De la Garza Toledo, Enrique, ed. 2001b. *Democracia y cambio sindical en México*. Mexico City: Plaza y Valdés.

Eckstein, Susan. 1977. *The Poverty of Revolution: The State and the Urban Poor in Mexico*. Princeton, NJ: Princeton University Press.

Espinosa Valle, Victor Alejandro. 1998. *Alternancia política y gestión pública: El Partido Acción Nacional en el gobierno de Baja California*. Tijuana, Mexico: COLEF.

Executive Director of Labor Studies, Mexico City Government. 1999. "18% a los tranviarios: Se evitó la huelga." *Informe de Política Laboral*. Vol. 2, No. 7 (February 15), pp. 1–2.

Fernández Allende, Emilio. 1995. "El Sindicato Único de Trabajadores del Gobierno del Distrito Federal." *Trabajo*, Issue 10: 17–23.

Foweraker, Joe. 1990. "Popular Movements and Political Change in Mexico." In *Popular Movements and Political Change in Mexico*. Edited by Joe Foweraker and Ann Craig. Boulder, CO: Lynne Rienner Press, pp. 3–20.

Foweraker, Joe, and Ann Craig, eds. 1990. *Popular Movements and Political Change in Mexico*. Boulder, CO: Lynne Rienner Press.

FPFV. 2000. *Frente Popular Francisco Villa: Estructura Orgánica*. Mexico City: FPFV.

Garcia del Castillo, Rodolfo. 1999. *Los municipios en México: Los retos ante el futuro*. Mexico City: CIDE.

Gilbert, Alan, ed. 1989. *Housing and Land in Urban Mexico*. Monograph Series #31. La Jolla, CA: Center for U.S.–Mexican Studies.

González, Susana. "Se requieren 129 mil viviendas al año para satisfacer demanda en la ZMCM." *La Jornada*. Mexico City. 9 October 2001: 49.

Grayson, George. 1989. *The Mexican Labor Machine: Power, Politics, and Patronage*. Washington, DC: Center for Strategic and International Studies.

Greene, Kenneth F. 2007. *Why Dominant Parties Lose: Mexico's Democratization in Comparative Perspective*. New York: Cambridge University Press.

Guillen López, Tonatiuh. 1996. *Gobiernos municipales en México: Entre la modernización y la tradición política*. Tijuana: COLEF.

Informe Mensual: Junio 1998. 1998. Coordinación General de Participación Ciudadana y Gestión Social, Gobierno del Distrito Federal.

López Castellanos, Nayar. 2001. *Izquierda y Neoliberalismo de México a Brasil*. Mexico City: Editora Plaza y Valdés.

Loyzaga de la Cueva, Octavio. 1987. *El estado como patrón y árbitro: El conflicto de la Ruta 100*. Mexico City: Ediciones de Cultura Popular.

"Marchan en el DF para pedir trabajo." *Reforma*, 12 December 2001: 8B.

Martínez, Fabiola. 2003. "Rompen 17 sindicatos con la FSTSE." *La Jornada*. Mexico City. 6 December 2003: 8.

Mendez, Patricia and Rodrigo León. "Manifiestan apatía por juntas vecinales." *Reforma*. Mexico City. 8 January 2003: 5B.

Merino, Mauricio, ed. 1995. *En busca de la democracia municipal: La participación ciudadana en el gobierno local mexicano*. Mexico City: El Colegio de México.

Middlebrook, Kevin J. 1989. "The Sounds of Silence: Organised Labour's Response to Economic Crisis in Mexico." *Journal of Latin American Studies*. Vol. 21, No. 2 (May): 195–220.

Middlebrook, Kevin J., ed. 1991. *Unions, Workers, and the State in Mexico*. La Jolla, CA: UCSD.

Middlebrook, Kevin J. 1995. *The Paradox of Revolution: Labor, the State, and Authoritarianism in Mexico*. Baltimore: Johns Hopkins University Press.

Olvera, Alberto, ed. 2003a. *Sociedad civil, esfera pública y democratización en América Latina: México*. Mexico City: Fondo de Cultura Económica.

Olvera, Alberto. 2003b. "Conclusiones y Propuestas." In *Sociedad Civil, Esfera Pública y Democratización en America Latina: Mexico*. Edited by Alberto Olvera. Mexico City: Fondo de Cultura Económica, pp. 410–438.

Preston, Julia, and Samuel Dillon. 2004. *Opening Mexico: The Making of a Democracy*. New York: Farrar, Straus and Giroux.

Ramírez, Bertha Teresa. "El GDF ha realizado más de 60 mil acciones de vivienda en dos años." *La Jornada*. Mexico City. 27 March 2003: 47.

Ramírez, Bertha Teresa, and Gabriela Romero. 2001. "Con base en los resultados de la consulta, AN a favor de regulamentar marchas: Luege Tamargo." *La Jornada*. Mexico City. 1 February 2001: 36.

Ramírez Sáiz, Juan Manuel. 2002. "La política, lo politico, y el Movimiento Urbano Popular." *Ciudades*. No. 55: 3.

Ravelo, Patricia, and Sergio Sánchez. 2001. "Protesta de bases y restauración del poder sindical." In *Democracia y cambio sindical en México*. Edited by Enrique de la Garza Toledo. Mexico City: Plaza y Valdés, pp. 73–91.

Regalado, Jorge. 1991. "Elecciones, partidos y organizaciones populares." *Ciudades*. No. 14: 49–55.

Rendón, Teresa and Carlos Salas. 2000. "La evolución del empleo." In *Trabajo y trabajadores en el México contemporáneo*. Edited by Graciela Bensusán and Teresa Rendón. Mexico City: Miguel Ángel Porrúa.

Reveles Vázquez, Francisco, ed. 2004. *Partido de la Revolución Democrática: Los signos de la institucionalización*. Mexico City: Ediciones Gernika.

Rodriguez, Victoria, and Peter Ward. 1995. *Opposition Government in Mexico*. Albuquerque: University of New Mexico Press.

Ruíz, Jonathan. "Frenan protestas a las inversiones." *Reforma*. Mexico City. 12 May 2003: A1.

Salazar, Claudia, and Carlos Reyes. "Viven burócratas cisma." *Reforma*. Mexico City. 6 December 2003: A1, A4, A5.

Samperio, Ana Cristina. 1996. *Se nos reventó El Barzón*. Mexico City: Edivisión.

Sánchez Mejorada, Cristina, and Lucia Álvarez Enriquez. 2003. "Gobierno Democrático, Sociedad Civil, y Participación Ciudadana en la Ciudad de México, 1997–2000." In *Sociedad Civil, Esfera Pública y Democratización en America Latina: Mexico*. Edited by Alberto Olvera. Mexico City: Fondo de Cultura Económica, pp. 205–283.

Schwarz, Mauricio-José. 1994. *Todos somos Superbarrio: La verdadera y asombrosa historia del luchador social más enigmático de México*. Mexico City: Editorial Planeta Mexicana.

Serna, Leslie. 1995. *Aqui nos quedaremos: Testimonios de la Coordinadora Única de Damnificados*. Mexico City: Universidad Iberoamericana.

Serna, Leslie. 1997. *Quíen es quien en el MUP*. Mexico City: Unidad Obrero y Socialista.

Trejo Delarbre, Raúl. 1990. *Crónica del sindicalismo en México (1976–1988)*. Mexico City: Siglo Veintiuno Editores.

Ward, Peter. 1989. "Political Mediation and Illegal Settlement in Mexico City." In *Housing and Land in Urban Mexico*. Edited by Alan Gilbert. La Jolla, CA: UCSD Center for U.S.-Mexican Studies, pp. 135–155.

Williams, Heather L. 2001. *Social Movements and Economic Transition: Markets and Distributive Conflict in Mexico*. New York: Cambridge University Press.

Vega Hernández, Rodolfo, et al., eds. 2001. *Reforma político-electoral y democracia en los gobiernos locales*. Santiago de Querétaro, Mexico: Fundación Universitaria de Derecho, Administración, y Política.

Zapata, Francisco. 1989. "Labor and Politics: The Mexican Paradox." In *Labor Autonomy and the State in Latin America*. Edited by Edward C. Epstein. Boston: Unwin Hyman, pp. 173–193.

Zapata, Francisco. 1995. *El sindicalismo mexicano frente a la restructuración*. Mexico City: El Colegio de México.

Zermeño, Sergio and Aurelio Cuevas, eds. 1990. *Movimientos sociales en México*. Mexico City: UNAM.

Ziccardi, Alicia. 1998. *Gobernabilidad y participación ciudadana en la ciudad capital*. Mexico City: UNAM.

Selected Sources – Brazil

Abers, Rebecca Neaera. 2000. *Inventing Local Democracy: Grassroots Politics in Brazil*. Boulder, CO: Lynne Rienner Press.

Alcántara, Manuel. 1999. *Sistemas politicos de América Latina: América del Sur*. Volume I. Madrid: Editorial Tecnos.

"Apoio ao GDF divide eleição para o Sinpro." Jornal de Brasilia. Brasilia. 2 June 1995.

Arretche, Marta, and Vicente Rodriguez. 1998. *Federalismo no Brasil: Descentralização das políticas sociais no Estado de São Paulo*. São Paulo, SP: FUNDAP

Assies, Willem. 1993. "Urban Social Movements and Local Democracy in Brazil." *European Review of Latin American and Caribbean Studies*. Vol. 55 (December): 39–58.

Avritzer, Leonardo. 2000. "Democratization and Changes in the Pattern of Association in Brazil." *Journal of Interamerican Studies and World Affairs*. Vol. 42, No. 3 (Fall): 59–76.

Baiocchi, Gianpaolo, ed. 2003a. *Radicals in Power: The Workers' Party (PT) and Experiments in Urban Democracy in Brazil*. New York: Zed Books.

Baiocchi, Gianpaolo. 2003b. "Radicals in Power." In *Radicals in Power: The Workers' Party (PT) and Experiments in Urban Democracy in Brazil*. Edited by Gianpaolo Baiocchi. New York: Zed Books, pp. 1–26.

Benevides, Maria Victoria, Paulo Vannuchi, and Fabio Kerche, eds. 2003. *Reforma política e cidadania*. São Paulo: Editora Fundação Perseu Abramo.

Bezerra Ammann, Safira. 1991. *Movimento popular de bairro: De frente para o Estado, em busca do Parlamento*. São Paulo: Cortez Editora.

Biazzi, Luis Augusto et al, eds. 1999. *Descentralização e privatização nos setores de infraestrutura no Estado de São Paulo*. São Paulo: Edições Fundap.

Biehler Mateos, Simone. "Paulistano apoia greve mas rejeita ação radical." *O Estado de São Paulo*, 29 May 2000: A10.

Bonduki, Nabil, ed. 1997. *Habitat: As práticas bem-sucedidas em habitação, meio ambiente e gestão urbana nas cidades brasileiras*. 2nd edition. São Paulo: Livros Studio Nobel.

Bonduki, Nabil. 2000. *Habitar São Paulo:Reflexões sobre a gestão urbana*. São Paulo: Estação Liberdade.

Branford, Sue, and Bernardo Kucinski. 1995. *Brazil: Carnival of the Oppressed*. London: Latin America Bureau.

Brasil de Lima Junior, Olavo, ed. 1997. *O sistema partidario brasileiro: Diversidade e tendencies 1982–1994*. Rio de Janeiro: Fundação Getulio Vargas.

Brasileiro, Anísio, and Etienne Henry, eds. 1999. *Viação Ilimitada: Ônibus das cidades brasileiras*. São Paulo: Cultura Editores Associados.

Bueno de Azevedo, Clovis. 1995. *A estrela partida ao meio: Ambiguidades do pensamento petista*. São Paulo: Editora Entrelinhas.

Burdick, John. 1992. "Rethinking the Study of Social Movements: The Case of Christian Base Communities in Urban Brazil." In *The Making of Social Movements in Latin America: Identity, Strategy, and Democracy*. Edited by Arturo Escobar and Sonia E. Álvarez. Boulder, CO: Westview Press, pp. 171–184.

Caldeira, Teresa. 2000. *City of Walls: Crime, Segregation, and Citizenship in São Paulo*. Los Angeles: University of California Press.

Calderón, Adolfo Ignacio, and Vera Chaia, eds. 2002. *Gestão Municipal: Descentralização e participação popular*. São Paulo: Cortez Editora.

"Camara decide bloquear projetos de Erundina." *Folha de São Paulo*. São Paulo. 9 August 1990: C5.

Câmara Municipal de São Paulo. 2001. "Habitação na area central." Final report of the Commission for Studies on Housing in the Central Region. São Paulo: Câmara Municipal de São Paulo.

Câmara Municipal de São Paulo. 2003. *São Paulo Plano Diretor Estratégico: Cartilha de formação*, second edition. São Paulo: Câmara Municipal de São Paulo.

Cardoso, Adalberto, and Alvaro Comin. 1997. "Centrais sindicais e attitudes democráticas." *Lua Nova*. No. 40/41: 167–192.

Cardoso, Ruth Corrêa Leite. 1992. "Popular Movements in the Context of the Consolidation of Democracy in Brazil." In *The Making of Social Movements in Latin America: Identity, Strategy, and Democracy*. Edited by Arturo Escobar and Sonia E. Álvarez. Boulder, CO: Westview Press, pp. 291–302.

César, Benedito Tadeu. *PT: A contemporaneidade possivel*. 2002. Porto Alegre: Editora da Universidade Federal do Rio Grande do Sul.

CMP. 2002. *Políticas públicas com participação popular*. São Paulo: Central de Movimentos Populares.

Costa Ferreira, Marcelo. 1999. "Associativismo e contato político nas regiões metropolitanas de Brasil: 1988–1996." *Revista Brasileira de Ciências Sociais*. Vol. 14, No. 41: 90–102.

"CUT articulou negociação." *Folha de São Paulo*. São Paulo. 20 May 1992: C3.

Da Silva, Ana Amelia. 1994a. "Dimensões da interlocução pública: Cidade, movimentos sociais e direitos." In *O Brasil no rastro da crise: Partidos, sindicatos, movimentos sociais, Estado e cidadania no curso dos anos 90*. Edited by Eli Diniz, José Sérgio Leite Lopes, and Reginaldo Prandi. São Paulo: Editora Hucitec, pp. 204–224.

Da Silva, Ana Amelia, ed. 1994b. *Moradía e cidadania: Um debate em movimento*. No. 20. São Paulo: POLIS.

Da Silva, Ana Amelia. 1994c. *Urbanização de favelas: Duas experiências em construção*. No. 15. São Paulo: POLIS.

Da Silva Prado, Eleutério, and Eli Roberto Pelin. 1993. *Moradía no Brasil: Reflexões sobre o problema habitacional brasileiro.* São Paulo: Companhia Brasileira de Metalurgica e Mineração.

Dagnino, Evelina. 2002. *Sociedad civil, esfera pública y democratización en América Latina: Brasil.* Mexico City: Fondo de Cultura Económica.

De Campos Gouvêa, Luiz Alberto. 1998. "Una política habitacional de interesse social para o Distrito Federal." In *Brasília: Gestão urbana, conflitos e cidadania.* Edited by Aldo Paviani. Brasilia: Universidade Nacional de Brasilia, pp. 253–270.

De Castro Andrade, ed. 1998. *Processo de governo no município e no estado.* São Paulo: Editora de la Universidade de São Paulo.

Diario Oficial do Municipio de São Paulo. 2002. Vol. 47, No. 16 (January 24).

Dillon Soares, Gláucio Ary. 2000. "Em busca da racionalidade perdida: Alguns determinantes do voto no Distrito Federal." *Revista Brasileira de Ciencias Sociais,* Vol. 15, No. 43: 5–23.

Di Tella, Torcuato. 1995. *Estructuras sindicales en la Argentina y Brasil: Algunas tendencies recientes.* Buenos Aires: Editorial Biblos.

Dos Reis Velloso, João Paulo and Leôncio Martins Rodrigues, eds. 1992. *O futuro do sindicalismo: CUT, Força Sindical, CGT.* São Paulo: Instituto Nacional de Altos Estudios.

Encarnación, Omar G. 2003. *The Myth of Civil Society: Social Capital and Democratic Consolidation in Spain and Brazil.* New York: Palgrave MacMillan.

Figueiredo, Rubens and Bolivar Lamounier. 1997. *As cidades que dão certo: Experiências inovadoras na administração pública brasileira.* Brasilia: Editora MH Comunicação.

Filipini, Flavia. "A luta agora e por 75.48%." *Correio Braziliense.* Brasilia. 22 January 2001.

Força Sindical. 1993. *Um projeto para o Brasil: A proposta da Força Sindical.* São Paulo: Geração Editorial.

Força Sindical. "Paulinho filia-se al PDT." *Jornal da Força.* July 2003: 1.

Frúgoli, Heitor Jr. 2000. *Centralidade em São Paulo: Trajetorias, conflitos, e negociações na metrôpole.* São Paulo: Edusp.

Gay, Robert. 1994. *Popular Organization and Democracy in Río de Janeiro: A Tale of Two Favelas.* Philadelphia: Temple University Press.

Genro, Tarso. 1997. "O modo petista de governor: Balanço e legado da terceira geração de prefeitos (1993–1996)." In *Desafios do governo local: O modo petista de governar.* Edited by Antonio Palocci, et al. São Paulo: Editora Fundação Perseu Abramo, pp. 14–31.

Gianotti, Vito. 1994. *Medeiros visto de perto.* São Paulo: Brasil Urgente.

Gohn, Maria da Gloria. 1987. *Lutas pela moradia popular em São Paulo.* Unpublished doctoral thesis. Faculty of Architecture and Urban Studies, Universidade de São Paulo.

Gohn, Maria da Gloria. 1995. *Historia dos movimentos e lutas sociais: A construção da cidadania dos brasileiros.* São Paulo: Edições Loyola.

Goldsmith, William. 1994. "Introdução à edição americana." In *As lutas sociais e a cidade*. Edited by Lucio Kowarick. São Paulo: Paz e Terra: 17–43.

Gonçalves Couto, Cláudio. 1995. *O desafio de ser governo: O PT na prefeitura de São Paulo (1989–1992)*. São Paulo: Paz e Terra.

Graham, Lawrence, and Pedro Jacobi. 2002. "São Paulo: Tensions between Clientelism and Participatory Democracy." In *Capital City Politics in Latin America: Democratization and Empowerment*. Edited by David Myers and Henry Dietz. Boulder, CO: Lynne Rienner Press, pp. 297–324.

"Greve perde força e dá espaço a negociação." *Folha de São Paulo*. São Paulo, Brazil. 20 February 2003: B10

"Habitação na area central." 2001. Final report of the Commission for Studies on Housing in the Central Region. São Paulo: Câmara Municipal de São Paulo.

Hagopian, Frances. 1994. "Traditional Politics Against State Transformation in Brazil." In *State Power and Social Forces: Domination and Transformation in the Third World*. Edited by Joel Migdal, Atul Kohli, and Vivienne Shue. New York: Cambridge University Press, 37–64.

Harnecker, Marta. 1994. *O sonho era possível*. São Paulo: MEPLA/Casa América Livre.

Hellman, Michaela, ed. 1995. *Movimentos sociais e democracia no Brasil*. São Paulo: Marco Zero/ILDESFES.

Hewitt W. E. 1998. "From Defenders of the People to Defenders of the Faith: A 1984–1993 Retrospective of CEB Activity in São Paulo." *Latin American Perspective*. Vol. 25, No. 1. (January): 170–191.

Jácome Rodrigues, Iram. 1994. "Perspectivas do sindicalismo no Brasil: O caso da CUT." In *O Brasil no rastro da crise: Partidos, sindicatos, movimentos sociais, Estado e cidadania no curso dos anos 90*. Edited by Eli Diniz, José Sérgio Leite Lopes, and Reginaldo Prandi. São Paulo: Editora ANPOCS, pp. 39–90.

Jácome Rodrigues, Iram, ed. 1999. *O novo sindicalismo: Vinte anos depois*. Petrópolis, Rio de Janeiro: Editora Vozes.

Jakobsen, Kjeld, et al., eds. 2000. *Mapa do trabalho informal: Perfil socio-econômico dos trabalhadores informais na cidade de São Paulo*. São Paulo: Editora Fundação Perseu Abramo.

Jard da Silva, Sidney. 1999. "Companheiros Servidores: Poder politico e interesses económicos do sindicalismo do setor público na CUT." Masters' thesis. São Paulo: FFLCH-USP.

Jard da Silva, Sidney. 2001. "Companheiros servidores: O Avanço do sindicalismo do setor público na CUT." *Revista Brasileira de Ciencias Sociais*. Vol. 16, No. 46: 130–146.

Keck, Margaret. 1992. *The Workers' Party and Democratization in Brazil*. New Haven, CT: Yale University Press.

Kowarick, Lucio, ed. 1994. *As lutas sociais e a cidade*. São Paulo: Paz e Terra.

Ladosky, Mario Henrique, and Roberto Véras. 2001. "Tendencias recentes do sindicalismo CUT em São Paulo." In *Ação sindical no espaço local*.

Cuaderno de Formação 2. São Paulo: Central Única dos Trabalhadores (CUT), pp. 55–88.

Levine, Daniel, and Scott Mainwaring. 1989. "Religion and Popular Protest in Latin America: Contrasting Experiences." In *Power and Popular Protest: Latin American Social Movements*. Edited by Susan Eckstein. Los Angeles: University of California Press, pp. 203–240.

Lopes de Souza, Marcelo. 2000. *O desafio metropolitano: Um estudo sobre a problemática socio-espacial nas metrôpoles brasileiras*. Rio de Janeiro: Editorial Betrand Brasil.

Macaulay, Fiona. 1996. "Governing for Everyone: The Workers' Party Administration in São Paulo, 1989–1992." *Bulletin of Latin American Research*. Vol. 15, No. 2: 211–229.

Macaulay, Fiona, and Guy Burton. 2003. "PT Never Again? Failure (and Success) in the PT's State Government in Espírito Santo and the Federal District." In *Radicals in Power: The Workers' Party (PT) and experiments in urban democracy in Brazil*. Edited by Gianpaolo Baiocchi. New York: Zed Books, pp. 131–154.

Mainwaring, Scott. 1999. *Rethinking Party Systems in the Third Wave of Democratization: The Case of Brazil*. Stanford, CA: Stanford University Press.

Marques, Eduardo Cesar, and Renata Mirandola Bichir. 2001. "Investimentos públicos, infra-estructura urbana e produção da periferia em São Paulo." *Espaço e Debates*. No. 42: 9–30.

Martins Rodrigues, Leôncio. 1990. *CUT: os militantes e a ideologia*. São Paulo: Paz e Terra.

Martins Rodrigues, Leôncio, and Adalberto Moreira Cardoso. 1993. *Força Sindical: Uma Análise Sócio-Política*. São Paulo: Paz e Terra.

Mazzei Nogueira, Arnaldo M. F. 1999. "Emergência e Crise do Novo Sindicalismo no Setor Público Brasileiro." In *O Novo Sindicalismo: Vinte Anos Depois*. Edited by Iram Jácome Rodrigues. Petrópolis: Editora Vozes, pp. 51–72.

McDonough, Peter, Doh C. Shin, and José Álvaro Moisés. 1999. "The Churches and Political Mobilization in Brazil, Korea, and Spain." In *Comparative Political Parties and Party Elites: Essays in Honor of Samuel J. Eldersveld*. Edited by Birol Yesilada. Ann Arbor: University of Michigan Press, pp. 197–237.

MMC. 2003. *Informativo do Movimento de Moradia do Centro-MMC*. August/September/October 2003.

Monteiro de Souza, Fernando Luiz. 1997. *A Construção da Central de Movimentos Populares: Uma Experiência da representatividade popular*. Unpublished masters thesis. Universidade de São Paulo.

Moreira Alves, Maria Helena. 1989. "Trade Unions in Brazil: A Search for Autonomy and Organization." In *Labor Autonomy and the State in Latin America*. Edited by Edward C. Epstein. Boston: Unwin Hyman, pp. 39–72.

Moreira Cardoso, Adalberto. 1999a. *Sindicatos, trabalhadores e a coqueluche neoliberal: A era Vargas acabou?* São Paulo: Editora Fundação Getulio Vargas.

Moreira Cardoso, Adalberto. 1999b. *A trama da modernidade: Pragmatismo sindical e democratização no Brasil.* Rio de Janeiro: Editora Revan.

Mouteira, Bonança. "CUT perde terreno para a Força, diz IBGE." *Folha de São Paulo.* São Paulo. 20 February 2003: B15.

Nicolau, Jairo, ed. 1998. *Dados eleitorais do Brasil (1982–1996).* Rio de Janeiro: IUPERJ/Editora Reván.

Noronha, Eduardo. "A explosão das greves na década de 80." In *O sindicalismo Brasileiro nos anos 80.* São Paulo: Paz e Terra, p. 135.

Nunomura, Eduardo. "Sem-teto querem 15 milhões de moradias." *O Estado de São Paulo.* 17 May 1997: C5.

Palocci, Antonio, et al. 1997. *Desafios do governo local: O modo petista de governar.* São Paulo: Editora Fundação Perseu Abramo.

Partido dos Trabalhadores. 1987. *'Relação partido/movimento popular/ movimento sindical' e 'Estado e movimentos populares.'* Cajamar, Brasil: Instituto Cajamar.

Partido dos Trabalhadores. 1993. *O PT discute a Central de Movimentos Populares.* São Paulo: Partido dos Trabalhadores.

Partido dos Trabalhadores. 1998. *Resoluções de Encontros e Congressos (1979–1998).* São Paulo: Editora Fundação Perseu Abramo.

Paviani, Aldo, ed. 1996. *Brasilia: Moradia e exclusão.* Brasilia: Editora Universidade de Brasilia.

Paviani, Aldo, ed. 1998. *Brasilia: Gestão urbana: Conflitos e cidadania.* Brasilia: Editora Universidade de Brasilia.

Perfil socioeconómico do Municipio de São Paulo. 2001. São Paulo: Secretaria Municipal de Planejamento.

Pochmann, Marcio. 2001. *A Metrôpole do Trabalho.* São Paulo: Editora Brasiliense.

Pochmann, Marcio. 2002. *Desenvolvimento, trabalho e solidariedade: Novos caminhos para a inclusão social.* São Paulo: Cortez Editora.

Políticas públicas com participação popular. 2002. São Paulo: Central de Movimentos Populares.

Puls, Mauricio. 2000. *O Malufismo.* São Paulo: Publifolha.

Rossiaud, Jean, and Ilse Scherer-Warren, eds. 2000. *A democracia inacabável: As memorias do futuro.* São Paulo, SP: Editora Vozes.

Rudner Huertas, Mauricio. "Crise da Prefeitura de SP atinge a moradia." *Folha de São Paulo.* São Paulo, 4 August 1997: C1.

Ruscheinsky, Aloísio. 1997. *Cidade, política social e participação popular: Movimentos de Moradia e administração do PT.* Cadernos Cedec. No. 64. São Paulo: Centro de Estudos de Cultura Contemporânea (CEDEC).

Sachs, Céline. 1990. *São Paulo: Políticas públicas e habitação popular.* São Paulo: Editora da Universidade de São Paulo.

206 *Selected Sources*

Sader, Emir. 2005. "Taking Lula's Measure." *New Left Review*. 33 (May/June): 50–79.

Sader, Emir, and Ken Silverstein. 1991. *Without Fear of Being Happy: Lula, the Workers' Party, and Brazil*. New York: Verso.

Sandoval, Salvador A. M. "The Crisis of the Brazilian Labor Movement and the Emergence of Alternative Forms of Working-Class Contention in the 1990s." *Revista Psicologia Política*. 173–195.

Santos, Fabiano, ed. 2001. *O poder legislativo nos estados: Diversidade e convergencia*. São Paulo: Fundação Getulio Vargas.

Santos, Milton. 1996. "São Paulo: A growth process full of contradictions." In *The Mega- City in Latin America*. Edited by Alan Gilbert. New York: United Nations University Press, pp. 224–240.

São Paulo Plano Diretor Estratégico: Cartilha de formação. 2003. 2nd edition. São Paulo: Câmara Municipal de São Paulo.

Secretariat of Housing and Urban Development. 2003a. "Mutirões beneficiam 68 mil pessoas." *HabitaSampa*. Vol. 2, No. 2 (April). São Paulo: Secretariat of Housing and Urban Development.

Secretariat of Housing and Urban Development. 2003b. "Paulistanos elegem 16 para Conselho de Habitação." *HabitaSampa*. Vol. 2, No. 2 (April). São Paulo: Secretariat of Housing and Urban Development.

Shidlo, Gil. 1998. "Local Urban Elections in Democratic Brazil." In *Urban Elections in Democratic Latin America*. Edited by Henry A. Dietz and Gil Shidlo. Wilmington, DE: Scholarly Resources, pp. 63–90.

Simões Junior, José Geraldo. 1991. *Cortiços em São Paulo: O problema e suas alternativas*. No. 2. São Paulo: POLIS.

Sindicalismo no setor público paulista. 1994. São Paulo: FUNDAP.

SINDSEP. 1991. *Resoluções: III Congresso dos Servidores Públicos Municipais de São Paulo*. São Paulo: SINDSEP.

SINDSEP. 1995. *Resoluções do V Congresso*. São Paulo: SINDSEP.

SINDSEP. 1997. "Um Sindicato Nascido das Lutas," *SINDSEP 1987–1997: 10 anos de Lutas*. São Paulo: SINDSEP, p. 6.

SINDSEP. 2002a. "SINDSEP. Feito uma jovem que cresceu, ganhou asas e voou." *SINDSEP 15 Anos: Fazendo história*. São Paulo: SINDSEP.

SINDSEP. 2002b. "Parabéns trabalhador municipal de São Paulo: Os primeiros passos de um sindicato de lutas." *15 anos: Fazendo História! Commemorative Journal of the SINDSEP*. São Paulo: SINDSEP, p. 26.

Singer, Paul. 1980. "Movimentos de Bairro." In *São Paulo: O povo em movimento*. Edited by Paul Singer and Vinícius Caldeira Brant. Petropolis: Editora Vozes/CEBRAP, pp. 83–107.

Singer, Paul, and Vinícius Caldeira Brant, eds. 1980. *São Paulo: O povo em movimento*. Petropolis, Brasil: Editora Vozes/CEBRAP.

"Sinpro é disputado por partidos." *Jornal de Brasilia*. Brasilia. 13 May 1995: 15.

Soibelmann Melhem, Celia. 1998. *Política de botinas amarelas: O MDB-PMDB paulista de 1965 a 1988*. São Paulo: Editora Hucitec.

Stedile, João Pedro, and Bernardo Mançano Fernandes. 1996. *Brava gente: A trajetória do MST e a luta pela terra no Brasil*. São Paulo: Editora Fundação Perseu Abramo.

Tatagiba, Luciana. 2002. "Los Consejos Gestores y la democratización de las políticas públicas en Brasil." In *Sociedad civil, esfera pública y democratización en América Latina: Brasil*. Edited by Evelina Dagnino. Mexico City: Fondo de Cultura Económica, pp. 305–368.

Teixeira, Marilane, and Arilson Favareto. 2001. "Mapeando o emprego, a atividade económica e os indicadores sociais do Estado de São Paulo." In *Ação sindical no espaço local*. Cuaderno de Formação 2. São Paulo: Central Única dos Trabalhadores (CUT), pp. 13–54.

Tomatis Petersen, Aurea, et al., eds. 1999. *Política brasileira: Regimes, partidos, e grupos de presión*. Porto Alegre, Brasil: EDIPUCRS.

UMM. 2003. *Estatuto da União dos Movimentos de Moradia da Grande São Paulo e Interior*. Printed from the UMM computer, August 2003.

Véras, Roberto. 2001. "O CUT e o poder local: Riscos ou oportunidades?" In *Ação sindical no espaço local*. Cuaderno de Formação 2. São Paulo: Central Única dos Trabalhadores (CUT), pp. 165–181.

"Vereadores eleitos." *O Estado de São Paulo*. São Paulo. 7 October 1996: A5

Vieira Machado, Leda Maria. 1995. *Atores sociais: Movimentos urbanos, continuidade e gênero*. São Paulo: Annablume.

Villas–Boas, Renata. 1996. *São Paulo: Conflitos e negociações na disputa pela cidade*. No. 23. São Paulo: POLIS.

Von Mettenheim, Kurt. 1995. *The Brazilian Voter: Mass Politics in Democratic Transition, 1974–1986*. Pittsburgh: University of Pittsburgh Press.

Selected Web Sites

http://africanelections.tripod.com
http://cdp.binghamton.edu/era/index.html
http://dss.ucsd.edu/~proeder/elf.htm
http://freedomhouse.org/
http://www.antorchacampesina.org.mx
http://www.asambleadf.gov.mx
http://www.broadleft.org
http://www.camara.sp.gov.br
http://www.cidcm.umd.edu/inscr/mar/
http://www.cl.df.gov.br
http://www.electionguide.org/
http://www.electionworld.org
http://www.europeanforum.net
http://www.finanzas.df.gob.mx
http://www.georgetown.edu/pdba/
http://www.ilo.org
http://www.mmoradia.kit.net

http://www.psephos.adam-carr.net
http://www.pt.org.br/site/assets/carta_ao_povo_brasileiro.pdf
http://www.socialistinternational.org/
http://www.stanford.edu/~jfearon/

Interviews

In addition to those cited from published sources:

Mexico City:

10 confidential interviews with party and government officials, fall of 2000 and summer 2001.

10 confidential interviews with labor leaders, 8 of them in the SUTGDF, fall of 2000 and summer 2001.

14 confidential interviews with leaders from urban popular movements, fall of 2000 and summer 2001.

Attendance at numerous party, public, and urban popular movement organizational meetings.

São Paulo:

5 confidential interviews with party and government officials, summer of 2002 and 2003.

4 confidential interviews with labor leaders in the SINDSEP, summer of 2003.

1 interview of SINDSEP president Leandro Valquer Leite de Oliveira, summer of 2003.

1 confidential interview with a labor leader in Força Sindical.

8 confidential interviews with leaders from urban popular movements, summer of 2003.

Participation in the series of discussions about urban development, held in São Paulo in the summer of 2003, in preparation for the "Conference on Cities" sponsored by the national Ministry for Cities.

Attendance at numerous urban popular movement organizational meetings.

Index

public goods, 134, 164

Quadros, Jânio, 139

repression, 10, 15, 32, 38, 152, 155
resource mobilization, 8, 46, 162,
  164
Robles, Rosario, 33
Roriz, Joaquim, 34, 38, 44, 73, 119

selective incentives, 85, 97, 100–1,
  115, 133–5, 149, 159, 164–5
self help, 121, 126, 141, 151
SINDSEP
  foundation of, 80
  leadership competition, 75
  membership, 74
  political culture, 80, 83
socialism, 1, 79, 81, 126, 139, 141
solidarity, 9, 59, 135, 143, 168
Stedile, João Pedro, 82
street blockages, 44, 97
street vendors, 157, 167
strikes, 8, 63, 69, 72–4, 78–80, 83,
  85, 88, 97, 100, 105, 165
students, 121, 125–6, 128
Suplicy, Marta, 34, 74, 83–4, 153
SUTGDF
  foundation, 95
  leadership competition, 95, 98,
  103
  membership, 95
  political culture, 96, 99, 101

target switching, 23, 116, 118, 135,
  148, 152, 159, 161, 164
Tarrow, Sidney, 5, 7, 8, 10, 12, 59,
  162
teachers, 31, 72, 77, 93–5
Tilly, Charles, 4, 8–9, 162, 168

ULC, 147, 154
UMM, 144, 152, 154
UNAM, 46, 121, 125–6
União de Movimentos de Moradia.
  See UMM
unicidade, 74
Unificação das Lutas de Cortiço.
  See ULC
Union of Bus Drivers and
  Conductors in São Paulo.
  See MOCO
unions
  legal privileges of, 52, 85, 96
  public versus private, 67, 69, 91
  relationship to parties, 69, 71
  relationship to PRI. *See* PRI,
    union linkage
  relationship to PT. *See* PT union
    linkage
  versus non-unions, 36, 51,
    55–6, 107, 165
urban popular movements
  definition, 115
  leadership competition, 115
  relationship to PRD. *See* PRD,
    urban popular movement
    linkage
  relationship to PT. *See* PT,
    urban popular movement
    linkage
  versus unions, 36, 115, 148, 158

violence, 10, 14, 23, 24, 54–5,
  77, 115, 127, 174

windows of opportunity, 15, 60,
  114, 159, 167
Workers' Party. *See* PT

zapatistas, 20